# Happily
# Ever
# Older

# Happily
# Ever
# Older

*Revolutionary Approaches to*
*Long-Term Care*

# Moira Welsh

Purchase the print edition
and receive the eBook free.
For details, go to ecwpress.com/eBook.

LIBRARY AND ARCHIVES CANADA CATALOGUING IN
PUBLICATION

Title: Happily ever older : revolutionary
approaches to long-term care / Moira Welsh.

Names: Welsh, Moira, author.

Description: Includes bibliographical references
and index.

Identifiers: Canadiana (print) 20200382209
Canadiana (ebook) 20200382217

ISBN 978-1-77041-521-8 (SOFTCOVER)
ISBN 978-1-77305-661-6 (PDF)
ISBN 978-1-77305-660-9 (EPUB)
ISBN 978-1-77305-662-3 (KINDLE)

Subjects: LCSH: Older people—Institutional care.
| LCSH: Older people—Long-term care. | LCSH:
Old age homes. | LCSH: Long-term care facilities.

Classification: LCC HV1451 .W45 2021
DDC 362.61—dc23

ISBN 978-1-77305-752-1 (AUDIO)

*To Beverly and Jim*
*For the laughter and the books*

*To Daniel and David*
*For inheriting your grandmother's humor*

# Contents

# *Prologue*

I WRITE THIS IN THE MIDDLE OF A PANDEMIC.

There is much that we don't know. Scientists are racing to create a vaccine. Immunity from a second round of COVID-19 is unclear. The virus's timeline in our lives remains a mystery, although public health officials say it could last a few years.

Here is what we do know.

When COVID-19 landed in North America, we had already witnessed its death march through seniors' homes in Italy, Spain and France, killing thousands — retired teachers, accountants, electricians and bakers. The parents and grandparents of Europe.

We knew that elders, winners in the lottery of long life, were vulnerable.

When the virus arrived, in cities large and small, nursing-home deaths surged and soon, New York, Chicago and Los Angeles became COVID-19 hotbeds. In Ontario and Quebec, infections decimated long-term care homes, but not before a young geriatrician tweeted a warning: seniors' homes will blow up like a tinderbox.

Dr. Samir Sinha was right. So were countless others, from

AARP, the influential advocacy organization for older adults, to the Registered Nurses' Association of Ontario, all telling governments to focus on COVID-19 in nursing and retirement homes. Give all staff masks, test everyone, not just those with symptoms because, as we soon learned, the telltale signs in older people were as innocuous as an upset stomach or nothing at all. The virus used stealth.

Those were the infection control actions, but the bigger crisis, the spark to the tinder that Dr. Sinha cited on Twitter, was the system that controls seniors' homes. For decades, long-term care has operated on a tight budget, draining the life pleasure of the people who reside within while devaluing the work of staff, forcing many to work in two or three locations just to make a living wage. This is how a virus spreads from one home to the next.

As I write this in June 2020, we still don't know how many elders will die.

We do know that the coronavirus-related deaths of older people are forcing the industry and politicians to confront reality, even though it was there to see all along. Going into the pandemic, governments mostly viewed nursing homes as a second-tier system for residents whose frailties were similar to those in acute care hospitals.

It remains to be seen if these flaws laid bare will lead to improvements, but the suffering will not soon be forgotten. Families were banned from visiting, a policy meant to keep residents safe, even though workers unintentionally brought COVID-19 inside, infecting the people in their care. Without proper protections, the virus spread. As weeks passed, and staff grew sick or terrified, families realized that parents and grandparents were dying, alone.

There will be a generation of adult children who live with the trauma of knowing their mother or father spent the final moments of life with no one to hold a hand or speak quiet words of love.

As a journalist with the *Toronto Star* newspaper, I have spent the pandemic writing about seniors' homes, speaking to families that were emotionally destroyed. People who had the means to employ private caregivers for a father in a privately operated retirement home now had to go begging for a worker, anyone, qualified to go inside. And still parents died. Some didn't have COVID-19 but withered with extreme loneliness. What sad deaths they had.

Suddenly, the isolation of elders became a talking point.

Geriatricians who spent their careers warning about the impact of loneliness on older people now had a new audience. And while I'm reluctant to claim that emotional fulfillment will deflect a virulent virus, most homes I visited for this book, all focused on individualized care, did well in controlling COVID-19. There were many reasons, perhaps even a bit of luck, but all shared a philosophy that placed the resident at the top of their organizational pyramid.

Early in the pandemic, the home I visited just outside of Atlanta, Georgia, wrapped itself in a bubble, asking staff to "shelter in place" by living inside the home, blocking infections from the outside world. Sixty workers volunteered.

"We did it because we just felt it was the right thing to do, which is usually your best decision," said Andy Isakson, of Park Springs. "I think our relationship-based model [of care] was the foundation; that's why we got the volunteers."

In Saskatoon's Sherbrooke Community Centre, the daily buzz in the art studio or wine-tasting club was silenced as people isolated in their "neighborhoods," but activities continued inside, with safe distancing.

As the weeks turned to months, it became clear that there is a deep desire for new ideas, and I hope the stories told in this book offer inspiration. Nothing will change unless citizens and advocates push for true innovation, creating a different approach to the way we live in our older years, focusing on friendship, purpose and the potential to flourish at any age.

# Introduction

IN HIS DAY, MY DAD WAS AN ATHLETE, making local headlines for baseball, sprinting and soccer in his hometown of Windsor, just across the American border. As a young man, he'd slip over to Detroit to watch the Tigers play and dreamed, probably a few years too long, of making it to the big leagues, preferably in Boston, where Ted Williams was creating magic.

I'm sure my dad thought his youth would never end and later, in middle age, that his strength would always last. The truth was, it did last, powering him through life until at age 88, tiny and still immaculately dressed, he was starting to fall. He'd trip at home, grab a bookcase for support, and heavy volumes of Second World War history would crash beside him. Sometimes, a rebel with a cane, he'd march out of the house to mail letters, and when my mom peered out the window, she'd see him rolling on the sidewalk, trying to get up, while a neighbor ran to help.

"There your father was, on the ground again," she'd say over the phone.

And yet in small-town Ontario, my parents kept strolling, with canes or less jaunty, sturdy metal walkers. When they didn't walk, local volunteers sometimes offered rides for haircuts, visits to the downtown bookstore, exercise classes or, my mom's one weekly excursion without her husband of 61 years — the book club where discussions ranged from American politics to the scandals of #MeToo.

Like the millions of elderly parents of boomers and Gen X children, they were still here, still hanging on. Even if I shuddered at the thought of my father's walk to the grocery store, he would not be deterred. It was a risk but it was his choice, his risk, and after losing his driver's license two years ago due to a series of mini strokes, it allowed him to stay active in his world.

In summer 2018, a few weeks before my mom's 90th birthday, I was about to publish a *Toronto Star* newspaper investigation into an Ontario nursing home that was transforming itself from a traditional institution into a place of warmth, friendship and, dare I say, love. My colleague, videographer Randy Risling, and I spent a year visiting the Redstone dementia household in a nursing home operated by the Region of Peel, just west of Toronto. This was the first nursing home in Ontario to add the U.K.-based Butterfly Model, trying to extricate itself from the old task-focused culture by changing the way staff envision care, from leadership all the way to the housekeeper.

My parents sat together on their red settee and, each holding a corner of my dad's iPad, watched the video. Nearly 15 minutes in, when the film showed a man with dementia sitting at the keyboard, playing the British wartime song "It's a Long Way to Tipperary," my mom put her hands up to her face and wept. For all the vulnerability exposed by the people in the video, this story gave my parents hope.

When I left that day, they stood side by side, so small now, and looked up at me. My dad said, "If we ever need to move to a home, will you find us one like that?" I remember feeling so sad because as they stood there, trusting me to find another nursing home like the one they had just seen, I could not make that promise.

After the series ran, I spoke with Dr. Samir Sinha, a fast-talking geriatrician and Rhodes Scholar who had worked at Johns Hopkins University School of Medicine in Baltimore before he was lured north to Mount Sinai Hospital in Toronto. He told me about an elderly couple, both patients, who had read my investigation before going to check out a different Toronto long-term care home for the husband. "It was considered a good home," Dr. Sinha said. "They walked in, saw staff talking to each other on one side of the room and residents sitting in chairs, alone, on the other. They left. When they came back to see me, the woman said, 'Can't you get us into a home like Redstone, the one that was in the *Star*?'" As Dr. Sinha told me this story, he stopped speaking and shook his head. "I'm pretty sure that home has a long wait list," he said. All the good ones do.

I've written about nursing homes for 18 years. The stories always exposed the negative — neglect, abuse and isolation — with the goal of improving the system. My first investigation included the story of a woman named Natalie Babineau who had a deep pressure ulcer on her tailbone and suffered for weeks before her family discovered the reason for her pain. After the *Toronto Star* series was published in 2003, Ontario's health minister promised a revolution in nursing home care and eventually passed new legislation with rules for tougher oversight. Journalists across North America have exposed similar problems, each investigation creating outrage among readers that led to new laws or promises for improvement.

By 2018, that promised revolution was long forgotten. Then the Butterfly story came along, offering a new way forward. While that particular model was far from the only answer, it showed that people can live well in their elder years.

Reactions from readers exposed a hunger for more stories of change, of living happily as we grow older. This book grew out of that experience. It became a quest, of sorts, to find more of those stories, more people taking chances, more proof to hold governments and industry to account, showing we can transform the way older people live.

The focus of my research turned toward people with memory loss, although the intention was not to overlook the stories of those who are frail but still mentally sharp. In many ways, it is in the field of dementia care where innovation is happening.

Industry leaders who created homes that focused on emotional happiness in the 1990s or early 2000s are now turning their attention to the people who have been ostracized within institutions and communities because they are living with cognitive decline. These new ideas for multigenerational inclusion, for those with or without memory loss, can create more vibrant communities for all.

"We are seeing so many different options now, because of dementia," says Penny Cook, president and CEO of the Pioneer Network, a Rochester-based organization that promotes innovation in seniors' care. "It's really pushing us to look at different ways of doing things and it's having a positive impact on the culture change movement."

No matter how ideas change, the progressive philosophies or programs still share a collective DNA, a predisposition toward emotional intelligence of staff and the happiness of residents, with or without dementia. There are differences in the architectural design of the homes, the way staff are trained or even ideas about family-style meals versus smaller dining room tables. The one constant is the focus on resident well-being.

Some of the homes I visited have been scrutinized through independent research, while others relied on qualitative surveys, citing anecdotes from families, physicians and staff.

After my Butterfly story ran, the City of Toronto wanted to improve care in its nursing homes and hired York University professor Dr. Pat Armstrong to assess the merits of different approaches, such as Butterfly, the Eden Alternative and the Green House Project, which are included in this book. In her report, Dr. Armstrong and her team noted the challenges of examining these models based on the traditional medical research practice that uses double-blind, randomized controlled trials with a focus on specific measurements that can be collected and compared. "One of the main challenges in the evaluation of models may well be precisely what is intended to make them successful — variability, a holistic approach, dynamism and adaption," Dr. Armstrong reported.

She found that some models, like the Green House Project, had been studied more than others, like Butterfly, which had no independent, quantitative research, although in Ontario there are plans for a full study. Dr. Armstrong concluded that all approaches offered benefits over the old institutional style of care but said it wasn't clear that the improvements last. It's important that homes and governments find ways to inspire and uphold change. Dynamic leaders don't always last, either.

My book began as a search for good nursing homes but soon opened wide to explore other new concepts of living, such as the Golden Girls, co-owners of a detached house; the young people who live in a seniors' home in the ancient city of Deventer in the Netherlands; and Toronto's HomeShare Program that matches university students with seniors. I visited a 1950s-style day program in San Diego that helps families with respite, delaying the need for residential care. And, finally, I met the residents of an aging-in-place community in North Carolina. It was built within acres and acres of soaring oak trees, where seniors run 80 programs and committees, and everyone seems to have a pet or a garden or both.

It was as if a door had opened to an unexpected world populated by health professionals and care workers and members of the population at large who share a passion for elders and for social justice. It helped that a taste for a bit of rebellion was often in the mix. There were early morning flights across North America, into Europe and back to Toronto where the Gen Xers have taken up the cause, raising big money for Alzheimer's music programs from rock concerts, pushing innovation, speaking at one another's gigs or partying over pizza and champagne.

Laura Tamblyn Watts is the host of the Friday night champagne gatherings. A lawyer, Tamblyn Watts founded CanAge, a Canadian seniors' advocacy group, and teaches law and aging issues at the University of Toronto. She talks to her students about the value of the "longevity dividend." If medical advances keep us alive longer, she tells them, those extra years must have value, they must be worth living. Tamblyn Watts believes society is entering a time of fresh thinking about the act of aging, a time of great possibilities.

"There is a fundamental shift toward well-being, in the community, in retirement homes, long-term care — everywhere," she says. "That is where the longevity dividend is supposed to be. We have to see these changes — otherwise there is no point.

"There's a good word in French that I have never been able to properly translate to English: bientraitance. It's a more infused notion. It's the opposite of maltreatment and it comes from an idea of personal well-being, engagement and inclusion. This is what we are seeking."

◎   ◎   ◎

Before we step into the good stuff, let's back up and figure out how we got here.

In North America, homes for the most vulnerable elderly people emerged in the late 1800s from the "alms houses," where the old and impoverished lived alongside orphans and sometimes adults who struggled with mental health, according to Paul O'Krafka, a longtime member of the not-for-profit seniors' housing association AdvantAge Ontario. Old and young lived together in poorhouses, which sounds like an unintended version of the intergenerational communities that advocates are now promoting. Back then, though, it was a Dickensian scene transplanted from England to North America. Some children grew into adulthood and old age without ever leaving the poorhouse. Over time social activists pushed for separate homes; institutions were created specifically for the elderly, some run as charities, others as municipal homes, and later many would be privately owned.

If you had family, you were lucky. People who weren't destitute or alone relied on relatives, because for centuries that was how aging was done. When my grandmother came to Canada from England as a young woman in the early 1900s, she lived with her mother, her sister, her maternal uncle and later her husband, all in one little house on Windermere Road, in Windsor, Ontario. She soon moved across the street with her husband, a hard-core Glaswegian who taught his youngest granddaughter how to land a punch, the way it was done in the housing tenements back in "God's Country." (Aim the first blow just beneath the lower ribs, and as the perpetrator conveniently doubles over in pain, provide a swift uppercut to the chin. He never explained what to do *after*.) My grandmother made the 30-second walk to her mother's house every day, gardening and baking as a family, until my great-grandmother, who coiled her long, braided hair like a crown on the top of her head, took to her bed well into her 90s. Her daughters cared for her until she died.

In the early decades of the 20th century, this was the way many people lived, with the built-in support of family. That doesn't mean there weren't fights created by life in close quarters. And it doesn't mean that elders lived in bliss, or that abuse did not exist. But the idea of shipping off grandma to the nursing home and visiting once a month, or never, was not yet a part of our culture. After the Second World War ended, the way we lived started to change. The suburbs were the place to be, so families scattered away from the city core and extended family into single-family homes to raise their children who are now the boomer generation. For many, the days of living on the same street, like my grandparents and their parents once did, became part of our past.

Some nursing homes improved and became accepted as the place to go after retirement, even for otherwise healthy adults who were not yet in decline. Lisa Levin, AdvantAge Ontario's CEO, describes sifting through old mid-20th century photographs that show people driving their cars to the home and waving goodbye to family as they moved in for regular meals and laundry service. Now most homes are locked from the inside. Only those with the code to the keypad have the freedom to leave.

In the 1990s, long before Butterfly (now called Meaningful Care Matters) arrived in North America, tiny households for eight or so people living within a larger nursing home were an up-and-coming concept. They're still novel today. As the 21st century loomed, the idea of a cozier, homier lifestyle captivated a few leaders, such as Suellen Beatty at Saskatchewan's Sherbrooke Community Centre and the managers of a Dutch nursing home called Hogewey, who hired Eloy van Hal to help design tiny homes in a "village" called de Hogeweyk.

It's hard to pinpoint the origin of any specific idea. America's culture-change movement, as it was called, began in earnest in the 1980s with the U.S. National Citizens' Coalition for Nursing Home Reform. In Dr. Armstrong's assessment for Toronto, she noted the coalition's report, *A Consumer Perspective on Quality Care: The Residents' Point of View*, started a new trend by arguing that quality of life was just as important as medical care. "Grassroots organizations were formed," Dr. Armstrong wrote, "most notably among them the Pioneer Network, which brought providers, researchers, consumers, and regulators together to promote what the Network called 'culture change.'"

In an industry of opinionated thinkers, the Pioneer Network is known for its fearless invitee lists. "At our conference, we welcome everyone," says Cook. "We have varying opinions, varying ideas that people present because our belief is that, just like we talk about individualized person-centered care, that each person is different, there is no one right way to do things. It really depends on your community, your organization, the residents who live there, the staff members who work there. And there is not one model to do that."

Among some there is pushback against ideas that don't fit their philosophy. The gerontology bubble, as insiders call it, is not for the faint of heart.

Like any other culture, there is a star system at play. In varying ways, the geriatricians, academics or nursing home leaders who appear in this book, people like Dr. Bill Thomas, Suellen Beatty, Dr. Allen Power, Dr. Jennifer Carson, Eloy van Hal, Pat Sprigg and David Sheard, all attract attention when speaking at industry events. A few have appeared at the Pioneer Network's annual conferences. Cook chuckles when I describe some as gerontological celebrities. "I call them visionary changemakers — who have a following," she says. "And they don't always agree with each other."

At the 2019 Pioneer Network conference, Butterfly founder David Sheard talked about his ideas, while Dr. Allen Power, a geriatrician, and Dr. Jennifer Carson, an academic, presented a very different approach. "We knew there may be some controversy," Cook says. "But our position is that people should have all the information. We wouldn't put out there, for example, a program that uses restraints on their elders. However, with some of these different models and some of these different ideas, we really do think it is important that people know about options.

"And so, just like the Butterfly Model is a more exclusive model, in that you almost segregate people with dementia, we had Al Power and Jennifer Carson promoting the inclusive model. And you know what? That is okay. There are still homes in the United States that are building the more segregated models of memory care. And there are a lot of them. And then there are communities that are building a more inclusive model. From everything that we are discussing at Pioneer, from everyone we've been talking to on the research side of things, or people whose parents are receiving support, there is mixed thought about what people want. We think it is important for people to have the opportunity to hear about the different models, so they can choose what's best for them."

These debates and openness to diverse ideas matter more than ever. Today, most people in long-term care don't arrive until well into their 80s, almost always in a vulnerable state with serious health problems that often include cognitive decline. Without multiple health issues, they won't qualify for a nursing home bed, so assisted living, retirement homes or home care, mostly paid out of pensions or savings, are the only other options.

In Ontario, where I live, and generally across North America, there are waiting lists for long-term care — at least for the better homes. Most people are accepted after exhausting other options, including their caregivers. Once inside, many will be prescribed multiple pills, including antipsychotic drugs to control the so-called "behaviors" that the system claims are a symptom of dementia but which advocates say are mostly the result of boredom, loneliness and a life without meaning.

Right now, research shows that every five years after the age of 65, the odds of developing dementia will double.

Think about that.

In the U.S., nearly six million people have Alzheimer's disease or other types of dementia. In Canada, with a population one-tenth the size of America's, there are 564,000 people with some form of cognitive decline, according to the Alzheimer Society of Canada. The cost to society is both personal and financial. In the U.S., in 2018, the direct costs of caring for people with Alzheimer's and other conditions that cause dementia was $277 billion. In Canada, it was $10.4 billion. Globally, the number has reached $1 trillion — and it is only going to grow as the boomer demographic ages.

Dementia is the umbrella term for disorders that can lead to neurological decline, including Alzheimer's disease, Lewy body dementia and Parkinson's disease. Almost two-thirds of people diagnosed with Alzheimer's are women. The reasons for this are complicated. Women typically live longer than men, which may slightly increase the odds, but researchers are examining other potential causes, such as depletion of estrogen.

Alzheimer's is unique in each person but often begins with loss of memory and judgment or a declining awareness of place and time. It always marches forward. Families can manage it, even hide it for a time, but eventually it must be faced. Mom might get lost while driving. Or she might forget to take the chicken out of the oven before it turns to charcoal. At a relatively late stage, usually after caregivers can no longer handle the complexities, or a senior is alone and incapable, most will end up in a nursing home.

No matter how the individual lived in earlier days, as a CEO of a private equity firm, as an artist who painted sunsets off the Florida coast or a calculus teacher who opened minds to the joy of infinite sequences, people who once controlled their own world are now forced to exist on a predetermined schedule.

Walk into a traditional nursing home and often you'll see a row of people slumped in chairs, staring at the floor. Some are frail or sick. Others have memory loss. Many of those with dementia walk endlessly, seeking something they cannot find. In a Toronto home I visited, an elderly lady in a wheelchair cried, "Daddy! Daddy! Daddy!" every night, struggling to get out of the restraint that held her in place. Others called for mother. "When is she coming to take me home?" Research shows that many people with cognitive decline revert to their original language. I was spirited into a "specialized dementia unit" in Toronto, where a beautiful woman, her hair still dark and long, spoke Portuguese to her personal support worker while he stared at his computer screen, filling in hourly data reports, looking up occasionally to say, "Speak English. Speak English." Many advocates say these people were likely seeking the *feeling* of being safe at home with Daddy, yearning for the times when they were loved, when the people around them cared.

In Canada the average length of stay before dying in the nursing home, not a hospital, is 2.3 years, according to analysis done for the *Toronto Star* by the Canadian Institute for Health Information. Depending on the perspective, that is either a long time to live in abject boredom or mercifully short.

Data shows that most Canadians will live long enough to need extra care. Our average life expectancy is growing, according to Club Vita LLP, which uses pension plan data to analyze longevity. Its findings show the average life span of an American with a pension is marginally lower than their Canadian peers. In Canada, an average female who turned 65 in 2019 will likely reach the age of 89.4. A man who turned 65 in 2019 is expected to reach 86.5 years of age. There is a caveat: those who have the best lifestyle, with the highest pensions and non-manual jobs, will, on average, live the longest. Based on Club Vita's data, the most advantaged men have a life expectancy of 89.8, while the least advantaged (among those with pensions) are expected to get six years fewer, reaching the age of 83.8. For the most advantaged women, the life expectancy is 92.4 years, while the most disadvantaged is 88 years. We need to start now on creative planning for the future.

In Canada, the cost of long-term care is expected to jump from $22 billion in 2019 to $71 billion by 2050, when the number of Canadians over age 85 will triple. These projections come from a report by the National Institute on Ageing. Its researchers defined long-term care the way I did, using the broader European definition, which means nursing and retirement homes, along with community supports that help people live at home. Its conclusions are dire.

"With baby boomers starting to turn 75 . . . [in 2020] time is running out to improve system sustainability and the availability and quality of long-term care options in Canada," the report said. It's hard to imagine the situation is any different in the United States.

Dr. Bonnie-Jeanne MacDonald, the actuary and PhD who co-authored the report, says many seniors risk running out of money for care, in part because the availability of unpaid family and friends to help is expected to drop by 30 percent by 2050. It's a social problem created by aging family caregivers and low fertility rates. If all those unpaid hours were covered by the government, it would cost another $27 billion by 2050.

"The aha moment was that it is not going to affect just seniors," Dr. MacDonald says. "I believe it is going to affect all levels of society. People can't be constructive at work if they feel like their parents aren't being cared for adequately, if they can't do it themselves because they have so much financial pressure, if they don't live near their parents, if there aren't enough of them or if they are having their own kids later. There are so many reasons. This is going to affect boomers' children and their children as well."

It's no surprise that within the boomer generation, the 80 million North Americans born between 1946 and 1964, many are doing their best to avoid the nursing home fate. Researchers tell us that healthy eating, learning a new language and a lot of exercise will play a huge role in the way we age, physically and cognitively. Even hearing loss, now linked to dementia, likely due to social isolation, doctors say, can be a simple fix if caught early enough.

The difference between the "old seniors," people born in the 1920s and 1930s, and the "junior seniors," born in the 1940s, is profound. Medical professionals are among the first to see the attitude change. Dr. Susan Vandermorris, a clinical neuropsychologist at Toronto's Baycrest Centre, has watched it evolve. "People used to come to me and say, 'My doctor sent me here, and I don't know why.' Now, it's much more common to hear, 'I went to my doctor because I'm worried about my memory. I wanted to do something now to promote my brain health,'" Dr. Vandermorris says.

The stoic acceptance that marked the generation that grew up during the Great Depression is giving way to a younger demographic's aggressive determination to stay fit. The first wave of boomers is turning aging into a competitive sport, with retired 72-year-old pickleball players so hardened by their hours on the court that 55-year-olds are afraid to play them. In community centers across North America, pickleball, a combination of tennis, badminton and table tennis, is one of the fastest-growing sports. It is transforming the older years, creating physical and mental agility and, unexpectedly, new friendships — all key ingredients to escape the dreaded finality of a nursing home.

Dr. Bill Thomas is a Harvard-trained physician, famous in the world of elders for developing the nursing home philosophy called the Eden Alternative, the Green House Project, a "rock 'n' roll" bus tour called Changing Aging and, later, tiny Lego-like homes so older people can continue to live in the community.

During the Butterfly story, I interviewed Dr. Thomas twice. Each time he repeated an idea that seemed outrageous to a reporter trained to uncover the worst.

"What's most dangerous to the status quo," Dr. Thomas said, "is reporting that shows it can be different. That there can be joy. There can be love. There can be dignity. There can be privacy. That older people don't have to be denied those things just because they are living in this particular building. To the degree that the public sees that and understands that, it undermines the entire poor-me argument of the industry, that 'Oh, we are doing the best we can. What do you expect?' Well, we are not doing the best we can! And we should expect better.

"The positive story," he said, "is the most dangerous story you can tell."

CHAPTER ONE

# The Butterfly Effect

D AVID SHEARD MAKES PEOPLE CRY.
With his spiky hair and enormous, youthful cheeks, Sheard
works the stage at a downtown Toronto conference center, talking
about emotional awakenings.

Sheard and his partner, Peter Preidnicks, began their journey
to Toronto a few days earlier, starting with the hour-long train
ride to London, England, from their home near Brighton, a
seaside resort town with a laid-back breeziness from the ocean
air. Tourists come for the beaches and the Palace Pier, a carnival
of roller coasters and merry-go-rounds on a wharf shaped like
a lollipop, built into the rolling water of the English Channel.
Sheard's business, Dementia Care Matters, is in an office building
close to the summer frivolity, but his real work is done with
people living inside long-term care homes in the United Kingdom,
Australia, and Alberta, Canada.

Sheard boarded the airplane at Heathrow Airport and sat in
his usual spot, the front row in economy, where he has a few extra
inches of room to stretch his legs. After suffering a heart attack
ten years earlier, his doctor wants him to keep the blood pumping

to avoid the fate of his father, who died on the street when Sheard was a child.

Today, a Monday in late April 2016, Sheard is in a Toronto conference room, telling the 500 long-term care leaders that their system is killing elderly people. He's got the face of a cherub and the delivery of a man who doesn't give a damn who is offended. In Ontario's conservative care industry, some react with antagonism to critiques. We could be innovative too, insiders say, if the rules here weren't so regimented. Some lash out against change agents. You can be too dynamic, too radical, too entrepreneurial. It raises the question: Who is acting in the best interests of the vulnerable people living in nursing homes? At this conference that role is filled by AdvantAge Ontario, the non-profit seniors' housing association whose leaders want innovation on the agenda and invited Sheard to speak. It's the subtle art of the dance, adding the radical guy to the mix of speakers, hoping his ideas will inspire those seeking full-on change without infuriating the others.

Sheard already has quite a profile. Twenty-five years ago, he was the general manager of old-age psychiatry in a British National Health Service trust, who came home one day, looked at Peter Preidnicks and said, "That's it, I'm out. I'm done warehousing people." Like all good partners, Preidnicks started a conversation about possibilities, the work that could be accomplished if, perhaps, it was done differently. That led to a new partnership of sorts with a woman running an English care home, who shared Sheard's ideas about coziness, color and, most importantly, deep emotional connections with the people who lived there.

Sheard worked with Anne Fretwell in her care home in the English town of Atherstone from 1996 to 1999, sowing the seeds for what would one day become the Butterfly Model. They inspired each other, appearing together in the 2009 BBC2 documentary show *Can Gerry Robinson Fix Dementia Care Homes?*, which created a major discussion about nursing home care in the United Kingdom.

Sheard went on to create the Butterfly Model, which focused on changing the way nursing homes care for people with dementia. In the U.K., and in Atlanta, Georgia, Butterfly runs a similar All Care Matters program for residents who are frail or sick but don't have memory loss. It is his work with dementia that receives the most attention and the reason why he is speaking at the conference. Within eight years of the documentary's release, Fretwell was diagnosed with dementia, eventually living as a resident in the care home she had run. Ten months after Sheard's Toronto visit, her obituary would appear online with a request that no one attending her funeral wear black.

◎   ◎   ◎

Today in Toronto's concrete-gray downtown, Sheard speaks into a microphone, telling the crowd that people who work in homes need to learn how to connect with the feelings of people living with cognitive decline.

If 88-year-old Mr. Jones thinks he is still a boy, let him have his moment, Sheard says. Don't feel the need to tell him he's an elderly man living in a nursing home. What if Mr. Jones can't handle the truth? You'll just scare him or, worse, he'll lash out in panic and fear. Just let him live in his moment, meet him there, even if he's locked in a memory from 1942.

Two women sit at the front of the room. One looks like she stepped out of a *Vogue* street-style photo montage. The other is tiny and wears wire-rimmed glasses. Both are long-term care executives from the Region of Peel, just west of Toronto, who have spent the last two years searching for another way.

Onstage, Sheard is promising joy, his voice rising and falling as he describes warehouses turned into homes where residents get on with living instead of dying. In his Butterfly program, uniforms are banned as symbols of one person's authority over another. Hallways are painted in vivid blocks of tangerine, purple,

3

green and blue to help people with visual problems navigate the tunnels created by long hallways.

He talks about filling homes with what he calls "the stuff of life," teacups, boas, soft blankets, dolls, a desk, a typewriter, a piano, family photographs, all chosen to reflect the lives and interests of the people living in the home. Bring the world inside, he says, for people whose existence shrinks as dementia progresses.

All good speeches have a narrative thread, like a short story that drives home the overarching point, and for Sheard, that theme is leadership. Nothing on the front line changes without a cultural shift that is embraced, nourished and demanded, starting at the top. Without that shift, and it's a dramatic one, transformation will not succeed.

The Peel Region women have been wiping away tears but now they are looking at one another. It's a moment of shared epiphany. To them, Sheard is describing the missing piece, the reason why so many other well-meaning programs in Peel's dementia units didn't stick, why residents always ended up sitting alone, staring at the floor.

The two women have the power to push for change in Peel's five municipally operated nursing homes. When his speech is finished, they walk to the stage and greet him.

◎　◎　◎

Six months later, in the Malton Village nursing home boardroom, the home's director of care is sobbing. At the head of the table sits Nancy Polsinelli, one of the two Peel Region bureaucrats who had met Sheard at the Toronto conference. Sheard is also at the table, delivering the results of an observational audit on social interactions he has been asked to conduct in the Redstone dementia unit of this nursing home. Polsinelli is naturally poised but, locked in this moment of reckoning, she struggles to keep her face calm, worried about her staff. She watches the lines furrowed in Sheard's forehead, the intensity in his eyes. The excitement, the exhilaration of her first meeting with him seems a long time ago.

All the women at the table are managers at Malton Village, except for Polsinelli, who works with her Butterfly co-conspirator Cathy Granger at the head office in Peel, the regional government that oversees the fast-growing cities of Mississauga and Brampton and the town of Caledon. Sheard tells the women that he reached his conclusions by watching staff with Redstone residents, monitoring their social and emotional interactions, in minute-by-minute intervals. He watched as two workers ignored residents like Maxwell McCoy, a long-retired cop, and spoke to each other as if the people in their care didn't exist. He saw a 94-year-old lady named Inga Cherry sitting alone at the end of a long corridor, clutching her red leather purse, staring out the window. "I'm in a cage," Inga told everyone. "In a cage."

In the dining room, Sheard looked at the flat, bare tables. Touchscreen computers were attached to the wall. With backs turned to the people in their care, workers filled out the government-mandated documentation, tapping icons that denote food eaten and bodily functions taken. Mr. Jones ate breakfast. Click. He had a bowel movement. Click. His mood was agitated. Click.

Meals were the most exciting time of the day. Residents lined up at least half an hour early, hovering. When it was time to eat, they sat obediently at tables as workers served food, cajoling some to eat, then whisking away plates, on schedule. Most residents spent the afternoon in the TV room, sitting, with the local CP24 news and crime running in the background.

"People are parked liked cars in a parking lot," he tells the managers.

Scattered across the boardroom table are copies of his report that hold one sliver of good news: there are no signs of intentional abuse. That is a relief, except the report goes on to say that the odds of actually committing abuse are limited by the fact that there are next-to-no interactions *at all*. Polsinelli knows that neutral care is a form of abuse, emotional neglect, even if it isn't intentional. She is struck by the way Sheard speaks. He is powerful, but there is no drama, none of the emotion he exudes at his stage presentations. Sheard reads from the report. He gives Redstone his second lowest rating, a nine.

Except for the sobbing, Polsinelli and her managers are silent, stunned. Ontario government inspectors usually found few problems within the nursing home, at least by ministry standards. For a moment, she wonders why he gave the home such a bad rating, but reality hits quickly as she realizes that every negative observation is true. People living there might be clean and safe, but they were lonely and bored, left with meaningless activities, month after month after month. She knows it isn't the workers' fault. They follow the schedule, are trained to keep up with the set tasks, always rushing from one to the next. She knows the activity board offers a thin gruel of entertainment. Lunch is always a chore to get everyone fed on schedule. And the big, ugly medication cart is pushed around the dining room during meals with drugs dispensed like a hospital, not a home. Redstone has never been evaluated on emotion-based care, so this territory is painfully new. Polsinelli realizes that Sheard is making her see reality through the eyes of the people who live in the home.

Sheard asks for comments. The room is silent.

Polsinelli speaks.

"We can't go back," she says. "Now that we know, we're not going back."

◎ ◎ ◎

Around the same time that the leaders at Malton Village were being handed the worst review of their careers, I was having a debate with my editor. I've known Kevin Donovan for as long as I've worked at the *Star*, more than 25 years. We became friends after working together on a few stories, and later he became my editor, a hierarchical shift that did not preclude creative disagreements.

This time we were debating a story idea. It was related to the case of the registered nurse who had killed eight long-term care residents in southern Ontario and got away with it until she confessed. In October 2016, I got a late afternoon call from a health-care source who told me the Ontario Provincial Police would hold a press conference the next morning, announcing a murder investigation into the nurse for the seniors' deaths. I pulled together a story that night on deadline. Now, as the media frenzy lessened, Donovan wanted me to look at the big picture by examining the Ontario inspection reports for all 629 nursing homes.

I've done that story at least 30 times over the past decade, I told him. It's the same, horrible story every time. Soiled briefs. Abuse. Bedsores. And, most frustrating, nothing ever changes.

"Then find a good home," he said and walked away.

An unusual suggestion. Especially from a man known for his ruthless investigative reporting. I started making calls. There *were* nice stories out there. One home allowed residents to eat meals on a flexible schedule. Another let residents tinker on the decommissioned engine of an old van or fold laundry to keep busy. It was all lovely, but nothing jumped out as the subject matter for an in-depth story until Debbie Humphreys from AdvantAge Ontario called with a tip.

"Have you heard of David Sheard?" I had not. She sent me his email address, and within hours, Sheard and I were messaging back and forth across the time zones. It's a coincidence, Sheard wrote from his home in England, I'm going to be speaking in Peel Region next week. Maybe you should ask if you can come.

Polsinelli and Granger, the two Peel Region bureaucrats who had met Sheard months ago, were less than thrilled at the idea of the *Toronto Star*'s negative nursing-home reporter tagging along. But they said yes.

It's intriguing, the ripple effect that one forward-thinking person can create. Most communications staff are exceedingly cautious. They ask reporters for questions in advance and respond in writing, often offering a lot of words that say little.

There's always an outlier. On Twitter, Peel Region's Janet Eagleson calls herself, "Strategist. Fixer. Connector. Listener." She manages the occasional calamity, answering reporters' calls in off hours, while trail riding on her mountain bike or hammering shingles on the roof of her backyard shed. Eagleson doesn't read from a script, she talks bluntly, often with a digression in which she will "bastardize" the words of a long-dead philosopher or a trendy podcaster. She once paraphrased French-American historian Jacques Barzun (who published what was considered his greatest work at age 93) telling a reporter, "Compassion is not a lost art, but the regard for it is a lost tradition."

So when Peel's long-term care leaders pushed for change in the Redstone dementia home but recoiled, in understandable horror, at a reporter's request to cover the transformation, Eagleson challenged her bosses with a new idea: use the power of journalism to show other nursing homes that bold ideas are possible, that vulnerable, fragile people can live in happiness. Be an advocate for change.

"You can only feed one thing — courage or fear," Eagleson told them.

And that's how we know Inga Cherry blossomed in her final year of life.

◎  ◎  ◎

In leather pants and a tiger-striped blouse clasped at the neck with a gold brooch, 94-year-old Inga saunters, carefully, into the dining room of the Redstone dementia unit, her red leather purse held tight, swollen with lipstick, pots of powder and photographs.

"What have you got in there? It looks like it weighs a ton!" says a lady in a wheelchair, pointing to the bag.

"The kitchen sink — but no money!" Inga says. She laughs quickly, although Inga has been known to rage at workers who mistakenly touch her purse. She excuses herself, sliding into the chair at the window table she shares with Peter, the former nuclear technician who once worked in Russia. She speaks English. He speaks Polish. They chat, politely and in different languages, as she places the napkin on her lap, awaiting dinner served by support workers who float around the dining room, trying to get residents settled.

When painters arrived five months into the Butterfly pilot program, young men in T-shirts and white pants, Inga got her energy back. Instead of sleeping in her room or sitting alone at the end of a hallway in a narrow doctor's office chair, Inga grew curious. She began flirting with a dark-haired man until his cheeks burned, and he sought out Redstone management for advice.

"She doesn't realize she's 94," the manager told him. "She just wants to talk." The young man started to listen. Inga told stories of the bombs in the Second World War, working as a butleress on an estate in England after the war and later, living in Canada, driving her white Chevy Vega to New York City or the forests of northern Ontario.

Her stories sounded so fresh, alive with detail, as if her adventures were new. "It's funny," Inga says, "I can remember what happened decades ago but I can't remember what happened yesterday."

As summer turns into fall, Inga feels free, not from the nursing home, but from the structured rules that had forced everyone to awaken, eat and even watch TV at a certain time. Now Inga chooses. Sometimes she bakes bread with Chelsea, a Redstone worker. Inga kneads the dough, her purse clutched at her side. Later, after a mini fridge arrives in the fall of 2017, she'll walk into the dining room and peer into the glass door of the fridge. The Butterfly project manager, Mary Connell, insisted that Peel Region's money managers free up the cash for a fridge with glass, so residents could see the milk and jam. "Otherwise," Connell says, "no one would know what's inside, and they'll never open the door."

Bread, jam, butter and cream for tea are there for the taking. Inga pulls out two slices of white bread, drops them into the toaster that sits on the counter beside the shiny fridge. She says hello to a worker. Up pops the toast. Picking up a butter knife, she spreads butter, then marmalade, across the golden-brown slices, just like she did at home. Then Inga sits with a former engineer, a Scotsman, chatting over toast and tea.

It's a lovely connection between two adults who would otherwise be sitting in the TV room, staring at the floor but, if David Sheard were here, he'd be annoyed. Not at the conversation, but by the design of Redstone's dining room, which remains stuck in the old ways, impersonal, like a hospital cafeteria. Across the room is a smattering of Formica tables, with food spooned onto white plates by dining staff who don't emerge from behind the stainless-steel hot table. There are negotiations going on with the leaders of the Canadian Union of Public Employees. The union wants more staff, and possibly more pay, for workers who are expected to stop and chat with residents while still doing the rest of their tasks. Peel has hired more workers, though Butterfly's stance is that extra staff is not a program requirement, since everyone from managers to housekeepers is expected to spend more time with residents, a "flattening of the hierarchical structure."

In September 2017, halfway through the year-long Butterfly project, Sheard arrived to conduct his second audit of the home's care. Food is everything in Sheard's program. He wants people holding vegetables, talking about cooking and tasting little snacks long before the meal is actually served. That way, he says, people will eat, gain weight and stay hydrated, all of which supports health and possibly helps avoid the dreaded pressure ulcers.

Sheard chastised Peel for its delay in creating a smaller, more intimate dining room. He had wanted to see a long communal table with meals served in big bowls, all passed around the table by residents and staff. He did not want to see workers standing and serving, as if the people living here were helpless.

During my research, I spoke with a lot of leaders who have paid for multiple programs in their care homes, but the good work always ended up absorbed, molded, by the institution's system. That system has been designed to support the needs of the doctors, nurses and frontline workers, rather than the people living in the so-called home.

If big change is to happen, there has to be a structure created to help people get there. Not too rigid. Staff must be empowered to take what they have learned and run with it, but there must be enough structure to see the changes through, to make sure they stick. That's the tough part, the reason why so many good programs just disappear into the nursing home industry's focus on tasks. Unless the leaders of the home are fully onside, or governments offer incentives, the old system will prevail.

I interview a consultant from Australia, Daniella Greenwood, who tells me about her work trying to help nursing homes improve care. Greenwood is hired by operators who want her to show staff how to connect with residents but often don't plan any changes to that task-focused system. She describes visiting a "very well respected" nursing home in Canada that rushes people out of bed to get to breakfast on time. The residents, adults who have had careers, raised children and put their mark on the world, are forced to wear bibs during meals. After breakfast or lunch, they are placed in a circle, facing one another, and every once in a while, she said, someone comes in and throws a ball for entertainment.

"I'm doing a walk-through, and I don't know where to look," Greenwood says, "because I'm thinking, you want to train staff to look at these people as if they are human beings, and this is what you give them to work with?"

She spends most of her time trying to help frontline staff. "I tell them, 'Everything we are sharing in this session, I don't know your managers but I'm going to bet they are not on board with it. I'm going to bet . . . there are different nurses in charge and they are going to tell you the exact opposite of what I am saying. But whoever has the most contact with the resident has the power.'"

That influence can be wielded subtly, she tells me. Often a worker or relative will speak down to a resident, as if they were a child. "When they leave, you can go over and have a joke about it. Or a family member walks in saying, 'Hi Mom, don't you remember me?' And you see the person panicking. So when the staff sees that family member coming, they can go to the resident and say, 'Hi, isn't it wonderful that your daughter Samantha is here. Hi, Samantha!'"

Frontline staff can make all the difference.

Butterfly — the very name denotes a sort of friendly airiness, which is the ultimate goal but getting there is not easy. From the start, Butterfly asks the administrators and staff to take intense emotional training, a work-related therapy, to help staff connect with their own emotions. Some have spoken of the death of a child or a beating by a spouse. Many have wept.

The goal is to help workers connect with their vulnerability, to better empathize with the people living in the home and to throw off the traditional detached style of care that kept a safe, impersonal distance. Over time, they are expected to become emotionally connected to residents whose dementia leaves them dominated by feelings. Long after logic disappears, our memories remain, and many people with dementia relive trauma from decades earlier.

If a husband died in a car accident as a young man, Sheard says his 90-year-old widow might see those memories as clearly as if it happened last week. "What if you are living in a nursing home and no one knows what you are feeling? Imagine how alone you would feel."

◎   ◎   ◎

It runs counter to the growing philosophy against separation based on a diagnosis of dementia, but Sheard has said that people with relatively equal levels of cognitive decline should live together in small households. Since Peel Region hired Dementia Care Matters, the company behind Butterfly, it was sold and renamed Meaningful Care Matters. It has started reviewing its model as evidence and practices evolve.

Sheard rejects the traditional wards of 30 or more residents, saying large numbers of people living in one space can lead to conflict, anger and violence, particularly if those residents spend their days in boredom. "It's not rocket science."

Before Butterfly, Maxwell McCoy spent his days sitting with eyes closed. Little changes began as Audrey Sinclair, his personal support worker, sat beside him, massaging the palms of his hands. "Hello, Max," Sinclair would say, "how are you today?" One day, his eyes opened. He watched her. He squeezed her hand. Sinclair beamed, her eyes grew misty.

Staff didn't know much about Maxwell. They had heard he was once a police officer and tried to piece together bits of information to create a history for him, even if it was not entirely accurate.

In fall 2017, when the retired cops first visited Maxwell, they brought a pair of old police uniform pants, with a red stripe down the side. Connell, the project manager, had asked the men to bring symbols of policing, hoping it would spark happy memories from his years as an officer in Jamaica.

When Constable Dave McLennan arrived, he said, "Maxwell, look what we brought you." He held out the police pants and placed them, gingerly, on Maxwell's lap. Maxwell grabbed the pants, his grip tightening, as his fingers rubbed the thick red stripe that ran down the side. Half an hour later, when it was time for the officers to leave, Maxwell wouldn't let go. His reaction, his emotional response to the uniform, came as such a surprise that the officers promised to return with the pants. Their second visit led to a third, and soon it was a regular date, every other Tuesday at 10 a.m.

As the months passed, retired Detective Sergeant Lonny Blackett got the doctor's permission to give Maxwell a drop of Appleton Rum, from Jamaica. Sometimes, when he pulled out the bottle, Maxwell bellowed, opening his mouth in ready position. When Blackett mentioned the names of Toronto's old-time police chiefs, Maxwell squeezed his hand. "See!" Blackett said. "He's in there!"

On the active side of Redstone, where people were still walking and talking, the man workers affectionately called "the professor" spent his days playing a keyboard that was delivered to the home and placed in the TV room. Sheet music appeared. Sometimes, when he played church hymns, a man known for his crankiness stopped scowling and listened. He wept, and after he seemed calmer.

Sometimes the professor played old war tunes, like, "It's a Long Way to Tipperary," that cheery First World War song that became popular, as the story goes, after a *Daily Mail* war reporter heard Britain's Connaught Rangers singing it while marching through the French town of Boulogne. The reporter filed a story. The song became a hit, although its uplifting message may have been a better fit with the early days of the war, when Britain expected a mere skirmish, not four years of brutality. The Second World War raised its profile once again, and the professor played it from memory.

When he finished, raising his hands with a flourish, the ladies applauded. He paused, then started anew, this time choosing a church hymn.

The doors to the Redstone unit are now unlocked, so it is no longer a "secure unit" with a keypad and secret code to enter or depart. This unlocking of the door seems radical to some who are worried their loved one will get out or worse, get lost. Others are angry that the people with advanced dementia are living separately within Redstone without the interactions with the more active residents. As it turns out, the doors between the two units are easily pushed open, so the engineer, the artist and Peter visited, sometimes seeking the quiet space.

In the dining room, a long communal table appeared. Instead of serving individual plates of food from the cafeteria-style hot table, the elders and workers sit together, passing around bowls of food, talking and eating like family. Peter, Inga's earlier tablemate, has started regaining words from his second language, English. One day, when an outside group came for a tour with Mary Connell, Peter told one of the women, "You look nice." The lady smiled. "You just made my day," she told him.

Among most workers, early cynicism was falling away. Kenroy Foxe was one of the first to let go of his old hospital-style uniform, the green scrubs. Now he wears jeans, neon orange golf shirts and Polo running shoes in red leather and suede.

Like the others, Foxe went through the intense empathy training and decided to put his new thinking to practical use. He was tired of getting hit every day, usually by Fred, who got scared when it was time to have his briefs changed. Fred didn't like it when Foxe pulled down his pants, which makes sense. Who would? He'd ball his hands into hard fists and swing, usually catching Foxe in the cheekbone.

One day in August, as his 3 p.m. shift began, Foxe pushed open the door to Redstone. He stepped into the dining room. A little crowd was gathered there, including Fred.

He walked toward Fred at the far end, near the window. The other staff watched. Foxe took slow steps. Fred saw him coming. Fred stood upright.

Foxe did something that could get him fired in another home.

He spread his arms wide, stepped forward and wrapped Fred in a bear hug.

Fred hugged him back.

"Let's go to the toilet, Fred," Foxe said. They walked, arm in arm, down the hallway to Fred's room, where the older man waited as his friend changed his briefs. As Foxe tells it, Fred never hit him again.

◎   ◎   ◎

A year after the pilot project ended, Redstone feels relaxed. More like a regular home. Most of the men sleep in now, arriving for breakfast long after the old days, when food was served at 8 a.m. sharp. The retired lawyer usually appears at 11 a.m., eats two bowls of porridge and returns to his books or the communal couch, where he stretches out, feet up on the armrest. His supine pleasure annoyed some of the ladies who hold a different theory on chesterfield etiquette, so Connell arranged for a new sofa just for the lawyer and his feet.

The women are up early. They sit together at the end of the long table. One knits, while her friend holds the ball of yarn. When Connell first saw the ladies gathering at the far end, she was worried the staff had separated everyone by gender, but the workers insisted it was the women who chose to be together.

There is a hot plate near the coffee maker, and one of the residents, a woman who speaks Italian, cooks eggs and sausages for the others. She loves feeding the people in her life. While she flips sausages, another lady stands and chats, telling workers she likes to watch but no longer has an interest in scrambling eggs. "I've worked all my life," she says.

After the pilot ended, Inga Cherry's daughter Rhonda arrived at the Peel council meeting to speak about Butterfly, wearing her mother's black shoes. Inga had died in hospital a few days earlier.

"It's a bit of a selfish reason why I am here," Rhonda told the councillors. "Because it could be me when I am older. It could be any of us when we are older. A place that is more like a home and a family is where we really want to be."

Peel council, including its notoriously tightwad members, voted in favor of adding the program to the four other regionally operated homes and a specialized behavioral unit, where people with dementia are sent when the health care system declares them troubled or violent. Mary Connell, the project manager, spent most of her career as a public-health nurse. She was trained to bring about change and inspired by her father's dementia diagnosis, would lead the implementation.

In Ontario, the Butterfly program stirred up controversy. Every now and then, someone calls to complain. Some critics said Peel chose a "foreign" program that competed with local business models. In the course of criticizing the Butterfly Model, others promoted another privately operated program as the only way to go. The cost of Butterfly — $100,000 for the first year — was a concern. Public health dollars are tight. The lack of independent peer-reviewed research into the Butterfly's claims was a criticism of many. Early on, Sheard pointed to his public record in homes across the U.K. "Who says academics are the judge and jury against 23 years of action-based evidence?" he said in an email. Those comments fit with his disruptor persona, but didn't help push the Butterfly Model in Ontario, where "evidence-based practices" are key to funding decisions.

When Ottawa's Glebe Centre added the program to its home in September 2019, Glebe's administrator emailed an announcement saying their model is based on what was previously known as the Butterfly Model of Care but had been "designed to meet the needs of the Canadian experience." Now called Meaningful Care Matters, the new CEO, Peter Bewert, said he wanted to "lessen the cost" and relax some of the rules to make it easier for homes to create the eating experience that works for their residents. Some people living in homes want formal dining. Others are happy with relaxed family-style tables. Bewert said the new program would give homes the freedom to follow individual needs or inclusive ways of living, such as shared space among those with or without cognitive decline.

In Peel Region, Connell pushed for a local, independent, peer-reviewed evaluation. So did Jill Knowlton, a registered nurse and chief operating officer of Primacare Living Solutions, a small privately owned nursing home chain that saw what Peel had done and decided to add the same program to its homes. Like Connell, Knowlton had a reputation for making change happen. Before even applying for the research funding, she started planning for an 18-month quantitative study to be conducted by researchers at Western University. "Governments like data," says Knowlton, "so we really have to do this, otherwise in five years (the momentum) will be gone."

She asked Dr. Karen Campbell to lead the research. The women were already working together on another study that looked at the use of virtual reality (VR) for people with moderate to severe dementia in long-term care.

Dr. Campbell started her career in 1976 as a registered nurse. She went on to get her master's in nursing at the University of Toronto, focusing on geriatrics and mental health. She rose quickly in the mental health field but decided she didn't want to spend her career in management meetings, so she went back to the bedside as a clinical nurse specialist, focusing on wound care and incontinence. She became one of Ontario's first nurse practitioners, an advanced medical role, and was the first nurse practitioner specializing in geriatrics at the London Health Sciences Centre's emergency department. At first there was concern about physician acceptance. "And you know what? There was absolutely no problem," Dr. Campbell says. "I think because I had a lot of gray hair and I had been around the block a few times and I wasn't there to take away their role as emerg docs." She developed best-practice guidelines for the Registered Nurses' Association of Ontario, for hospitals or long-term care homes. In her 50s, Dr. Campbell went back to school, this time at Western University to get her PhD, specializing in rehabilitation science and wound healing.

Since then, she has been immersed in a few carefully chosen research projects and traveling, hiking around Lake Louise or taking a walking trip through Italy. "Life is short," she says.

As a researcher, Dr. Campbell is deeply aware of the demand for proof that programs actually work, particularly when public dollars are involved. "One of the big complaints about Butterfly is that there is not a lot of evidence," she says. "A lot of it is anecdotal. There are publications, but those are personal stories, which are interesting, but funders want to see strong evidence."

Dr. Campbell and Knowlton plan to start with a small study due to delays created by COVID-19 and later apply for research money, hoping for a grant from an organization like Baycrest's Centre for Aging + Brain Health Innovation. They've hired a research methods expert who designed a plan to study people living in Butterfly homes at both Knowlton's Primacare Living and Peel Region homes, along with 600 nursing home residents who do not live in Butterfly homes. At Butterfly, now Meaningful Care Matters homes, researchers will focus on hard data that answers the question: Does the use of antipsychotic drugs decrease? It is a measurable outcome. Researchers will also examine changes that are harder to measure, at least definitively. As people become more mobile, do falls go up or down? Does depression, agitation or aggression diminish? What about weight? Do people eat more in a program that wants them to peel carrots or smell food cooking to whet the appetite?

It's a study that requires complex data collection. One proven way to capture details on emotional turmoil, Dr. Campbell says, is the Cohen-Mansfield Agitation Inventory, which records how often, for example, a resident hit, kicked, bit or made sexual advances. Under the nonaggressive section, it collects details on aimless walking, intentional falls and hiding or hoarding items.

It also asks if a resident screams or makes verbal sexual advances, swears or asks repetitive questions or is constantly seeking attention.

The bigger challenge, Dr. Campbell says, will be the measurement of happiness. Researchers need a way of measuring the emotion that has been tested and is valid, reliable. The difficulty is recording changes in people with cognitive decline who can't communicate their emotions, at least for a research study. If that is the case, then there has to be some other method for accurate measurement with a proxy, either relatives or staff who know the person well.

"As you can imagine, it is always, always, always better if you can get an individual to report these things," Dr. Campbell says. "A proxy is second best. There are some outcome measures that have been developed for proxy, just because of the issue with dementia. But there aren't a lot of good ones. The issue in this case is that there is anecdotal evidence to say that this [Butterfly] is helpful and it is just another way of organizing care that is person-centered, which, you know, kind of makes sense.

"There is a debate in the research world: Do we need research for everything? The example they give is, 'Do we need to study whether you need to wear a parachute if you jump out of a plane?' It's a good analogy because, for God's sake, it's common sense if you don't want to die. Now, someone could say, 'Show me the research study.' That is taking it to the extreme.

"I'm not opposed to looking for evidence. When I was working clinically, I always tried to make it evidence-based. Sometimes, when nothing works you end up trying anything to help people. Generally, I think we need to look at evidence but does it have to be evidence from a medical model?"

She's referring to the randomized controlled trial model designed for medical research like drug studies, measuring, say, blood levels or hypertension. The struggle, says Dr. Campbell, is found in documenting medical-grade proof of happiness, contentment or, as Laura Tamblyn Watts would call it, bientraitment.

"The randomized controlled trial doesn't work as well for quality of life," Dr. Campbell says. "How do you look at some of these things that are softer but just as important?"

◎　◎　◎

Long after Redstone's pilot project ended, the retired cops kept visiting every second Tuesday.

Like any good detective, Lonny Blackett was curious. He wanted to know more about Maxwell's life, so he made some calls to his Toronto police contacts and discovered that Maxwell had worked as an officer in Jamaica, from 1967 to 1970. In July 1973, he started working for Toronto Police Service as a parking ticket officer.

Maxwell was a Green Hornet, named for the color of the uniform, one of the guys who drove a "pie wagon," a three-wheeled motorbike to hand out parking tickets. Blackett connected me with one of his contacts, a parking ticket officer turned career cop. It turns out Maxwell was a charmer.

"He was a jolly fellow," the retired officer emailed from somewhere warm. "I will always remember Max as a people person. He gave a ticket to a lady who became furious and berated Max. He smiled his winning smile and spoke to her in his soft Jamaican accent. The lady calmed down and as she left [with the ticket] she actually smiled and wished him a nice day. That was what he was all about. An all-round sweet guy."

When I last saw Blackett, he had been visiting Maxwell for more than a year. That day, Blackett held Maxwell's hand and watched him sleep. Blackett started talking about his personal experience, years earlier, with a close family friend, a father figure who had developed early dementia. He spoke of his sadness, of watching the man who meant so much to him sit frozen in a chair, eyes closed, silent. No one thought to massage his hands or bring him symbols of his past. Eventually, Blackett decided it was pointless and stopped visiting. That was years ago.

Now he shakes his head, sadly. "I've learned so much since I started coming here," he says.

"I always thought these guys were just vegetables, taking up space, waiting for the grim reaper to show up. But they're alive in there. They're listening."

After the story was published in June 2018, John Tory, the mayor of Toronto, mused about creating similar changes to city-run homes. Toronto councillor Josh Matlow wrote a motion for a Butterfly-like pilot project and, later, the transformation of care in all ten city-run homes. Both won unanimous votes from council, no easy feat. Instead of choosing an established approach, Toronto decided to move forward with its own programs designed to focus on the diverse needs of people in each residence, recognizing, for example, the large population of LGBTQ2S residents in downtown homes.

In Ottawa, the not-for-profit Glebe Centre signed up for Butterfly. A nursing home in nearby Renfrew Country did too, along with the Sunnyside municipal home in Kitchener.

Word spread, and it wasn't long before I received an email from Linda Hong, the executive director of the China Alzheimer's Project, a social enterprise organization, who said the *Toronto Star*'s series resonated with her members, who are trying to promote emotion-focused care. Roughly ten million people in China have dementia.

"In China," wrote Hong, "the aged care industry is still dominated by the old culture of care, just like what [researcher] Tom Kitwood described as 'malignant social psychology.' Many of the care providers can't even provide good clinical care. Can you imagine that the old Redstone is much better than many of the care homes in China?"

While the stories highlighted one home's experience, it did so with the goal of launching a much bigger conversation about seniors' care and the rights of elders to engage in their world, not just wait to die.

As it turned out, Peel's communications director Janet Eagleson was right. By offering a glimpse into the possibilities, Redstone's experiment gave voice to a hunger, among all ages, for a better way.

It was a beginning.

◎　◎　◎

My parents grew old, living in their home, with a certain pride that they had lasted so long on their own. A few months after my mom's 90th birthday, all that changed.

She fell late at night, and my dad, 88, tippy with Parkinson's, stumbled around in the dark, until he leaned over, unsteadily, and grabbing her hand, tried to pull her up.

"If you fall on me, we'll never get up!" my mom told him. "Call the ambulance!"

The paramedics arrived, lifting my mom onto a stretcher. On the way out, one grabbed her medication from the washroom sink, knowing exactly where to find it because, well, they'd been there before. My dad was ordered back to bed, and in the morning, his telephone rang with a call from a hospital nurse saying the blood tests showed an increase in troponin levels, a possible indicator for heart trouble.

When my cell rang a few minutes later, my dad bellowed, "Your mother had a heart attack!"

I was at my desk in the newsroom. It was one of those calls I had always dreaded.

"I hope they don't keep her in there long," he said. "What's going to happen to me?"

By the time I drove the 90 minutes to their town, picked up my dad and took him to the hospital, it became clear that my mom had been hiding what should have been obvious. Even though he could talk baseball, Second World War history and the machinations of MI6, my father seemed off his game . . . almost innocent, definitely impulsive. And boy was he fast. We went out for coffee, and when I turned to tap my debit card, he would march out the door, toward the street. I'd race out to catch him just as he stepped off the curb.

I spent the next four days chasing after my dad, whose remaining athletic agility propelled him forward with a crazy momentum, until he'd teeter and start sidestepping on an angle. It looked like a slapstick routine from those old Laurel and Hardy movies that he made my sister and me watch as kids. We didn't share his appreciation for their bowler-hat humor, but it sure was fun watching our dad, who mostly hid behind his newspaper, weep with laughter on the couch.

It was a weekend of illumination. An alleged heart attack will do that. My mother, mistress of her domain, had always greeted suggestions of paid help with contempt. Now, lying in the hospital bed, drinking from ice chips, she looked fragile, worn down.

## CHAPTER TWO

# The Eden Alternative, The Greenhouse Project and De-Institutionalizing Eldercare

A T AGE 32, KYRIE CARPENTER IS A CRONE-IN-TRAINING.
It's a radical concept, this millennial embrace-of-age, particularly in a nation that spends $16 billion a year to stay young-ish and, according to Instagram, you can never start too early.

Carpenter is reclaiming the word crone, discarding its hollow negativity for a new definition, the way feminists took control of the other C-word, which Carpenter articulates in its entirety, while I am failing the sisterhood by following publishing etiquette here.

A coach in matters-of-life from San Francisco, Carpenter is here at the University of Southern Indiana (USI), home of the Screamin' Eagles, to teach a class on intergenerational living. The class is open to all ages, to USI students and older people living in Evansville, the local community. It's a one-credit course, taught over two eight-hour days in bursts of mind-expanding conversation all leading to one goal: inspiring activism that connects young and old, powerful and vulnerable. The students have spent the last 90 minutes discussing the intersectionality of race, religion, money, education, disability and the greatest equalizer of all, old age. "Even the most powerful will become less. *Slightly* less, as they age," Carpenter says.

For years university leaders here have embraced the concept of connections between young and older people. They have sent more than 1,000 students into the community to interview elders. It's an assignment that might build understanding, maybe inspire a career with elders or create a healthier view of aging among 20-year-old college students.

Now, USI is teaching housing inclusion in age and ability after a meeting with Dr. Bill Thomas, the Harvard-trained physician, elderly advocate, fighter of loneliness and nursing-home entrepreneur who is building tiny homes to help elders live with greater ease in the community. His 600-square-foot Minka home, with a soaring ceiling for the illusion of extra space, sits on the campus near the David L. Rice Library. Built in a flurry by Dr. Thomas and his team in fall 2018, the Minka home has a telepresence robot that roams around on wheels, while the screen beams in images of teachers talking to students and professors from afar.

The idea behind the Minka communities is getting attention, but it is new and untested by long-term research. Those who have bought into the concept see the houses as an opportunity for simpler living in a community that provides daily supports, much like assisted living or retirement homes. Instead of moving into an institutional setting, people would live in a cluster of individual, albeit very small homes, that are designed for accessibility and require a lot less housework.

The course is called MAGIC (Multi-Ability, Multi-Generational, Inclusive Community) written by Dr. Thomas and taught by Carpenter and Dr. Thomas's troupe of academics, actors and musicians who tour the U.S., offering community theater performances that promote healthy aging. Dr. Thomas is the headliner, known for his creations, the Eden Alternative and the Green House Project.

It's Friday night in January 2019 on the edge of Evansville, Indiana, a few miles north of the Kentucky border. A storm is raging outside, dumping five inches of thick, wet snow on a region that prefers its traditional winter over this white mess.

Outside on the Lloyd Expressway, cars without snow tires struggle to avoid the ditch. Inside USI's Health Professionals Building, the MAGIC students, mostly young women studying occupational health, biology or accounting, will worry about Snowstorm Gia after class.

I pull Carpenter aside and ask about her Twitter name, @cronetraining.

Carpenter is a direct talker, holding nothing back and standing tall, her eyes serious.

"Crone in our culture is only associated with the hag, the long nose, witch with warts and all of the terrible things in the Disney fairy tales," she says. "I studied Jungian psychology and that is where I first came across the crone, in those studies. The crone is actually a very multifaceted archetype. It holds both the enchantress and the witch, the hag. I love this idea of a woman being more than just beautiful but beautiful and powerful and able to create the witchy side too.

"Women can be villains and that is okay. We have permission to be ugly, we have permission to be naughty, we have permission to break things, and the really awesome thing about being a woman is that we can hold both at the same time. It's super dynamic.

"The trajectory is maiden, mother, crone, for a female throughout her life span. [Crone] is the capstone of being a woman . . . But the thing is, you don't lose the maiden, she is in there too. I think it's a really big misnomer that older women aren't considered beautiful. I think that's a cultural thing, and that we can find beauty in older women.

"In order to become a crone, we need to be intentional about it from a younger age, that is why I am a crone-in-training."

It's the new activism. Pro-age. Any age. Taken to its logical conclusion, that means promoting inclusive multigenerational communities, where the old interact with the young without artifice. It's a natural way to live, like families did before the mid-20th century, when older people were sent away to live separately, as if they were "others."

"I am radically pro-aging and dementia positive," Carpenter says, eyes flashing.

◎ ◎ ◎

Long before he built tiny homes with tall windows or traveled the U.S. in a rock 'n' roll tour bus performing shows about aging, Dr. Thomas — Dr. Bill, as his people call him — worked in an upstate New York nursing home.

"I really divide my life into two parts," Dr. Thomas says. "There is the part before I went to see her. And the part after."

She was tiny, with white hair and the lightest blue eyes. Nobody came to visit her. The staff asked Dr. Thomas, the tall Harvard grad with slightly unruly hair, to check the rash on her arm.

"I was very busy and very self-important," Dr. Thomas says. "I sort of gave her the doctor talk, but she took hold of my arm and pulled me down and actually made me look into her eyes. She said, 'I am so lonely.' Those words just shattered the illusion that I was living in. That I was a doctor and I am giving you the medicine and it is all good and I am very busy. It just shattered all of that."

Dr. Thomas went home that night and pulled out his medical books to investigate loneliness, long before researchers concluded it is detrimental to the health of all, young or old.

"There was nothing," he says.

He started visiting the nursing home in his downtime.

"I would get these black-and-white speckled notebooks, and just sit for hours and hours, and just watch and listen and write down what I was seeing. The whole place was like a different world. Because when I went to the nursing home in turbo Dr. Thomas

28

mode, it was like, I'm very busy, everybody is paying attention. But when I went there and just sat there, I just disappeared like everybody," Dr. Thomas says. "I could see what she was saying. It was just a building full of people who were lonely. Because all of the contacts they had with other humans were instrumental. Like me. The doctor is coming to see you about a rash on your arm. That doesn't do anything for loneliness. And nobody came to see that woman *for her*. To be with her."

Dr. Thomas was 31 years old. At that time, in the early 1990s, the New York State government announced a grant program for ideas that would improve care for people living with dementia. "I decided I was going to apply," says Dr. Thomas. "I had only one idea. That this place should be more like a garden and less like a hospital. That's all I had.

"Honestly, my whole career grew out of that seed. You have a choice. You can go this way or this way. And every time I just kept going this way. And that has just been the nature of my career."

Dr. Thomas decided to devote his career to abolishing what he defined as the three plagues of old age: loneliness, boredom and helplessness.

And so began the philosophy he called the Eden Alternative. He envisioned life in nursing homes that brought the calm of nature indoors, with green space and gardens. As the philosophy grew, there was a focus on kindness. Companionship. Dogs balanced on the arms of wheelchairs. Cats hung out wherever they felt like hanging out. The people who lived in these homes cared for those plants and pets. Children became natural participants, through school visits or day care. There was an expectation of purpose. Making art. Or talking about art. The point was, to offer a life of creativity, connection and ongoing personal development for the elders.

With his wife, Judith Myers Thomas, he expanded the reach of the Eden Alternative, its concept spreading across the United States, up to Canada and beyond. There were training conferences.

Dr. Thomas made speeches. With long-term care leaders across North America and beyond, they worked to transform traditional ideas about aging, attempting to erase institutional care from the home, improving the lives of residents and staff.

By the late 1990s, Dr. Thomas was restless, the upshot of an affliction he calls "persistent dissatisfaction." He started looking around, curious, wondering how to take his concept to the next level.

His restlessness would lift at a tennis ranch in Texas, where Dr. Thomas was corralled, so to speak, by Suellen Beatty, a registered nurse and leader of a nursing home in Saskatoon, Saskatchewan, on the Canadian Prairies. Like Dr. Thomas, Beatty was always pushing new ideas.

She had originally met him in the mid-'90s at an old nunnery in Minneapolis–St. Paul during a three-day Eden Alternative associate training program. Beatty brought seven workers to that course, all ready to transform their nursing home with new ideas. Dr. Thomas taught the second day. Beatty grabbed a few minutes with Dr. Thomas over lunch, where she told him about a new project in the planning stages at her nursing home, the Sherbrooke Community Centre. She tried to describe it to him, an interior "village" of small households, each with roughly ten residents, a huge change from the institutional units of 40 or 60 people living together.

"I kind of had his attention," Beatty says, "but I didn't *really* have his attention."

She attended another Eden Alternative training session in White Eagle, New York, this time with plans to become an Eden Alternative regional coordinator. "I told him again about the village." Dr. Thomas was busy, with people waiting to meet him. She could tell her words didn't quite stick.

Beatty flew back to Saskatoon, immersed in the final stages of the project. Sherbrooke's new addition of little homes opened, each with its own kitchen, a family room and a door to an outside garden. Most of the residents were older and frail, and while some had memory loss, their cognitive decline was still in the early stages. Workers had a different role than traditional staff. They cooked meals to the residents' tastes, cleaned and looked after the people in their care. Their role was so new, Beatty had to write a different job designation for the union.

Life in the little homes took on a familiar energy. People grew relaxed. They laughed around the dining room table. If the sun shone the worker might say, "Let's barbecue!" and turn the ground beef meant for meatloaf into hamburger patties. Beatty started taking pictures. She printed them in large format and created a photo album with images of home cooking, the communal living room and the people who now lived like a family, each with a bedroom of their own.

In 1999, she flew to Texas for another Eden Alternative conference, just outside San Antonio at the John Newcombe Tennis Ranch. This time Beatty came armed with her photo album. "Page after page, so he would clearly understand what I was trying to tell him," she says. It was a strategic move to capture Dr. Thomas's attention. Identify the obstacle, then disrupt.

"I followed him around . . . It was kind of like I was stalking him with this big photo album," she says, laughing. "Everybody wanted his attention, right? But I was pretty sure he wanted to see this."

Eventually she pulled him aside. Sat him down. Opened the book.

"He looked at it and said, 'Oh my goodness! This is it! This is wonderful.' Sort of like, Why hadn't I told him?"

A few months later, Dr. Thomas, his wife and young family flew from their home in New York State to Saskatoon, called the Paris of the Prairies for the multiple bridges that span the South Saskatchewan River.

"I was just blown away," he says of the little village homes inside Sherbrooke.

"They broke the frame. I had been through so many places where they were like, 'Oh, we'll paint the walls and it's good.' But this was . . . WOW!"

He visited the Ukrainian home (Saskatchewan has more than 120,000 people of Ukrainian descent) and ate traditional stew in Wicihitowin Place, where Indigenous people held healing circles and drumming ceremonies.

"The conventional nursing home," Dr. Thomas says, "is like a cultural meat grinder. It just grinds up every bit of culture and makes it into pureed culture. But these people were getting to live in a way that was aligned with who they really were. WOW. Super powerful. Clearly and without any question, Sherbrooke Community Centre was an inspiration for Green House."

That's what Dr. Thomas named his next idea: the Green House Project. Nursing homes with small households of six to ten bedrooms, focused around an open kitchen and living room where the elders are, in many ways, in charge of their day, particularly the choice of meals. Workers are called Shahbaz, which, Dr. Thomas says, is the Persian term for "falcon to the king," a sign of respect for the elders.

During my original *Star* Butterfly story, I visited a Green House home in Penfield, New York. Built in a residential neighborhood, the two bungalows operated by St. John's seniors' housing were connected by an outdoor garden. Inside, the kitchen had granite counters and rich brown cupboards. When we visited, buttery grilled cheese sandwiches were served for lunch. The elders and workers ate together, chatting, at a long wooden table.

"What is nice is that the [staff] have conversations with me," one lady said. "They don't talk to each other over my head, like they do in other homes, as if I don't exist."

The Shahbazim (plural for Shahbaz) are certified nursing assistants who take specialized training with a focus on creating a life of meaning for the elders. That old medical model of care, that put the efficiencies of the doctor and nursing staff before the well-being of the people living in the homes, does not exist here. The homes are intimate, and the Shahbaz are empowered to act as the caregiver, social convener or chef. The Shahbaz I spoke with, a young man who was preparing the lunch, talked about the value of work that has meaning. Instead of racing from task to task, he has long conversations with residents and takes turns cooking meals and shopping for food. He still looks after the showering and toileting of people who need help, but his days are more gratifying because the care and the relationships are not rushed, not the cursory "hello, how are you today?" conversations that leave everyone feeling empty.

No job is perfect, ever, but homes that want to attract and keep workers are more likely to succeed if those jobs are meaningful. Ontario, like many American states, has a shortage of personal support workers, called certified nursing assistants in the U.S. The COVID-19 pandemic exposed the need for a workforce earning a living wage, with full-time jobs in one home, instead of part-time shifts in two or three. As the demand for senior care grows, homes will be more successful if they offer a workplace that is generally happy, offering fulfilling work, especially when staff could make similar wages in retail jobs with a lot less stress.

While at the Penfield home, I spent time with two women, elders, who laughed as they described their political debates with another resident, a man, who provided a contrarian perspective. They felt engaged in their world here, and friends visited regularly. They stayed intellectually involved with the greater world by discussing the current state of affairs in the White House. They looked at me, a bit side-eyed, not stating their political opinions.

The Green House Project was one of the models that the City of Toronto considered for its homes, with its new focus on resident emotions. Dr. Thomas's Eden Alternative philosophy was another consideration, although the city later chose a made-in-Toronto model. Green House captured the attention of Dr. Samir Sinha, who, in addition to working on the Ontario seniors' strategy and the Canadian dementia strategy, co-chairs the Toronto seniors' accountability group with city councillor Josh Matlow. Dr. Sinha noticed that Green House had received funding from the Robert Wood Johnson Foundation, a measure of respect, he says, because the foundation makes decisions based on empirical evidence.

Known for funding advances and evidence-based research in health care, the foundation was created by General Robert Wood Johnson II (1893–1968), who built the medical company started by his father, Johnson & Johnson, into the massive enterprise it is today. (According to the foundation, General Johnson championed a minimum wage that the unions of the day considered generous.) When he died, Johnson left most of his considerable fortune to the foundation.

When Dr. Sinha looks around for evidence to improve the lives of older people in City of Toronto homes, he relies on studies funded by not-for-profit organizations like the Robert Wood Johnson Foundation. A foundation-supported study by THRIVE Research Collaborative (The Research Initiative Valuing Eldercare) made some positive conclusions about Green House homes. While it found some implementation inconsistencies among the different Green House homes, the study also said elders living in them were less likely to be bedridden, need catheters or suffer from pressure ulcers. The study also found lower health costs and more shared time between elders and workers. As the Green House concept spread across the United States with its evidence-based reputation, Dr. Thomas shifted his focus. He started a band, with a tall, laid-back guitarist named Nate Silas Richardson. They went on the road. Richardson wrote the music. Dr. Thomas spoke. The show kept growing. Dr. Thomas lined up performance dates across the United States extolling his themes about aging differently.

I met up with him in Montclair, New Jersey. Like Suellen Beatty, I had to travel a few thousand kilometers to get him to sit down for an interview. It was scheduled for 10 a.m. at the Montclair High School, but it would be hours before he settled in for a talk.

At 10:30, Dr. Thomas stood outside the auditorium, clutching a giant cup of iced tea, emphasis on the ice, when a woman who sings in his theater troupe said, "Here, Dr. Bill" and shoved a second enormous glass of the same drink in his left hand.

"I like my tea," he explained, laughing.

Thomas downed lemony caffeine as his traveling gang of academics and musicians assembled the set for the day's performance of Changing Aging, or as Dr. Thomas calls it, his rock 'n' roll tour about growing old. It would be easy to say this is the quintessential boomer act, to make aging cool, sort of like the septuagenarian Rolling Stones, except most of his fellow performers are millennials.

Dr. Thomas is now in his late 50s and the elder of this tour. The timing for disruption could not be better. To quote Dr. Thomas's posts on his Changing Aging website, the outgoing elders, the "quiet generation" who lived through the 1920s Depression and accepted life's circumstances with stoicism, are being replaced by the boomers, a vastly different demographic.

"These are men and woman who grew up questioning the dominant narrative of the time: sexism, racism, the Vietnam War," Dr. Thomas wrote. "They're looking for a new framework with which to understand aging. They're looking for a new story to tell. We believe in possibility, change, growth, optimism, spirit and soul."

Dr. Thomas walked down the aisle, surveying the auditorium in the Montclair High School, an old stone building surrounded by colonial homes, the kind with wide front porches and crisp wooden trim.

School in Montclair was closed for teacher training, and Dr. Thomas's tour had 300 tickets sold for afternoon and evening shows, exploring the realities of aging, or living with dementia, or isolation, which is relatable at any age, really. Over the years he has added University of Nevada, Reno, academic Dr. Jennifer Carson, and communicators Kavan Peterson and Kyrie Carpenter to the troupe.

Dr. Thomas also brought in Samite Mulondo, a musician originally from Uganda who now lives in New York State. Mulondo returns to Africa frequently, bringing his music as therapy to countries where child soldiers and many others have been traumatized by war. Mulondo and Dr. Thomas appeared in the Sundance-celebrated documentary *Alive Inside: A Story of Music and Memory* that documented the ability of music to connect with people who have dementia, tapping into the deep emotional memories that remain long after logic has disappeared.

Together, Dr. Thomas's troupe has traveled in a bus from Boulder, Colorado, to Oak Park, Illinois. Today they are a 45-minute train ride from New York City. When the first of two shows begins at 2 p.m. they will sing, perform monologues about old age (Dr. Carson grew up in a Nevada nursing home, where her mother worked as a nurse nicknamed Doris Day), speaking about loss, dementia, joy, family and love.

The tickets were snapped up by people looking for inspiration in their lives or work, seeking alternative ideas to the clichéd end of life in a dreary nursing home. Or, as Dr. Thomas describes the isolation of old-style care, "The house on the hill."

Nobody really wants to live in that house.

This is his 128th show. As always, Thomas is moving on to a new enterprise. Self-reflection ("a benefit of age," he says) has taught him that he has seven years of flat-out enthusiasm for any given project and then another idea emerges. His next plan is already underway, inspired by the questions that people ask him during the show's Ask Dr. Bill Anything lunchtime sessions.

"Nobody ever asked how to move into a nursing home," he says.

When I interviewed him for my *Star* series, Dr. Thomas made a comment that I've never forgotten, so counterintuitive it seemed to a journalist accustomed to hard-core investigations. We filmed him in Rochester, backstage at another theater. He told me that writing about the bad would never lead to the change that could be inspired by the good.

The more stories about healthy aging that people read, about a life phase of rich emotional growth, the more they will expect the same for their loved ones and, one day, themselves.

In Ontario, news of the Butterfly home's success in Peel Region, just west of Toronto, did exactly that. "You've given me hope," reader after reader said. Almost everyone I spoke to, it seemed, had a loved one with dementia. There are always revelations when writing a story, and this time, it was the sheer number of people whose parents or partners were living with cognitive decline.

At Peel Region, the Butterfly project manager Mary Connell gave dozens of tours for other nursing home leaders, advocates, politicians and researchers, all creating a groundswell of support for better care, no matter what the model might be.

When I saw Dr. Thomas that November morning in Montclair, I described the reaction to our "positive investigation." He smiled. "You caught the wave."

I have no idea what he meant by that.

There is, however, a rising tide, so to speak, of 80 million North Americans born between 1946 and 1964. Some will need nursing or retirement homes, while others will seek new ways to live well, very well, if the history of the boomer generation repeats itself.

If they demand it before their power ebbs, change will come.

◎　◎　◎

It is 6 p.m. November 2018.

We are backstage, left. Patrons are arriving for the show when my interview begins.

Dr. Thomas wants to talk about his new project.

"You do this, 130 times, and you get a different perspective," he says of the Ask Dr. Bill Anything lunch sessions he holds at every Changing Aging event.

"People are not asking about nursing home Regulation 42.J. There are some heartbreaking questions about real stuff. Individual situations differ, but the big, big, big struggle if you talk to families and older people is . . . what do you do about the house?

"The problem is in the United States, we give people a fork in the road. Keep the house. Or move into a facility. That is it. That's it! So very rational people say, 'Screw that, I'm keeping the house.' Then trouble ensues. People come up after, saying, 'What do I do? What do I do?' The housing industry is not providing those answers."

He leans in for effect.

"What *should* we do about housing?"

He leans back.

"Well, the house shouldn't crush you. How about that! That would be a good place to start. It shouldn't suck out your money and your health and your energy. It shouldn't isolate you. Let's agree on that."

He could be talking about my parents. I don't mention this personal connection but I could put a bright red check mark beside every point he just made. Is the house draining health? Check. Isolating? Double check.

Maybe we are all just creatures of our demographic, millions of people with aging parents who are trying to figure the next steps. It's almost freeing, what he says about the house, because it makes me realize that it might be okay for my parents to let go. Maybe living independently isn't the end-all, if they spend most of their days sitting alone. Not to mention my mom's exhaustion from cooking three meals a day.

But is there an alternative to institutional living?

"Compact houses that are exquisitely designed for people of different abilities that can be clustered together for neighborliness," he says. "Houses that are affordable. Houses that serve their owners, rather than being served *by* their owners."

Small homes like laneway homes, or those part of Dr. Thomas's latest entrepreneurial project called Minka homes, the Japanese word for "dwellings of the people."

Dr. Thomas took the idea for tiny, sustainable, smart homes to Copenhagen, Denmark, where housing philosophies bear no resemblance to North America's desire for the single-family home with a big garage. He created a partnership in design and philosophy, "pieces of architectural wisdom," with Ax Jensen and Goehring Architects. Together they designed small, accessible spaces, using materials that are manufactured with methods similar to 3D printing, then assembled on-site, like Lego blocks. For now, in the early stages, houses cost roughly $75,000 to $100,000. Dr. Thomas runs Minka with his son, Zachary, and help from Changing Aging writers and performers, like Kyrie Carpenter and Kavan Peterson.

It's a few days after my interview with Dr. Thomas. At the University of Southern Indiana (USI), Dr. Katie Ehlman meets me on campus for my first visit. A Minka home sits in the center of campus. Right now it's a classroom but off campus it is marketed as a home for elders or people with disabilities. It has an open-concept living room with a kitchen. If the ceiling was a regular height, the room would look claustrophobic, but it is at least 14-feet high, with wide windows across the front and sides, so the room is filled with natural light. In the back is a bedroom that opens into a washroom with a walk-in shower with no step up, so a wheelchair can easily roll inside.

Minka's presence is uniting disparate groups on campus, from the engineering students who did soil samples to find the right location for the house, to humanities students and the young people studying health professions, says Dr. Ehlman, professor of gerontology and director of USI's Center for Healthy Aging and Wellness.

"I have not seen momentum like that across disciplines before," Dr. Ehlman says. "I think we all have a touch point. Many of us have aging parents or aging grandparents. Or we know somebody who could even say, 'Yes, if I had a telepresence robot, I could say hi from afar to my great-grandmother who has dementia.'"

USI is using the Minka house as a smart home telehealth lab, responding to elders' desire to age in the community. Dr. Ehlman is leading a five-year project, with the Minka lab as home base, to improve the health of older adults in underserved communities. In Colorado, Minka homes are being considered for affordable housing and a seniors' community. Pennsylvania's Clearfield County Area Agency on Aging, has drawn up a blueprint for the future called the Village of Hope, with Minka homes for people with dementia and their families. "We are seeing some younger parents with dementia, some with children still in high school," said the agency's CEO Kathy Gillespie.

It is hard to get funding for big projects. When I interviewed Gillespie in 2018, she was hoping to break ground on her new community in spring 2019. That didn't happen. She is still fundraising, still pushing her plans forward.

It is difficult to bring new housing ideas, such as tiny houses or granny flats, into traditional neighborhoods. At the Montclair lunch, just after the Ask Dr. Bill Anything session, the local mayor spoke of the need for innovative elder housing, like Minka homes, added to residential yards. He also made it clear that he must listen to the homeowners who oppose the idea of those dwellings, worrying the little houses will change the look or value of their neighborhood.

As the theater seats fill on the other side of the curtains, I ask Dr. Thomas about the mayor's concerns and the challenges of exclusionary zoning for single-family homes. He looks at me the way Elon Musk might stare at someone who questioned the merits of galactic mobility.

The formula for success, Dr. Thomas says, is being written in Vancouver, British Columbia. In fact, since Vancouver's Laneway House Program began in 2009, the program has issued nearly 4,000 permits for laneway homes and granny flats. Those dwellings are increasingly a natural part of Vancouver's urban design. There are plans for another 4,000 homes over the next decade and a push by city planners to make them easier and cheaper to build.

Policymakers are now recognizing the need to adapt, for seniors or affordability. A new California law will allow additional tiny homes in single-family yards. And the City of Toronto recently started its own program for affordable laneway homes with a focus on green roofs and other sustainable materials, declaring little houses perfect for young adults or aging parents.

"Things are not possible," Dr. Thomas says, "until they are possible."

◎  ◎  ◎

It is time for the show to begin.

The Harvard-trained physician is huddled backstage with the bearded guitarist and a young woman whose face shines when she sings.

Before every performance on dementia and life they connect, sharing energy through hands held inches apart. Every show, just before they walk onstage, Dr. Thomas chooses a word or two of inspiration for his fellow performers, although his revelation would work just as well for the people in the audience, waiting for his wisdom on aging.

"Let's sparkle."

◎  ◎  ◎

It was sort of nice, taking care of my dad.

Before my mom was hospitalized, if he happened to pick up the telephone when I called their house, he passed me to my mom. When I visited, my mother held court while my father sat in his chair, not saying too much, other than quizzing me on my knowledge of "the best baseball player in the history of Major League Baseball." All answers led to the Red Sox and Ted Williams, who was the last MLB player to hit over .400. (In 1941, Williams's batting average was .406.) I couldn't tell if these repetitive questions indicated a baseball obsession (true) or the bored mind of a man who has spent years alone in his house with his wife (understandable) or a flicker of decline. Something was off.

It seems odd to say, but this new connection, this kindness for one another, while my mom awaited the heart tests, felt good. It was also terrifying, watching him. I didn't think he was capable of staying on his own, not after seeing him try to walk onto the busy downtown street as cars whizzed past. Was he just impatient? Or not processing the need to wait for the entire red light? He clearly did not think that he needed help. All he wanted was a ride to the hospital to find out when his wife could come home and cook for him. So, on a Saturday afternoon, when he sat with my mom in her hospital room, I chatted with the hospital workers in the hallway, confessing that I didn't know how to manage him alone.

I've always said nursing staff are problem solvers. They told me that he could be admitted to the hospital for tests if I brought him through emergency and told staff the truth, just what I had told them, about a crisis situation and a father who might be confused.

To be fair (to myself) I had been trying, for several months, to get my mom to hire a part-time personal support worker to come by their home, maybe cook some meals, or help with cleaning, someone who could be there in case of an emergency like this. Maybe my mother was not willing to let another woman in her home. Maybe she was proud of her independence. I'm not sure why she refused, but she did.

I slept over that night on the big couch in their living room. The next morning my dad rose early, laid the table with linen placemats, silver spoons and bowls for cereal, in his case, Bran Flakes. They had a vast collection. It was 7 a.m. He was already wearing dress pants and a suit jacket. I checked the valise that was packed on his bed. He had clothes for two nights. I suggested extra socks and underwear, just in case. He refused, looking at me like I was a bossy child, and I got the feeling the temper I saw in him when I was a child, might rush to the surface. We left quickly.

Given what I know about hospital overcrowding, this seemed a risky proposition. When we walked through the emergency department doors at 8 a.m., there was just one other person in the waiting room. Maybe it was a slow weekend. I explained the situation to the intake nurse, repeating the exact words the women in the hallway the day before told me to say. Crisis. Health issues. Can't stay on his own. Wife had a (possible) heart attack.

Four hours later, the one emergency doctor on shift said he would admit dad to a room upstairs to have him checked out. "Can I have the empty bed in my wife's room?" Dad asked. The doctor's eyes narrowed. I suggested that we not be so presumptuous. The doctor told us to wait.

Another four hours passed. Any minute now, a nurse said. I decided to get my father's overnight bag from the car and told him I'd be back in a few minutes.

When I returned, Dad was sitting on the edge of the bed, his skinny legs swinging angrily.

"The other doctor came in and told me to go home," he said loudly.

"What?" I asked.

It was the tall guy who had seen my mom in her room the day before. Instead of speaking to my mom, who sat upright in bed, he listed her health issues to me. At the time, I said, "My mom likes to speak for herself." Frankly, my mother has honed the art of self-advocation to a virtuosic skill. The public health care system owes her nothing

Dad said the doctor from yesterday arrived for his shift and, walking by, pointed at him, saying, "Why are you here?"

"I told him I'm going to stay here so my daughter can go back to work in Toronto."

Oh dear.

Of course, there was some truth to my father's statement. I did have to go to work. Toronto is a 90-minute drive from my parents' town (two-and-a-half hours in gridlock), and later that week I had to fly to New Jersey. But it was just as true that my mother's stay in the hospital exposed an even greater problem: my father seemed confused and at risk of hurting himself. Where else, in a crisis situation, could a family go for help? There was nowhere else to turn in this small town. The whole situation made me feel sick and terrified. Suddenly I understood what other families have gone through all of these years, people who called the *Star* when there was nowhere else to turn, crying into the phone, asking for help.

Feeling very Scottish, I approached the doctor, suggesting he explain his decision. Before he could begin, I told him of my father's confusion, fragility, lack of balance, and surprised myself by succinctly quoting statistics on the overall cost of falls among the elderly to the health care system, even providing the source of those statistics.

His eyes rolled upward toward the fluorescent lights.

I noted a crisis situation, with nowhere to turn. "Haven't you planned for this?" he asked. Well, I had tried to get them to hire a personal support worker, but I couldn't really throw my mom under the bus for completely ignoring those suggestions, not when she was upstairs after suffering a possible heart attack.

The doctor said there might be a room, but we'd have to wait and we would likely be charged for the stay, instead of using Ontario's universal health insurance plan. How much would that cost? He couldn't say.

I had no idea if I should authorize what could be thousands of dollars in expenses. My mother would be displeased. The adrenalin that initiated this emergency-room confrontation disappeared. Left with no additional facts with which to press my father's case, I started repeating myself, aware that this was not a winning tactic but unable to stop. "I think we should end this conversation," he said, not unkindly.

He left.

I sat with my father, who looked so small, so forlorn. I felt tears on my face, a surprise, as I was not expecting this depth of emotion. The doctor moved on with his rounds, looking into our little room with a bit of a smile. I turned away, furious with myself for giving in to emotion.

"I'm so sorry I've done this to you," my dad said, his head hanging.

A few minutes later I stood at the nurses' station, trying to find out how much a night in the hospital might cost. No one could answer. A social worker in a handknit sweater approached. The doctor, she told me, was not aware that a room was available in the rehabilitation wing. Dad could go there and over the next few days, specialists would do some tests. Her eyes were kind.

And off he went, following a nurse to the rehab unit, which looked a bit like a nursing home. Dad had a shared room and a new nurse asking him questions.

"Do you know why you are here?" she asked him.

He nodded.

"So my daughter can go back to work in Toronto."

## CHAPTER THREE

# Park Springs and Pebblebrook:
## Making Dementia Care More Humane

EVERY TIME JULIA GREW MORE FRAGILE and her dementia a little bolder, her three children had to find a new home to care for her. It didn't take long, usually a year, before the administrators told the family that Miss Julia's needs exceeded the services offered. It is hard to imagine that a family of their stature would have such a struggle, since her eldest son, Johnny, would soon enough be elected to the United States Senate and her youngest, Andy, was a commercial property developer who built shopping malls and offices across their hometown of Atlanta. The DNA that made the Isaksons want to build was a family legacy. Andy's paternal grandfather came from a family of carpenters in Östersund, Sweden, a city close enough to the Arctic Circle to share the radiance of its midnight sun. In 1903, a young Andrew Isakson left Sweden, choosing his destination by pointing to a map of the southern United States. His finger fortuitously landed in the subtropical locale that would become the town of George West, Texas, founded by George West, a venture cattle rancher. Andrew created his own job, erecting sturdy brick houses and later his son, Edwin, discovered he had a gift for selling homes.

Ed Isakson went on to run Atlanta's Northside Realty, a brokerage with 1,000 agents selling houses across the region. His eldest son, Johnny, joined him in real estate before Georgia politics called, and his youngest, Andy, built his first mall at age 25. The emerging Isakson dynasty was an American immigrant success story, proving that hard work and a bit of good fortune can lead to a very comfortable life. And it lasted for a long time.

There was no drama in the way life changed, just old age and its unexpected frailties. There are term limits in politics and, unexpectedly, in parents too. They surprise us by growing frail and suddenly a gentle spouse is left confused when her husband is diagnosed with cancer and within months, gone. Julia's Alzheimer's disease was already part of her life, but now the man she met as a young woman, who wooed her with hand-written notes of love, whose personality consumed every room he stepped into, well, he was no longer at her side. Her dementia intensified, taking up the space that Ed once filled.

The Isakson children, two sons and a daughter, took turns sleeping at the independent-living home where Julia and Ed had moved a year earlier. It was a beautiful space, two apartments renovated into one, with dark hardwood floors and room for her antiques. Julia stayed with a live-in helper and a year later, when that arrangement ended, her children could see she needed a higher level of care. The search began. The homes they found were never great, just the best available. There is a difference. She would move five times in her final years of life, and each new home would last about a year before the administrators would say, "We can't care for your mother any longer." The search would begin anew, always with a hope of finding a home that would give a bit of love too.

It was the first move that worried her children the most, leaving behind the apartment she had shared with her husband. It had her thick, beautiful rugs, her red-and-pink sets of heavy china and the wooden table that, for decades, held the weight of her meals, the fried chicken, turnip greens and the cornbread she'd cook like pancakes in a frying pan, butter melting on top. Now, in the mid-1990s, the Isakson children had to tell their mom that she needed to leave most of her possessions and move into a new, tiny home. This facility offered a type of "memory care" for people living with dementia. Julia's room was painted a shade of hospital white, with baggy curtains. Their greatest fear was that Julia would refuse to leave her home, traumatized by the separation of her old life and the next chapter that held the promise of being a lot less vibrant. Her world was shrinking. Julia was leaving a 3,000-square-foot apartment and moving to a 600-square-foot room in the best home her children could find. As Alzheimer's diminished her brain's functions, Julia's vocabulary shrank, and her spatial skills declined, leaving her lipstick a touch askew. Researchers say that people with dementia lose their ability to reason but hold on to their feelings, and Andy noticed that his mom still seemed attuned to her children's emotions. She might have felt their fear over this transition, because even with few words, Julia seemed to calm her children, accepting her new home graciously.

One problem emerged. Something was missing, left behind. She wanted to return to her old apartment. She struggled to pull out the words, but could only say, "It's mine." Sometimes she grew angry, becoming a person Andy did not know. Something was missing, something that mattered.

In the first few weeks after her move, Julia's children organized a schedule to keep her busy. One weekend, she stayed with her eldest son and his family at their lake home. Later Andy invited her back to his house in Atlanta's historic Roswell community. Andy's home was once his parents' summer house, built by his dad in 1963 on the edge of the Chattahoochee River, the slow, southern waters that emerge from the Blue Ridge Mountains and meander through Atlanta to the Florida Panhandle.

It was a magical childhood place, too special to let go, so Andy rebuilt it, making it his family home. On a Sunday in the mid-1990s Andy brought his mom here for the day, spending most of the

48

afternoon with her, sitting on the deck beside the river. At dinner they stood in the kitchen, leaning against the white countertop that was built like a bar, watching Andy's wife as she cooked. Andy and his mom, still so pretty, were trying to have a conversation. Julia, who had always been a sweet mom, was getting agitated, her brow furrowing and fingers fluttering as she tried to find her words. Andy was growing increasingly worried that she wanted to move back into the apartment, or bring all of her antiques, her china place settings and crystal bowls to her tiny new room. That night Julia had something to say and eventually, she said it.

"I want to go back."

*Oh no*, Andy thought.

Julia looked at her son. "It's mine . . . You took it."

Andy didn't know what "it" was. "What do you want, Mom? What is 'it'?" he asked. She was silent, staring at the countertop.

Andy tried to use logic to at least deduce the size of "it." Is it bigger than a bread box? Smaller than a shoebox? None of those questions led to the answer, only his mother's insistence that she be returned to her old apartment, where her possessions remained in various stages of packing. Andy sighed. He helped her into the passenger seat of his SUV, and they drove for ten minutes in silence to the brown brick building. As he opened the door to her old apartment, a bit shaky, Julia breezed past him and, paying no mind to her china plates and antiques, she disappeared into the bedroom. By the time Andy caught up to her, she had climbed onto a little step stool and was reaching deep into the closet. She soon emerged triumphantly with a small metal box.

Without a glance at her candlesticks and crystal bowls, Julia marched straight out the door of the final home she had shared with her husband. As they drove to her new home, Andy looked side-ways at his mom, clutching that little box, smiling. He was curious. But he was also patient. He waited until his mom was safely inside her little room at the memory care center.

"Okay, Mom," he said. "What's with the box?"

They were standing beside her bed, with its crisp white comforter, when Julia opened the lid, turning the box upside down. Out spilled page after page of notes, love letters, written by Andy's father 50 years earlier after they met on a double date and he arranged a change of partners, charming his way into the heart of Miss Julia Baker. All these years she had kept the letters written by a young man in love.

And Andy realized, this was what mattered to her, more than any of her beautiful possessions. When she read those letters, Julia could feel her husband's love again as if their courtship was starting anew. His words tapped into deep, emotional memories that gave her joy.

When Andy tells that story now, his eyes redden, filling with tears.

"She looked like she was holding up thousand-dollar bills or gold coins," he says.

"It was a lesson in what really matters, at the end. You know, at the end of the day, the bottom of the barrel, the jumping-off place, whatever you want to call it, it makes you think about what really matters.

"That was the gift she gave to me."

◎ ◎ ◎

Andy Isakson made his money in bricks and mortar.

He avoided his father's invitation to join the residential side of real estate. Instead, he built shopping malls like his grandfather and, later, millions of square feet in low-rise office buildings. He recalls his dad telling him to stay away from commercial real estate, saying it was too complicated, but as Andy likes to say, "I like complicated."

Life has its complexities too. His dad died in 1993, and his mom followed in 1998. "When your parents are both gone, it makes you realize — you're next," he says.

He started feeling an inner push to do more with his life, something that might help others sliding into their later years. It didn't matter where he was, driving to work, or sitting on his deck with a beer, Andy's mind was working, thinking about the fleeting passage of time, about his father, a man "you wouldn't want to cross," who died within a few months of his cancer diagnosis and his mom, Julia, who spent her final years in an imperfect system, even if she had her children's love.

"I feel good about my mother and what I did with her in all those years," he says. "If you don't feel good, it can come back and haunt you. It wasn't haunting me. But I learned a lot by going through it, I learned a lot from a consumer standpoint. I saw it as an opportunity to do something that would help a lot of people. And I wanted to have a purpose in my life."

So, he did what the Isaksons do. He started building.

In 2004, the Park Springs retirement community opened its doors. It looks like a ski resort designed by architects from Europe. It is tucked away from the Atlanta suburb of Stone Mountain, winding rows of yellow and gray villa apartments, with peaked gables and dark shingled roofs. It started as a retirement campus where seniors bought into the community and paid a monthly fee for an all-inclusive lifestyle, choosing homes, cottages or apartments. Most people arrived in their 70s after financially rewarding careers. One man, Fred, captained a nuclear submarine and later worked as the facility manager for the Pentagon. Andy speaks of him with reverence, saying, "Fred knows everything anyone would need to know about satellites and fiber-optic cables." When the cable company comes to Park Springs, Fred and another 80-year-old get in there, splicing the cables, making sure the job is done properly. "It's their hobby, it gives them purpose," Andy says.

It's a successful demographic, with enough money to pay the entrance fee starting at roughly US$200,000 to US$550,000, which, Andy says, is "90 percent refundable when you leave."

(Usually, to the individual's estate.) There is also a monthly fee ranging from $3,000 to $5,000. That fee covers some meals and all the recreation offered on site. It's basically an all-inclusive resort, minus the beach. When Andy started building Park Springs, the campus-style communities were unusual, at least in Georgia. Now they are starting to catch on in the United States and Canada. Some are costly, others less so. The goal among seniors' advocates is to make sure that people without the means to afford a fabulous lifestyle still have options. At Park Springs in Atlanta in 2018, it all feels like living on a luxury cruise ship that never leaves port. There are four restaurants, including a dining room with 50-foot vaulted ceilings and fireplaces built into each of the three walls that partially divide the room. Women dress for dinner. One tall lady arrives in a long narrow dress, glittering with black sequins, gliding into the dining room with her husband. Down the hall is a pub with dark wood tables and a rich, abstract oil painting hanging behind the bar. Andy collects art, and there's a small fortune hanging here. In the pub, people sit at round tables with a glass of wine or a rum, sometimes meeting the same group, sometimes switching it up for new conversation. The ladies at my table describe the activities here: the painting, the woodshop, tai chi, pickleball and swimming. There are water volleyball teams that compete regularly. There are guest lectures, including resident speakers, who've had careers at the Centers for Disease Control and Prevention, in banking, theology and the arts. There are book clubs and monthly breakfast clubs. It's almost exhausting to hear their daily schedule. "It's giving me extra years of life," says one woman.

After the independent living community opened, Andy watched the friendships flourish and deepen as the years passed, and he realized he was not finished building.

Park Springs was fine for those who could live on their own, even if they needed a bit of extra help. But what happens when some of those people develop dementia? Or need more extensive nursing care? The odds are that many residents will experience some type of cognitive decline. The Alzheimer's Society of America says the disease is the sixth leading cause of death in the United States and so far it cannot be prevented or cured.

The constant uprooting to a new home, one that can handle advancing medical needs as age progresses, is painful for residents and their families. It hurts to say goodbye to friends, or even a spouse, as one person grows frail and has to move to another institution. So Andy made a business decision: he would create a new home on the same piece of land, smaller than Park Springs, with households for people living with moderate and advanced dementia. Pebblebrook, as it would be called, would have a skilled nursing floor for the very sick or people in a palliative stage of care. On the main floor, just off the entrance, where he'd later hang an original Dr. Seuss print, would be the rehabilitation center, stocked with exercise machines and free weights. Physiotherapists would work with people recovering from injuries, strengthen legs that grow weak without regular exercise. People would practice the skills of daily living, how to get in and out of a car or walking on different surfaces, such as carpeting or cement. There would be a kitchen too, with jars and twist tops to strengthen hands. Even though the original building had an area for memory care and skilled nursing, Andy wanted to expand it and make it better in his new creation.

In real estate vernacular, Pebblebrook is the dealmaker. People want to be able to age in place. Memory care is expensive and, Andy says, despite the $7,000 monthly fees for each resident, it doesn't boost the overall profit margin of his company. Still, Andy believes the addition of nursing home levels of care is worth the investment.

"No matter if you are for profit or non-profit, the business has to work," Andy says. "There is a business side. This is not all from the bottom of the heart. Good care is good business. People want good care.

"We have a large campus, and a lot of people come independently. And they come in for the reason that they want to know if they ever need it, we have good health care. So we focus on good health care. Maybe it's not the highest-margin part of our business, but it really is an amenity that makes things go for us. When people see it, they know that we're on to something. I think that more people are seeing this and are getting ready to do it in their new projects. It's going to catch on. It is a better mousetrap."

It's the dementia household, downstairs, that captivates him.

Sometimes Andy comes here for lunch. He likes the vibe, the energy and laughter, ever since he hired David Sheard to bring the Butterfly program to Atlanta. It's the first appearance of Butterfly in America, inspired after Andy saw some women from Alberta, where several Butterfly homes exist, talk about their work at a conference held by the U.S. Pioneer Network. He had been looking for something special for his memory care households, something that could help the people living here feel love. After a lot of Skype sessions between Atlanta and Sheard's office in Brighton, England, Andy concluded that Sheard, more than anyone, would have understood his mother's yearning for her husband's letters. He hired Dementia Care Matters to transform the memory households. In spring 2018, two Pebblebrook memory care homes earned the Butterfly accreditation and its highest rating.

◎　◎　◎

The ladies and gentlemen in the moderate dementia home are streaming into the dining room with its huge built-in kitchen — a rarity in long-term care. And what a kitchen it is: open-concept, with stacked ovens and floor-to-ceiling Shaker-style wooden cupboards. The pièce de résistance, though, is the dark granite countertop long enough for three people to sit at the counter, deli-style, and drink sweet black tea, while Chef Trevon Johnson prepares lunch. Chef Trevon trained at the Le Cordon Bleu culinary school in Atlanta, drawn to the French training that inspired Julia Child. He smiles when he talks, which is often, one of the reasons Betty, who lives here, has a reserved chair at the counter. "She has it in her mind that me or my partner is her man," he says kindly, as he spoons a ball of scalloped potatoes onto each plate. Lunch today is two thick barbecue ribs or a pulled chicken sandwich in a homemade bun, served with a bowl of creamy Trevon-made coleslaw. It is all cooked in the kitchen, from scratch.

For most of the morning, the members have been dancing to Christmas carol videos playing on the television set. Everyone has their own beat, but Betty is among the best. "She can 'git' down," says Tim Knight, the executive director of health and wellness services Andy hired from Maine after a long search for a creative thinker who understood what he was trying to achieve.

Betty's arrival at Pebblebrook coincided with the home passing Butterfly's 12-month program. By the time Betty moved in, music was a regular part of the day, but for the first two, maybe three weeks, she would not leave her bedroom. She stayed inside, door closed, isolated. She refused to speak.

One day Knight arrived with a small collection of old records picked up at a local thrift store, including a few by a singer whose fans, back in the day, were prone to fainting, a man born in Mississippi in 1935.

Well.

As Knight tells the story, a worker pulled the Elvis album out of its sleeve, centered it on the turntable and carefully lowered the needle. Mercifully, there were no scratches. As the mesmerizing beat of "Jailhouse Rock" began pounding out of the speakers, Betty's bedroom door burst open. Seconds later she appeared, sashaying into the lounge. As Elvis crooned, Betty danced with abandon, doing the twist, up and down, round and round, belting out the lyrics.

Knight and the workers stood, frozen. "Our mouths dropped open," he says. "We actually started to cry. It was one of those moments you hear about. It was an awakening."

Now two black-and-white posters of young Elvis hang at eye level on the front door of Betty's room. A 1970s portrait of Betty and her husband, a good-looking couple, hangs off to the side.

This morning Betty did her share of shimmying and, like the others, she has worked up an appetite. She's sitting in her chair along the granite counter, sipping tea, quietly watching Chef Trevon get the lunch plates ready.

Nearby, Miss Patricia sits with her ladies at a long table. She's tiny, wearing a white jersey top and a navy-blue sweater. Her curls, soft brown, have kept their natural color all these years. From across the room, her dark eyes are shining so warmly, it's as if she's calling to a stranger, "Do come say hello."

"Will you join us for lunch?" Miss Patricia asks, motioning to the chair on her left. Four other ladies sit at the table, smiling. One winks.

Miss Pat, as the workers call her, has chosen Chef Trevon's barbecue ribs for lunch.

"Oh, I do love ribs," she says, placing a white linen napkin in her lap. The ribs, dripping with sweet sauce, sit on a white plate, with a scoop of the yellow potatoes and some of the coleslaw. It looks like an Instagram photo of southern home cooking.

While the other ladies choose pulled-chicken-on-a-bun, Miss Patricia looks down at her plate and smiles. She begins to eat. Between delicate bites she worries about bits of sauce landing on her white shirt.

"Delicious," she declares.

Chef Trevon slides past the table to make sure everyone is enjoying his creations before joining a caregiver named Musa Valentina and residents at a table nearby. At Miss Patricia's table, a worker named Culix Wibonele notices a lady isn't eating, so she chats with her about the food, coaxing her to take a bite of her sandwich. Wibonele slides in and out of conversation with the ladies, with Chef Trevon and her work friend Valentina. "We are a team," she says. "It's good."

Miss Patricia has eaten every last morsel on her plate and with the assistance of a small collection of paper napkins, her face and clothing remain pristine. Wibonele asks about her latest book choice and they discuss it for a few minutes, in detail. "What's it called?" Wibonele asks. "Oh, I don't remember the title," Miss Patricia says.

"What was the name of the book you wrote?" Wibonele says.

Miss Patricia smiles. *"This Dialogue of One."*

"Miss Pat was an English professor," says Wibonele. They smile at each other.

"I taught at Agnes Scott College," Miss Patricia explains. She started her career as a newspaper reporter but loved academia and earned a PhD before arriving at Agnes Scott College, a liberal arts college for women, in downtown Decatur, Georgia.

"What did you teach?" Wibonele prompts her.

"Oh, Shakespeare and Milton. The old boys," she says, with a toss of her head.

Wibonele disappears momentarily, returning from Miss Patricia's room with a copy of her book. *This Dialogue of One: The Songs and Sonnets of John Donne.*

"I don't know why it is here," Miss Patricia says. "My mother must have packed it in the box for me."

Chef Trevon appears with plates of cookies. "It's National Cookie Day," he announces. (Celebrated every December 4 since 1987.) "Miss Pat, would you like some cookies?" Why, yes, she would. The cookies are warm, baked in the oven a few feet away.

Miss Patricia slides her book across the table to protect it from greasy fingers. She has two cookies, chocolate and peanut butter. She bites into the peanut butter cookie. Her eyes flutter.

"Oh my," she says.

By the time she finishes the chocolate cookie, Miss Patricia is asking Wibonele to get the recipe from Chef Trevon.

"He won't give it to *me*," Wibonele says. "But he might tell *you*. TREVON!"

He peers around the kitchen wall.

"Tell him I want to know the name of his new girlfriend," whispers Miss Patricia. They laugh, their heads lowered together, co-conspirators. Chef Trevon awaits his fate.

"Number one," Wibonele tells him, "Miss Pat wants to know the name of your girlfriend. And number two, she wants the recipe for your chocolate cookies."

Chef Trevon smiles.

A few minutes later he slides a copy of the recipe next to Miss Patricia. It's written in blue magic marker, on a white paper towel.

"Three cups of chocolate chips!" she exclaims, taking in the ingredients. "No wonder they were so good."

She reads the rest of the recipe. "I can bake these."

With that, Miss Patricia places the napkin inside the cover of the book she authored about a 17th-century English poet and, taking her leave, delivers a final pronouncement.

"They are as good as cookies could be."

◎　◎　◎

TREVON JOHNSON'S CHOCOLATE CHIP COOKIES
2 ¼ cups of flour
3 cups of chocolate chips
1 cup of butter
1 cup of sugar
2 eggs
Bake at 350°F for 25 minutes

◎　◎　◎

Hanging on the wall in the entrance to Pebblebrook is a series of framed black-and-white photographs, professionally done, of the people who work in the home.

Andy calls the staff care partners. Most are nursing assistants, some are registered nurses or administrators, like Tim Knight. The images show them in moments of laughter, eyes crinkling, or staring into the camera, confident, the photographer catching each person in their moment. It's unusual to see a home celebrate its workers so . . . artfully. In the memory care center, each worker's life is detailed in a binder of pictures and personal stories, so families can see who is caring for their loved ones. Culix Wibonele immigrated years earlier from Kenya and is the mother of four boys. She lives here in Stone Mountain, where homes are still affordable and the commute to work is quick, a bonus that cannot be overstated. Gridlock is Atlanta's narrative flow. It's a conversation that unites, from business executives to Uber drivers, the same way Canadians complain about the weather.

Like the workers, the people who live here, the members, all have a personal photo gallery displayed on the walls outside their room. One gentleman has several perfectly aligned rows of framed university degrees, awards and professional citations. "Some families get a bit competitive," says Tim Knight, the executive director. Miss Priscilla was a schoolteacher. The walls outside her room are empty. "She keeps taking down her pictures and brings them in the room with her," he says. "She wants them close." For a long time Miss Priscilla wouldn't sleep at night. Instead she'd walk, endlessly, through the hallways. Every time the workers would put her to bed and turn out the light, she'd appear moments later, an apparition in a nightgown. Butterfly training gives workers the freedom to think intuitively about the people in their care, to be close enough to understand their needs and even to show love. Not every health-care worker is cut out for it, but those who are comfortable with it can shine. One night, says Knight, Miss Priscilla's care partner brought pajamas to work and changed into them after dinner. When it came time to put Miss Priscilla to bed, her worker climbed onto the mattress, curling up beside her. Miss Priscilla, comforted by the warmth of another person, fell into a deep slumber. Most of us spend at least part of our adult lives lulled to sleep by the breath or physical warmth of a person we love. Why would that desire for connection, for security, go away as the years pass?

It has become a bedtime routine, and Miss Priscilla now gets a full night's rest, leaving her happier during the day. Her family appreciates the kindness, Knight says. He chuckles, telling a story of the worker's new schedule. "One night, the other care partners were looking for her and found her in Miss Priscilla's room, both in their pajamas, both sound asleep. When we heard about it, we just laughed. It's hard to get upset about that."

◎　◎　◎

Freedom to innovate. It's a key part of the Butterfly program, now called Meaningful Care Matters, offering people comfort in their final years. Freedom allowed 87-year-old Marjorie Bittinger to feel at peace, while placing her husband of 64 years in the home.

Leaving a husband, wife or parent in a care home can lead to a world of emotional pain. In my years researching stories on long-term care, I've spoken with hundreds of families and even if those families gave selfless care or if jobs took them too far away to help, most feel a terrible guilt dropping off a parent or spouse and walking away.

Guilt is an emotion that can torment people, especially when care goes wrong. Even when it goes right. Some children feel shame over the ability of a caregiver, a stranger, to look after Dad when they couldn't. A wife feels resentment because a worker can bring out the humor in her husband when he hadn't laughed with her for years.

The act of letting go, it's never easy. Marjorie took an innovative approach.

When I meet her, she is sitting with her husband in the dining room on the advanced side of the memory care home. John Bittinger is 86 years old, with the face and shoulders of a man who spent his life taller and stronger than most. Now he has Parkinson's disease and Lewy body dementia.

Marjorie is dressed in slim dark jeans, a crisp striped shirt and a blue kerchief knotted at her neck. "I'm admiring your necklace," she calls out.

"It's the Celtic cross," I tell her.

"I have one too," she says.

"I have been living here with my husband, but I just moved out," she continues, seeking conversation.

Tim Knight is here. "How's that going for you?" he asks her.

"It's fine," Marjorie says, "but the commute is tiring, and my sons have been saying, 'Mom, you have to get home before it's dark.' I tell them, I'm not ten years old. But it's a half-hour drive — in the good weather."

Knight nods and sighs heavily. "I've been talking about the traffic." The disembodied voice of a worker, somewhere inside the kitchen, calls out, "It's a nightmare!"

Marjorie agrees with the voice. "It is a nightmare. I drove into Atlanta this week, and I hope I never have to do it again."

While John waits for lunch, Marjorie takes me to his room for a chat. A few pictures hang on the walls but most are packed away because John just moved here after living in a larger room with Marjorie until a month ago. She came for a tour of the memory care home in spring 2018 and asked the manager if she could move in with her husband, just to make sure. The manager said, Hmmm, interesting, yes.

"Eight months," she says, of her stay in memory care. "I was not ready to turn him loose and say goodbye.

"Well. Walk it back. We, Bitt and I, went to Peabody Demonstration School in Nashville. He started there in the sixth grade. I went there in the ninth grade. I have known Bitt since ninth grade. We dated. He was in a fraternity. I was in a sorority. We exchanged pins, so we were pinned in high school.

"I guess it was selfishness on my part. We had been married for 64 years. I wasn't ready to just drop him, so to speak. I wanted to know more about the daily schedule and just really wasn't ready to say goodbye in that sense."

Marjorie opens the door to his closet. She bends over, rummaging through a box. She seems agile and later tells me she and Bitt spent their later years working out at LA Fitness. She drags the white cardboard box out of the closet. Inside are framed photographs and snapshots of their life together, all 64 years. For half of that time John Bittinger worked for the First National Bank of Atlanta, while she taught elementary school and raised two sons. She's pulling out snapshots, speaking quickly.

"Bitt was an elder in our church. Here's a picture of his mother and father in Jacksonville. His father was a Presbyterian minister. Daddy Bitt. Now, here's one of our homes, at Lake Capri (a community of mid-century homes 20 miles east of Atlanta). We lived there for 36 years, and Bitt built the deck.

"This one, this is when he was in the navy." It's a black-and-white photograph, five rows of young men in dark uniforms and white sailor hats. They would all be in their mid-80s now, like Bitt. The men in the front are holding a flag that says *R.T.C. Bainbridge, 239th Co.*

She holds up a framed photo of her young husband in a tie at work, holding a ledger with a black dial telephone in the background. "This is Bitt, working at his desk. And here he was, in the American Legion.

"In recent years, what Bitt was known for is marathon running," Marjorie says, standing upright.

Impressive. "Which marathon?" I ask politely.

"Which?" she says. "He's run 27!"

Marjorie drags the box closer and pulls out a framed Marine Corps Marathon certificate, signed on October 28, 2001, by Joseph Composto, Brigadier General USMC. At age 69 Bitt ran the 26.2-mile course in Arlington, Virginia, with a time of 4:45:07. That race came six weeks after the terrorist attacks of 9/11, and organizers dedicated it to the "memory of our fellow citizens who lost their lives, the survivors of these tragic events and the selfless heroes who worked tirelessly to save lives on September 11, 2001."

Her voice is high. For so long, life unfolded nicely. Her marriage, her two sons and later her husband's retirement with the freedom to travel. Now those years are held in a box of photographs, and Marjorie is learning to let go, allowing new people to care for Bitt, giving him a new family.

"I wanted Bitt to be in a place where I felt like, above everything else, he would be cared for in the closest manner to being cared for at home."

She speaks slowly, carefully.

"So, thinking about the concept behind the Butterfly Model, it seemed the closest to 'home.' I like the idea . . . that there would be people . . . who not only would assume the responsibility of caring physically for Bitt, but they would care for him in an emotional way as well. And it seemed that the philosophy behind the Butterfly Model was one of embracing the member, as though they were a member of a family . . .

"We have always been a close-knit family, even though each of us, Bitt and I, are only children. So, family has always been very important. We knew we couldn't have just one child, we needed to have at least two. So, it was just the idea of family. It was the deciding factor. He would not just be somewhere — he would be a part of something."

She blinks quickly. She starts rummaging through the photo box, pulling out more pictures, setting them aside to hang on the walls of Bitt's new room over his single bed. She looks so youthful in her straight-legged jeans. We talked about exercising throughout all the years of life, and she says she misses her workouts at LA Fitness.

I tell her about visiting Montclair, New Jersey, where Dr. Bill Thomas, the traveling geriatrician, performed his theater show and how he told the audience that "motion is lotion," meaning that more than any drug, exercise keeps joints lubricated and mobile.

Marjorie nods enthusiastically.

"Now, I have talked your head off and I am so sorry."

She will pack up the box now but keep out the photographs of Bitt in his running shorts to hang on the wall of his bedroom. When she's finished, Marjorie will walk down the hall to find her husband, and before the evening grows dark, drive herself home.

◎ ◎ ◎

In a storage room, amidst the stacked folding chairs, Andy Isakson is talking about legacy.

It's a narrow room, painted white, near the main entrance to Pebblebrook. Leaning against the wall is a 26-foot oil painting, on three canvases, he commissioned from a South Carolina artist named Tarleton Blackwell. The mural was Andy's way of honoring those who live and work here.

Some of the images were inspired by photos that Andy shot on his phone, capturing the moments of, say, a man who lived here, surrounded by his grandchildren, smiling with pride. Or two women hugging, a worker and a daughter who came for a visit, six months after her mother died. The woman who comforted the mother, as she eased from this world, has her arms around the daughter. They are crying and laughing.

Andy leans against the wall, taking in the scene.

"When I look at this, from our perspective here, with our care partners, this is what we do, this is the purpose, and this is the legacy of our life. That's why people work in this business; they could work in a restaurant or retail. This is hard work, but there is purpose to it."

It hasn't been hung yet. For now it leans against the storage room wall, deft strokes of paint showing the passage of life and deep, meaningful connections created as time marches on. If the love letters written by her husband meant the world to Julia Isakson, this painting may be the possession, at least for now, that means the most to her son.

"It was impactful for me," he says of his mother's yearning. "It told me what is important in life.

A legacy. It can be as small as a box of letters. Or it can grow, spreading wide, creating art through the act of caregiving.

◎　◎　◎

As it turned out, my mother had not had a heart attack, a diagnosis that seemed increasingly unlikely after I watched my parents waltz in her hospital room. A few minutes after the dance, my mother announced that she felt a swoon coming on and collapsed, delicately, in bed. She shared this information with the doctor on rounds. He did not appear overly concerned, although he kept her in the hospital the entire weekend for the full cardiac workup when the specialist returned on Monday.

With the confirmation that she had the heartbeat of a 70-year-old, her focus returned to The Leg, as she called it, and the swelling that was now coming to the surface. It was the same leg she had injured six months earlier and, as we were occasionally reminded, more than a few times through the decades.

Like many daughters, I've received a lifelong master class on guilt. It was now time to use the fundamentals and insist she hire a private caregiver lest I be forced into another showdown with an emergency room doctor.

She agreed, or gave the appearance of it, and returned to an empty house, saying she was grateful she didn't have to cook. My dad stayed in the rehab unit, with a warning sign taped to the front of his walker that said *IMPULSIVE*, or so my mother claimed.

When I left my dad, he seemed pretty chipper as he sat for dinner at a table with two ladies and a couple of men. As he put the napkin in his lap, he was grinning and talking. When I drove back to Toronto, it made me wonder: What if he is just lonely? What if he is losing his social skills, sitting alone all day with no one to talk to but his wife?

In the meantime, Ontario's home care system kicked in, sending nurses to check on my mom's left leg. Mom provided us with condition updates. "The Leg is swollen." Or "The Leg is black from bruising."

I once suggested she stop calling it The Leg and just refer to it as her leg, which was an error in my way of thinking. She reminded me that The Leg had been through a lot, including the time she injured it falling through the wooden planks of a board-walk while volunteering for my grade four class trip.

"Not the boardwalk story!!!" my sister texted from her new home in California. "You cannot win!!"

I texted back. "I had blocked it until today."

She responded, "Now you will need at least a year of therapy."

I told her I was drinking an organic Ontario wine which, as the evening progressed, seemed to take off the edge, although probably not as nicely as her Napa Valley red.

When my dad was sent home a few days later, more nurses and personal support workers appeared. My mother scheduled their visits, and when they arrived, she entertained them all with stories of her various ailments, which she could recite in reverse chronological order, back to childhood. She claimed exhaustion from so much time in the spotlight. My dad grew annoyed when a worker sat on the couch and slept. My parents didn't need to be bathed by a stranger, but it sure would have helped if someone picked up groceries or ran errands, services that would make their continued independence easier to manage. Government-funded home care didn't offer personal shopping services, so it wasn't long before my parents had the workers reassigned.

My mom's leg took months to improve, mostly because she was 90 years old, but also because she insisted on cooking and cleaning, even though we found a paid caregiver she liked, a woman who once worked as a hairstylist in Europe.

We all had to insist that mom lie down, with The Leg elevated, to help it heal.

One day, she said something unthinkable, unimaginable even, especially for a woman with a vast collection of Royal Doulton china.

"It might be time to look at a retirement home."

CHAPTER FOUR

# The Little Blue House and the Glenner Town Square: New Ideas in Day Programs

THE HEADLINE ON HIS 1995 OBITUARY IN THE *New York Times* read, "Dr. George G. Glenner, 67, Dies; Researched Alzheimer's Disease."

Dr. Glenner, the *Times* said, had spent decades studying the beta amyloid protein, the plaque in the brain that is linked to Alzheimer's. He became ill from the same plaque, in his heart. After his death, researchers would continue to build on his pioneering work, exploring the degenerative brain condition that has impacted the lives of so many.

The *Times* focused on Dr. Glenner's work as a physician and researcher. He had graduated from Johns Hopkins University in 1954 with a degree in medicine, and later studied surgery and pathology at Mount Sinai Hospital in New York City and the Mallory Institute at Boston City Hospital. After 12 years at the National Institutes of Health in Bethesda, Maryland, he was recruited by the University of California, San Diego, as a physician and research pathologist.

Hard science was his focus but there was another side to his work, a softer story but equally powerful.

Dr. Glenner and his wife, Joy, had a published telephone number. Family caregivers struggling with the confusion, loneliness and heartbreak of Alzheimer's disease often cold-called their home for advice and a bit of solace.

Here is a story that didn't make it into the obituary:

It was nearly midnight when the phone rang on an otherwise uneventful evening in March 1982. Dr. Glenner and Joy were in his laboratory when their answering service patched through an emergency call. Dr. Glenner heard sobbing. On the other end, a man's words exploded: wife . . . dying . . . dementia . . . I have cancer . . . no one to take care of her . . . a loaded gun for both of us . . .

The caller was an elderly man who planned to end it that night, with a bullet for his wife and himself. Dr. Glenner kept him on the phone, passing a note with the man's name on it, asking Joy to call police for help. He kept the man talking with his soft Philadelphia accent, the kind of voice that makes people feel safe, and promised to visit the very next day. The police arrived at the man's home to find two people, one desperate, both critically ill. The Glenners saved the man and wife from a violent ending.

The next morning they drove to the couple's home in Julian, a little town in the Cuyamaca Mountains in San Diego County, and helped with arrangements to get both into a nursing home.

At the end of the day, Dr. Glenner looked at his wife and said, "What are you doing tomorrow?"

Joy recalls saying, "What do you mean?"

He said, "It's time we started taking care of the living."

Within a few days the Glenners found a little cottage in the Hillcrest neighborhood of San Diego and with friends from the community, began the renovation needed to create a daytime respite center for people with dementia, offering some hours of freedom and peace of mind to family caregivers. Volunteers painted the house blue with white trim. They built ramps to the front door and added a wide awning over the patio, so people could sit outdoors, enjoying the breeze.

At that time, Joy says, there were no day programs for people with dementia so when they applied for a traditional day-care license, the bureaucrat scratched out the word *children* and replaced it with *adults*. Months later, over the 1982 Thanksgiving weekend, the day program opened. It was a homey little place with registered nursing staff, and it offered people with dementia the opportunity to work in the garden, go for walks, bake cookies or dance to the music they loved. Equally important was its support for the families, the caregivers, who are often forgotten. It gave them a few unencumbered hours to relax or run errands. Joy understood their struggle. Her mother had had a series of small strokes that led to dementia, and her father, T.C. Sharp, a Hollywood expert in sound whose career exploded when technology moved from silent film to "talkies," helped to care for her at home.

"We were always the Glenner Alzheimer's *Family* Center," says Joy, now in her 80s. "We recognized that it was a family disease."

The Glenners missed the grand opening because they were invited to the White House to witness President Ronald Reagan sign the proclamation that named November as National Alzheimer's Awareness Month.

The center quickly filled with people. At first, "the little blue house" was simply a trusted place that offered caregivers a break, allowing a husband to keep his job or a daughter to watch her son's soccer game.

It became so much more.

Over the next 38 years the George G. Glenner Alzheimer's Family Care Centers created half a dozen different day programs in greater San Diego with weekly counseling and support groups for informal caregivers, some of whom forged friendships lasting long after their loved ones died. The Glenner husband-and-wife teamwork was recognized with a Presidential Commendation in 1988 during a ceremony with President Ronald Reagan, who was reportedly diagnosed with Alzheimer's six years later. By 2015 Joy was long retired, spending time with her family, and the Glenner organization was ready for a new direction. The incoming CEO, Scott Tarde, was also keen for change, ready to leave his leadership role with a private long-term care company that, he said, kept cutting costs to keep profits intact.

"How much is enough?" he'd asked his company executives.

After a 20-year career, starting as a caregiver and working his way up to a licensed nursing home administrator and, later, a regional director, Tarde had grown cynical that the industry was willing to provide a life of value for elders.

At Glenner, a not-for-profit with a higher calling, Tarde would have the opportunity to create a new vision. As Dr. Glenner and his wife did years earlier, Tarde found inspiration from an unexpected source. His 11-year-old daughter, Mackenzie, came home from school one day, talking nonstop about a trip with her fifth grade Junior Achievement class.

Mackenzie had spent the day in a 10,000-square-foot minicity in San Diego called BizTown, with storefronts posing as a credit union, a television station, a UPS office and a medical clinic, offering children the opportunity to step inside, pick up an order form or stethoscope and imagine a future career.

As Mackenzie bubbled with stories, her father grew curious. That night, he looked up BizTown online, quickly scrolling through the images of the storefronts as his mind clicked into creative mode. He grabbed a piece of graph paper and sketched a community built around an old-fashioned town square. He drew, knowing that people with dementia often live in their memories, and the families most in need of respite are those with parents or spouses in their 70s or 80s, who would have been young in the 1950s and '60s. He gave the square a vintage theme, harkening back to a time when the cars had chrome grilles, tires had whitewalls and the backside of vehicles stretched long past necessary with tailfins inspired by aerospace flight. It was a lot. The vintage style could be modernized, he decided, as a new demographic arrived. For now, if people didn't like overt 1950s styling, then this was probably not the place for them.

Tarde kept drawing. There was a diner with a jukebox, a Central Park outside the city hall, a library, beauty parlor, pool hall, department store, doctor's office (for a real nurse), a pet shop and theater.

Those tightly penciled sketches, with tidy names on each storefront, reflected Tarde's training in reminiscence therapy, a way to prompt people with dementia to connect with their strongest memories, created in their youth and early 30s. It's a period of big life events, the fun times with friends in university, tinkering on the engine of a new car, walking down the aisle to get married or holding a newborn child.

Research into reminiscence therapy has shown some promise, some evidence that it can improve cognition and the sense of well-being, however temporary. There are a lot of different ways to practice reminiscence therapy: individually, in groups, at a museum or a 1950s town square. In a systemic review published in the Cochrane Library in 2018, U.K. researcher and Bangor University professor Bob Woods and his team looked at 16 studies involving 1,749 people living with dementia and found the effects of reminiscence therapy were inconsistent, depending on where and how it was offered. Care homes had the "widest range" of benefits, the research found. The review concluded that reminiscence therapy can "improve quality of life, cognition communication and possibly mood" and called for more research on the benefits. Still, Britain's National Institute for Health and Care Excellence recommends its use along with activities like art, baking, gardening and music therapy. Its June 2019 updated quality standards for people living with dementia said, "Whether it's joining a choir, gardening or enjoying art classes, so many activities can help people live better and trigger precious memories and help reconnect them with their communities."

The next day, Tarde passed his sketch, carefully, to his colleague Lisa Tyburski, Glenner's chief marketing officer, whose mother had passed away from Alzheimer's disease a few years earlier. He described the storefronts, saying they had to be real, with doorways to walk through, chairs to sit on, artifacts for a museum and period costume jewelry in the department store. He wanted activities inside each location to give people a purpose. People would paint, make flower arrangements, create Christmas decorations or fold towels, like they used to do at home. In the theater, there would be films and music from their era, leading to conversations about memories that might emerge. It started to feel real. A mid-century town, for people with memory loss, much like those the other Glenner day programs served.

Serendipity played its hand when the San Diego Opera company's designers agreed to build theater-like sets that opened to 9,000 square feet of usable space inside a warehouse in the San Diego suburb of Chula Vista. Workers hammered and painted, applying the finishing touches in time for a tour with television journalist Maria Shriver and her *Today Show* crew. It was an important interview for Town Square in no small part because Tarde knew that Shriver would understand. Her father, Sargent Shriver, had lived with Alzheimer's disease before his death in 2011. In the years since, she has explored dementia through a documentary and created an association devoted to the significant number of women living with Alzheimer's. Almost two-thirds of those diagnosed with Alzheimer's are women, according to Shriver's website and the National Dementia Strategy of Canada. Men have higher rates of frontotemporal or Lewy body dementia.

It felt as if the paint was barely dry, but Town Square was finished just before the *Today Show* cameras arrived. When the story ran, Shriver introduced it, saying, "This idea could revolutionize the care you are getting and giving." It showed the diner with turquoise and white vintage-style seats and a working jukebox, along with the theater marquee announcing *The Greatest Show on Earth*. Cameras filmed Tarde and Maria Shriver talking in the tiny replica of the San Diego Air & Space Museum with old flight maps on the walls, routes in arched white lines reaching outward, from the United States to Europe and beyond. Behind a glass display case was a bright orange flight suit with a patch on the upper chest that said *Starfighter F-104*, the supersonic aircraft that first flew in the early 1950s.

The Lockheed-built airplane was called the "rocket with a man in it," which does not take into account a pilot named Jacqueline Cochran whose 1964 Starfighter flight reached a record 1,429 miles per hour. Cochran started flying as a young woman in 1932, piloting herself around the country to promote her cosmetics line. Marilyn Monroe endorsed her lipstick. She raced in flight competitions, delivered bombers to England during the Second World War and, later, fought to get more women pilots in the United States Air Force. She became the first woman to break the sound barrier. There's a photograph of Cochran in her later years on the San Diego Air & Space Museum website. She's wearing a flight suit, leaning against the Starfighter, arm flung commandingly across the sharp nose cone, her hair curly and white. They called her the Speed Queen.

It wasn't Cochran's uniform in the exhibit, but as Shriver said to Tarde when they walked through, "Everything in here is designed to trigger something in the brain."

"It's very intentional," he said.

After the story ran, families started calling, making appointments for assessments to see if their mom or husband or uncle would be a good fit for the program, which is licensed by California's Department of Public Health. It's not a drop-in center; people have to be enrolled. San Diego broadcast journalist Kimberly King visited with her mom, Jacki Taylor, a former theater performer and PBS broadcaster, still blond and beautiful in her 70s. A deputy sheriff named Joey Tennison and his sister, Sheri Tennison Berg, signed up their 70-year-old mom, Susie, who once worked as an office manager and accountant.

David Wallace, general manager of Senior Helpers in San Diego, was staffing the program and was as immersed in the project as Tarde. Years earlier he had served on Glenner's board of directors and he was a longtime operator of the local Senior Helpers franchise, in San Diego, part of a bigger company that has franchises across North America and Australia. Like other private companies that provide caregiving services, Senior Helpers workers are hired by families to care for people at home or to give extra service to residents in long-term care.

The Glenner Town Square officially opened on August 13, 2018, augmenting the existing Glenner day programs operating throughout the San Diego area, including the Little Blue House.

For Scott Tarde, Lisa Tyburski and David Wallace, it felt like a first day at college or an exciting new job. They joined the staff, greeting families, introducing clients to the theater, pointing out the sleek black Thunderbird, the pool hall and the full-service diner with framed black-and-white portraits of young Ingrid Bergman and Audrey Hepburn hanging on the walls.

Everyone settled in, except Susie.

She had been diagnosed with Alzheimer's in 2017 and now lived with her son Joey, the 37 year old deputy sheriff with San Diego County. Susie and her two kids were a tight family unit. Joey called his mom a "princess and a firecracker." She had won beauty contests as a young woman and in the 1980s, after divorcing their father, worked as an office manager and accountant in two jobs, at a parachute company and a Travelodge. Susie had never played team sports but was so determined to coach Joey's Little League team that she memorized the rules by reading baseball books borrowed from the library.

"She's the one who raised me," Joey says. "She made me who I am today . . . the everyday grind. That was my mom."

Eventually Susie had to stop working. She was not happy. Susie loved running the office, controlling the budgets, keeping order in her world. Joey and his sister, Sheri, tried day programs but found them barren, useless hours of bingo trying to pass for enriched programming. Susie started spending her days in Joey's home — a frustrated, anxious, isolated existence.

It was a struggle for the whole family. Joey put exercise and career advancement on pause to share his mom's care with his sister. He could see she was slipping. He wanted to offer more and spent most of his free time with his mom, yet he still felt a terrible guilt as she retreated further into her disease. As a police officer, he was accustomed to problem solving. Now, there was nothing he could do.

On that first day at Town Square, Susie stood outside the diner, clutching her son's arm.

He watched the other caregivers leave, as their moms or dads got comfy in chairs for yoga in-the-park or settled into a front row seat in the theater for a sing-along. Susie was having none of it.

Her hand tightened. David Wallace noticed Susie's grip and walked over to chat.

"I guess this is what people feel like when they're dropping their child off at nursery school for the first day," Joey said.

"Absolutely," Wallace said, "and, you know . . . in those situations the teacher tells the parent to go."

Wallace had worked with seniors for years. He was pretty sure he could handle this situation.

He saw Susie's GrandPad, an electronic tablet that acted as a cellphone, dialing her kids if she tapped their picture on the screen. Susie had two photos linked to phone numbers, one picture of Sheri and a selfie that she and Joey took together.

"If she calls you, don't pick up," he told Joey. "Your mom will be fine."

Joey told his mom he'd be back and left, wondering how the day would end. Susie was not pleased. For her, this was unfamiliar territory.

"What kind of a son would do this?" she said. Repeatedly. "What kind of son would just leave me here?"

Wallace tried to make conversation. He tried to empathize. To comfort. Susie tapped Joey's picture. He didn't pick up.

When Wallace stepped away, thinking she might want space, Susie dashed through an exit door, landing in a transition room that was designed for a few minutes of calm time before entering the lobby. Wallace joined her, and they moved toward the entrance, a sunny space with big glass windows. Tarde arrived, speaking lightly, trying to make conversation. Susie ignored them. She tapped Joey's picture. He didn't pick up.

As the clock ticked toward noon, a worker strolled by and said, ever so casually, "Hi Susie, everyone is having lunch. Want to come?" Susie joined her in the diner. A minor victory.

Lunch ended at 1 p.m. and at 1:01, Joey's phone started ringing again. His phone logged 100 missed calls.

"Where's Joey?" Susie asked Wallace, as she sat in Glenner Park. "When is he coming back?"

Wallace decided he'd better let Joey know that his mom was struggling when, as he later said, "The thought popped into my head."

Susie used to do accounting.

When they enrolled her at Glenner Town Square, Joey and Sheri described their mom's work history, including her repeated desire to go back to an office, to find a job, to be busy. She constantly asked if she could work again. It was all in her file, which Wallace had read.

He ran upstairs to the administration offices. On the computer, he typed invoices, one was the gas bill. Another was the electric bill. A bill for pencils was $3. Computer costs were $100. Some included dates and money owed. Working fast to get the papers printed, he cut them in half and raced down the stairs, bursting into Town Square. Susie was still sitting in Glenner Park.

In a loud voice, Wallace said, "Oh no. We just got off the phone with the Internal Revenue Service. We're being audited. Does anybody know a good accountant?"

Susie looked up. "I'm an accountant."

"Thank God," he said, "I really need your help. Where should we go?"

Susie said, "Let's go to my office."

She took him to the Town Square's replica of the Little Blue House, with a table and chairs, and Wallace gave her the invoices. He realized he needed more materials and ran back upstairs, returning with pencils and a paper tablet. Susie said, "Okay, give me some time to work on this."

He went up to Tarde's office, where he could see Susie through the window. For a long time, she had her head down, focused. Suddenly, she stood upright, holding her purse, marching toward the exit. Wallace raced down the stairs to meet her.

"Susie, are you leaving?" he asked, catching his breath.

"No," she said, "I was looking for you. I'm finished my work."

They walked back to the Little Blue House. On the table, all the slips of paper were laid out in chronological order. The sums were written down on the paper. "Everything is good and checks out," she told him.

"Thank you," Wallace told her. "I am so glad that I met you."

Susie eyed him. "If you want me to keep doing this, just make sure that everything is dated properly. Some of these invoices aren't dated, and I don't work like that."

Wallace nodded. "If you come back tomorrow, I will make sure everything is dated. Where would you like to set yourself up?"

She walked into the city hall, which had an office with a wooden desk, a filing cabinet and radio. She draped her sweater over the back of the chair.

"Susie, what would you like to do now? Would you like to go home?" Wallace asked, thinking he'd better stop while ahead.

Susie shook her head. "No, I'm on my break right now and

I am going to hang out with everyone else." She went into the library and chatted with the others.

The next morning, as people streamed through the front door for their second day, Wallace was surprised to see Joey and Tarde — with glistening eyes.

He watched them, puzzled. A cop and a CEO, both kind of crying? He made a beeline, asking, "What's wrong? Is Susie okay?"

Joey explained.

At 5:30 a.m., he awakened to see his mom standing over his bed, peering down at him. She was dressed in work clothes. She had her makeup on, her hair fixed, purse in hand. "Joey," she said, "I can't be late for work."

He got up, stalling a bit, since Town Square didn't open for another three-and-a-half hours. He took the long route to the industrial mall in Chula Vista. At one point, Susie insisted he pull over to buy a box of donuts for the people at work.

When Susie arrived at Town Square, she walked straight to city hall and, after hugging the caregivers, she fixed her sweater on the back of the chair. One of the staff invited her for coffee. Susie joined them.

Since that first day Susie has gone to Town Square's day program, every day, five days a week. It costs $95 a day which includes meals, exercise, conversation or music programs, including sing-alongs with a guitarist who performs in Spanish and English.

Susie spent most of her time in the programs with the others. She sat at the same turquoise booth with the same three friends, every day for lunch and coffee breaks. They were in the moderate stages of dementia, higher functioning than some others, still able to have conversations, share a story.

Wallace continued dropping by to say hello. Tarde negotiated the deal that he said would boost Glenner's funding, by giving Senior Helpers the rights to sell the Town Square concept to new franchisees. Handing off control to an outside company takes faith. Tarde said Glenner's board chose Senior Helpers because "we have confidence in their franchising abilities and support for their franchisees." In 2016, Senior Helpers was acquired by Altaris Capital Partners, a private equity firm with plans for expansion in health care. The care of senior citizens is a growth industry.

The staff that Wallace sends to Glenner Town Square are trained in occupational therapist Teepa Snow's Gems program, which equates people with cognitive decline as gemstones, each representing a different range of abilities. On a good day, Susie was a diamond, he says, which means clear and sharp, though stubborn and sometimes unwilling to accept change. On a slower day, she was an emerald, unsure and confused when things weren't going her way. As Wallace describes it, the right training helps workers or families understand how the brain changes with the disease, and the Gem designation is a good shorthand for where people are on the spectrum. Training makes it easier to predict some behavior, and it can help identify an individual's current abilities. With shared training and vocabulary, caregivers — families and workers — can communicate better and arrange activities that can bring comfort.

It's complicated, the human brain. In people with diseases that cause dementia, the brain shrinks over time, leading to changes in thinking or behavior, eyesight or mobility. It's different for each person.

If the front of the brain is damaged it can, for example, harm the ability to follow socially acceptable norms. What we sometimes jokingly refer to as the "inside voice," is really a filtering system that tells us what is better left unsaid. A person with dementia might lose that filter. Someone who never swore might now curse a blue streak or make comments that are insulting.

Research is shifting away from the belief that different compartments of the brain store certain types of information or are responsible for specific behavioral changes. Dr. Susan Vandermorris, the neuropsychologist at Toronto's Baycrest Centre, says there is an increasing recognition that the brain is more systems-based, sending signals throughout the brain, rather than module-based, where one region alone controls specific actions.

"A lot of the early cognitive neuroscience work was done trying to figure out which parts control which functions," Dr. Vandermorris tells me. Scientists mapped the brain, building a picture of how different regions are connected and what might happen if one area disconnects from the rest through trauma or disease. Advances in brain imaging have allowed a more nuanced picture to develop, she says. "The brain is a complex system talking to itself in complex ways, and things don't always break down as predicted. If you remove the red wire, things don't always blow up."

Frontline workers come to the same conclusions: each person with dementia responds to their disease in unique ways. The Gems guide, like other training, gives staff an understanding of what might happen. It helps workers feel prepared.

When I first visited the University of Southern Indiana, Dr. Katie Ehlman, the professor who gave me the tour of Dr. Thomas's Minka house on campus, spoke about the research she did, examining the impact of Snow's "positive approach to care" certification course. In the *Journal of Continuing Education in the Health Professions* in 2018, Ehlman and her fellow researchers noted that, among health-care workers, there is a "knowledge gap" related to the care of people living with dementia. They assessed 24 caregivers in skilled nursing facilities and found that Snow's training significantly increased their understanding of changes related to dementia, including vision, personal space and working memory.

Snow's work has come up frequently in conversations I've had with people in the aging field. Like others, she has focused on the value of empathy, understanding and social connections for people living with cognitive decline, which she has called "neurodegenerative change" instead of dementia. The word dementia originates from the Latin demens, according to the *Canadian Oxford Dictionary*. It's a negative word, for sure, even though it is used by some of the most progressive people in the industry.

Snow's empathic approach highlights another universal characteristic we all share, no matter what our cognitive abilities may be — the capacity for loneliness. The need to feel purpose is similarly universal; we all need a reason to get out of bed every day. None of this, whether expressed by Snow, Dr. Bill Thomas or Scott Tarde, would seem unusual or even radical if the care of older people wasn't narrowly focused on medicalized institutional models.

At Glenner Town Square, in the months that followed opening day, Susie was the one who decided how she would spend her day, not the staff. Maybe she'd join a yoga class or help Lisa Tyburski organize marketing material or coupons for supplies from Target or Walmart. Most days, when Wallace dropped by, Susie was chatting with her friends, listening to musicians or at her desk in city hall. Sometimes, when an elder walked past, Susie popped out, saying, "Can I help you?"

For Wallace, the decision to pull Susie into the program by asking for her assistance with accounting was a last resort, when all else failed. "In a moment of panic, the idea came to me of what her purpose could be," he says.

In the seniors' industry, a lot of good people have very different opinions about interactions with those who have memory loss. There are debates about safety versus the risk of independence, inclusiveness versus separation of people with dementia and truth versus the creation of a reality to meet an individual's emotional needs. A study published in the British peer-reviewed journal *Aging and Mental Health* in 2011 asked, "Do people with dementia find lies and deception acceptable?" The answer was complicated. Researcher Ann M. Day and her team focused on 14 people with dementia, living at home with a spouse or in a nursing home. The study found that the "acceptability of lies and deception" in dementia care in many ways depended on whether it was in the person's "best interests." Lying was considered negative, for example, when an individual was in the earlier stages of cognitive decline, and the deception blocked coping skills they might have otherwise learned. Lying could be considered in the best interest when the individual was in the later stages of the disease and unlikely to recognize the falsehood. "Lying, therefore, became more acceptable if, on balance, it promoted the most beneficial outcome," the researchers concluded.

When I mentioned Susie's experience to Suellen Beatty of the Sherbrooke Community Centre in Saskatoon, she said lying to people with dementia can lead to a devastating loss of trust if that lie is ever discovered. "He met [Susie's] need by doing what he did, which is wonderful. It would have been great if it was met in a way that was not fabricated . . . because I think what happens sometimes is if somebody figures that out, then you're really in trouble, man. They've lost trust. And trust is such a big deal," said Beatty, who is widely known and respected for her groundbreaking work with seniors.

Instead, Beatty said she would validate the emotions of an individual in distress, by saying, for example, "'You're very angry, aren't you? Yeah, I can see you're angry.' And then all of a sudden, somebody has empathy for you. And empathy is kind of a big key to get connected with someone with dementia."

It was a bit of a shock to hear this opinion, if only because Susie's story seemed inspiring. It is hard to know if any other approach would have worked with Susie that day. When faced with an extreme situation, Wallace created a scenario that made her feel comfortable.

I ask Wallace about Beatty's perspective. He's a thoughtful man, aware that there are strong opinions on truth telling. Some believe in telling the hard facts, always, even when an 89-year-old is calling for her mother. Others, like Beatty, rely on the validation of feelings, rather than recitations of blunt facts, never, for example, telling a woman that her mother was dead, believing that the repeat discovery of such a loss would be torment.

For Wallace, it's a balance between full truth and finding a way that helps someone like Susie feel safe in her surroundings, to give her a sense of familiarity, of purpose. "One of the biggest challenges that people with Alzheimer's have is the feeling of being ignored or overlooked or not understood. And so, by taking the time, and slowing down and interacting with the person, to really understand where they are in that moment, gives that person a sense of control, a sense of being understood and that in itself can help reduce a lot of the anxiety," he says. "It was connecting to her sense of purpose. She was able to see where she fit in, and an environment that was unfamiliar became familiar to her. I gave her a puzzle that she could solve."

When I ask Susie's son, Joey, for his thoughts on the differing philosophies, he hadn't considered those choices. Joey is quiet for a minute. Then he speaks.

"If there's a need to make everything honest, how do you make it honest when she has Alzheimer's? Her reality is already shattered. I'm just trying to make her quality of life better. If she thinks she's the president, I'm fine with that. As long as she's not aggressive or angry, that's more important," he says.

"Give her the right environment and she's a joy to be around. So, saying a lie, or playing into the lie, I would say that creates the environment that she needs, that she creates, that she is building in her mind. That way, she can deal with life."

It's an interesting dilemma. How far do we go, ethically speaking, to offer people a sense of value, the ability to contribute, a reason to get up like the rest of us and greet the day?

◎　◎　◎

Let's talk about guilt.

Scott Tarde, Town Square's CEO, has views. He has opinions on the entire seniors' care industry, among them the growing cost of assisted living or retirement homes. "Who can afford to pay $10,000 a month? What happens when you run out of money?" He talks as well about the need for purpose in late life. And his hope is that good day programs can help people with cognitive decline live longer in the community.

Among these other pressing concerns, Tarde has also thought a lot about guilt.

It's an emotion that hits hard when families put their loved one in nursing homes. He believes that Town Square's respite program will help alleviate caregivers' exhaustion, their guilt, so that they can give their loved ones more time before they must look for institutional care.

Tarde wants to build a network of Town Squares across the United States, to delay or even prevent nursing home admissions. Day program franchises that use the Glenner Town Square model are being purchased in Louisville, Las Vegas, Philadelphia, New Jersey, St. Louis and Austin, Texas. Tarde says Glenner, the not-for-profit, will get a percentage of the royalties.

The *Today Show* feature led to dozens of newspaper articles and television appearances. Some compared Town Square to de Hogeweyk in the Netherlands, a reference Tarde says he doesn't understand since de Hogeweyk, near Amsterdam, is a nursing home and Town Square is a day program. In his second-floor office, Tarde stands near his desk, talking. It's a wide space with a glass window overlooking the community he designed. The corner wall near the couch where I sit is lined with pictures. There's a poster of Captain America, holding his shield, blocking evil cartoon dudes. Below Captain America is a framed picture of Rocky Balboa, the fictional Philly boxer who never gave up, although the backstory of Rocky's creation, provided by Sylvester Stallone during publicity interviews, was just as compelling. In the '70s, when Stallone was an unknown actor and writer, he said he wrote the screenplay for *Rocky* in a room with windows painted black to block distractions. I used to tell that story to my son whenever he needed to rise with Herculean effort to achieve a goal in school. The point was pretty straight up. Through the sheer force of focus, anything is possible.

Tarde didn't paint any windows. But he did take a pencil sketch on a piece of graph paper and turn it into a daytime refuge where people have found a late-life purpose.

He smiles when I ask him about the significance of Rocky and Captain America. "They are all inspirational to me because they fight the good fight," he said. "They have a bit of the underdog."

That underdog theory does not explain his poster of the New York Yankees, the pinstriped American League team that crushed the hometown San Diego Padres in the 1998 World Series.

Speaking of guilt and baseball, at the 2019 season opener of the Toronto Blue Jays, I sat with a woman I knew when our sons played rep ball together in Toronto. She spoke of her cousin's deep remorse, her shame, over the decision to place her mom in a nursing home after years of caring for her.

Their family is originally from India. "Back home, we keep our parents with us," she said. She empathizes with her cousin's decision, knowing she'd probably have the same horrible feeling. "We spend all these years, raising our kids, and now that they are off in school, we have a bit of freedom to actually enjoy life before it's too late for us. Do we have to give up everything?" It was a rhetorical question.

In his years overseeing nursing homes, Scott Tarde saw that guilt every day. It took on a life of its own, darkening interactions between families and the nursing homes, correctly or not.

"There is nothing wrong with guilt," he says. "It is very natural. These are their parents and most people love their parents, and even if they have a bad relationship with one or both parents, they still want to try to find a way to make their remaining years as comfortable as possible. But they are dealing with the guilt of placing a loved one in a nursing facility or an assisted living facility — probably having promised them that they would never do that.

"What typically happens in a nursing home or assisted living is, I say, 'Here is my loved one, and guess what? I'm going to come back in a couple of weeks and most likely, something is going [to go wrong] and even if something doesn't happen, I haven't been there in two weeks and my loved one is going to look different to me, which is going to alarm me, and make me feel like you are not taking care of them because no one can take care of them like I can take care of them.' There is a built-up animosity that starts to brew. Even if you know inherently that you can't take care of your loved one, and this facility is helping them — I'm talking about good facilities — there is still this unconscious anger over the fact that you couldn't provide that care, which is almost an unrealistic expectation.

"And then you have the family members, multiple siblings, one that says the parent *shouldn't* go into a nursing home, another that says they *should* go into a home, and then there's the one who says, 'It's ridiculous that you had to put them in a home, couldn't you take care of them?' And they live 3,000 miles away.

"And then, oh, by the way, there's the dynamic that says, 'Well, we're now having to spend all this money that was supposed to be our inheritance.' So, this fundamental guilt issue. I've got all this mapped out because I have seen it hundreds of times in my career."

"I don't see that here," he says.

"It doesn't mean it can't happen. But generally, families drop their loved ones off at 8:45, they come back at 5:15. They've had a good day. They've had a chance to do some of the things they need to do."

For the year that Susie spent at Town Square, her son felt the freedom to relax. "On my days off work, I would hop on my bike and ride around San Diego, just to have time for myself," Joey says.

He laughs, describing one of life's unexpected twists. "At home, my mom was like, 'Hey, what are you doing?' I'm doing laundry. And she says maybe you can teach me how to do that.

"My mom taught me how to do laundry when I was in sixth grade. Now here she is, asking me. I can look at that, at my mom's deterioration, and feel sorry for myself, but that's not going to change anything. Might as well just have a fun experience, and teach my mom how to do laundry. It's a way to interact with her. And have an adventure versus anything else. My mom can iron like a champ."

Susie is no longer at Town Square. As her disease progressed, her behavior changed. During the evenings and weekends when she wasn't at Town Square, she became frustrated, angry and started lashing out. Tarde tried to help find solutions, but ultimately Joey says the stress of caring for her at home became overwhelming and unhealthy. Joey and his sister looked at seniors' homes but the cheapest was $3,900 a month, and when another home quoted $7,500, he stopped looking. Eventually Joey found a memory care home that accepted his mom with California medical insurance called Medi-Cal for older people with limited assets. "My mom didn't plan for her future," he says.

Susie is now living in a small home with nine other people. When she arrived, Joey and his sister told the staff to make her feel comfortable, give her something to do. She needs a sense of purpose, responsibility, because she loves to work. They spoke with confidence and had the right language because of the Glenner experience, because of a desk with Susie's name on it inside city hall.

"Glenner provided that comfort level where she could be herself and that gave my mom her sense of self again. It gave the whole family our mom back," he says.

"To give someone a sense of purpose, that is so powerful."

◎　◎　◎

For years, Kimberly King, a longtime San Diego television personality with a few Emmys to her credit, spent life stretched between her mom, raising teenagers and trying to build her media consulting company. "I'm the sandwich generation," King says with a smile.

After her mom's diagnosis of cognitive decline, King struggled to explain when well-meaning friends insisted her mom seemed fine. It's not easy to explain the constant challenges. King created a Facebook album, called "Jacki's Journeys: A Look at My Mom Fighting Dementia with Spunk and Spirit!" Like most social media posts, these photos don't show King's sadness; they show two pretty women, mother and daughter, laughing and smiling.

"You look at my mom, you can't see the dementia," King says. "I was with a group of girlfriends that I rarely get to see. They said, 'She looks good — what's the deal?' But you can't see the caregiver's heart. You can't see the stress and pain. How tired we are. Because it's my story too. Nobody is going to post something on social media that doesn't look good. Nobody knows the story behind the scenes."

Now, her mom spends several days each week at Town Square, and by the time King sees her at the end of the day, Jacki may not remember exactly what she did but she's more content and calm.

"This is her home away from home," King says. Like Susie, Jacki became deeply involved in Glenner Town Square, picking up a role she once had in her career. Years ago, she performed with the Starlight Musical Theater in San Diego. At the local PBS, Jacki Taylor had her own radio show called *Lunching in the Park*, interviewing the California movers and shakers. Later, after Jacki's radio show ended, she stayed with PBS to do promotional work, organizing the telethons and running tours at the station.

Every now and then, Jacki recreates the tour guide role, greeting visitors to Town Square.

"She becomes the ambassador. She puts her jacket on. She puts her little Jacki hat on and becomes the director, back to work again, saying, 'This is where I spend my days.'"

◎   ◎   ◎

Months after I left San Diego, Susie's story stayed with me. I encountered some who shared Suellen Beatty's philosophy, saying it is better to figure out the person's needs by affirming their anger or fear through conversation. Others said Wallace met Susie where she was in that moment of distress, and many felt he did what was necessary to connect. Dr. Allen Power, known for his advocacy for people with dementia, says he would have done something similar with a real task, such as taking attendance or tabulating records.

"I think the intent was very good. With a little more creativity, you can go a little farther, to find something real," says Dr. Power, a geriatrician who has written two books on elevating the lives of people with dementia — particularly without the use of antipsychotic drugs.

As an aside, he describes an encounter between two women in a nursing home and a psychologist named Dr. Richard Taylor who, after being diagnosed with Alzheimer's disease, spent time traveling, talking to other people with dementia for a book called *Alzheimer's from the Inside Out*. It was ultimately translated into multiple languages.

"He told a great story about going to a long-term care community and visiting two women who probably had moderate stage dementia, who were folding children's clothes and putting them in a laundry basket," Dr. Power says. "He asked if they were for a children's day care. One woman said, 'Oh, there are no children here. They bring us these clothes in a pile and we fold them and put them back and then they take them away and mix them up and bring them back again.' Richard looked horrified, and the other lady jumped in and said, 'Yeah, but it's better than a stick in the eye.' So, Richard's plea to the care community was to try to find activities that are better than 'a stick in the eye.' They have to have meaning."

It's a good point. In the last few years, I've seen a lot of folded towels.

Dr. Power's push for meaningful work makes sense. Still, it's a challenge for long-term care managers who could easily embrace a new perspective but who are generally wary of change, worried about the upheaval of their regulatory obligations.

Still, it's hard to conclude when interacting with people in demanding, escalating situations that there must be defined rules on how to engage. Susie's son and daughter credit Wallace for changing their mother's life for the better. In doing so, their lives improved too. Even though Susie ultimately declined, for a long time she found a place that made her feel comfortable.

A few months later, I met Laura Tamblyn Watts in a west Toronto coffee shop to catch up on a shared favorite topic, elders. It was a freezing late spring day in Toronto. Inside, a woman with a southern U.S. accent was talking into her phone with dismay, saying, "The weather here is shocking." A nun in a black habit sat at our usual table, so I joined Laura near the front window, overlooking Roncesvalles Avenue, my almond-milk latte beside her skinny vanilla.

I told her about Susie and asked her thoughts on the ethics of it all. She teaches law and aging to graduate students at the University of Toronto and, as a longtime advocate for seniors, Tamblyn Watts has the ability to step back for a wide perspective.

"We can hold preferences, we can hold things that are aligned to our values," she began, easing into the conversation. "If we were talking about education, I might think that Montessori is wonderful, but when I get into Montessori I find that my kid is not a Montessori kid. Or, I might go into the public school system and discover that my child has special needs and even though I have very strong views on public schools, in the end, my child needs private school and tutoring and so on.

"So. You're trying to get a key into the lock. You're trying to find an understanding. You're kind of searching for that education model, the thing that unlocks your mom or dad from a place of anxiety or a place of fear and gets them into a place of blossoming and engagement."

After countless interviews, I am starting to realize that there is no overwhelming agreement, no blueprint for behavior by experts in this field, although there are good ideas that offer inspiration, ways to challenge ourselves. Tamblyn Watts comes down on the side of do no harm, but do what works for each individual.

Or as she said, watching the nun walk into the cold rain with coffee cup in hand, "We need different ways to unlock wonder."

◎　◎　◎

My parents had a double room with his-and-her washrooms on reserve in the local retirement home. It was in a freshly constructed wing of a home that my mom liked because it was built like a long ranch-style bungalow, without the elevators she feared would break down or, more annoying, be unable to handle the space needed for more than three people with walkers.

"I've heard about lineups for 30 minutes, just to go downstairs for lunch," she said.

So, it was decided.

Their house was emptied, polished and staged, a project completed by a rotating cast of family and friends, with my mother as the director and my dad, the stagehand.

Every Saturday and Sunday, an open house was scheduled, from 1 p.m. to 3 p.m. I'd take them out for the afternoon, while the home hunters and the tire kickers walked through. My mother's purse was heavy with jewelry, the gold rings and earrings from her Aunt Isabel, who worked as a housekeeper for a wealthy automobile executive in Detroit with a sick wife. A few months after the wife died, Aunt Isabel, age 66, married the widower. It was 1951. "She looked so happy in the photographs," my mom said. Her husband died nine months after the wedding, and Aunt Isabel inherited everything, the best of which was now tucked inside my mom's purse. The rest of the family jewels, so to speak, were hidden inside the grandfather clock. "Don't let me forget them if I give the clock away!" she'd say, laughing, since she does not forget anything.

On open-house days, we'd go for lunch. I'd walk each parent up the steps to the restaurant and stand ready to block tumbles as they slid into a booth. They were tired and it showed. My dad ordered a BLT. He had mayonnaise on his face, so I suggested he might want to wipe it off. He didn't get it off the first time, so I told him to try again. I could see by his eyes that he was offended.

"I will look forward to 30 years from now so you can see how it feels to be like this," he said. He seemed feistier than my mom.

"We waited too long," she said. "We should have moved earlier. It just took me so long to get used to the idea."

She was talking about the retirement home, a sweet, if traditional, place with an atrium and a café where my dad could indulge with a coffee and a tart. He could watch baseball games with the Toronto Blue Jays fans, and Mom could hopefully find someone who was up for a debate on federal politics. Their room was 650 square feet, about the same size as a Minka home or a Vancouver laneway house, except it was in a building for seniors. The only other options in their town were retirement homes with elevators.

"I'm so tired," Mom said. "I feel like I'm going to die before your father."

The next weekend she was freshly energized, probably due to her excitement over the blizzard prediction on the weather channel, which she watched religiously and emailed updates that often forbid driving, although no such messages arrived that day.

A snowstorm was raging. It was minus 20 degrees Celsius.

By the time I arrived, they were dressed in coats and gloves but no footwear. This won't do. I asked each parent to take a turn sitting on the chair near the front door while I crouched down to put on their winter boots, insisting they keep their feet straight, not wiggle, so as to fit them inside.

After lunch, they demanded we visit three shops during the whiteout in the otherwise deserted downtown. On the slippery sidewalk, I stood in between my parents, and we all linked arms as we walked. I felt like Dorothy, with the Tin Man and Scarecrow, sliding down the yellow brick road.

My mom laughed at our reflection in the store windows.

"What a riot!"

## CHAPTER FIVE

# The Dutch Model

"I T'S DISNEYLAND FOR DEMENTIA!" chirped a seniors' advocate. "From what I've read, there may be some ethical issues," intoned an editor.

My heart sank, hearing these words a few days before flying to Amsterdam to visit de Hogeweyk, a Dutch nursing home "neighborhood" for people with severe dementia. Years earlier, it had made headlines around the world for its unique concept.

In 2013, CNN declared it a "dementia village." *The Atlantic* likened it to a benevolent version of *The Truman Show*, the 1998 Jim Carrey film about a man who discovers that his gleeful reality is, in fact, a TV show where he is constantly watched and controlled.

After some news stories described a contrived community, de Hogeweyk became a destination for people interested in long-term care, even if just for the bragging rights to say, 'Hey, I've been to that dementia village.' From around the world, journalists, academics and nursing home operators made the trek to the Netherlands for an official tour. Some even dropped in, unannounced.

In Canada, where we pay high taxes for our health care and social benefits, we look for inspiration to countries that have similarly high (or higher) taxes, such as the Netherlands, Finland, Norway or Denmark. They have a certain social credibility. Their health-care programs often appear more innovative, their philosophies about the collective good more progressive, their architectural design more communal, thoughtful, functional.

It seems odd, then, to assume that a Dutch nursing home suddenly went rogue.

Now, on a chilly March morning in the town of Weesp, an ancient suburb of Amsterdam, I wait for my interview with Eloy van Hal, one of the creators of the village concept.

Van Hal appears in the foyer precisely at 10:30 a.m. as arranged. He looks a bit like Jaime Lannister from *Game of Thrones* if the Kingslayer were to wear a crisp dress shirt and pants with sharp creases. I feel a bit sorry for him. Another reporter waiting for a tour.

We start our interview in the dining room of de Hogeweyk, an establishment that is open to the public, with a shiny display of wine and spirits on the wall behind the bar reaching up to the ceiling. It reminds me of Bar Buca, a trendy neighborhood hangout in downtown Toronto where my stepdaughter once worked, staying late to make sure all those bottles that touched the ceiling were polished and full.

Coffee arrives, each cup with a perfectly round sugary almond cookie. "You're not allergic to nuts, are you?" he asked. Almonds are my favorite, I tell him. "In that case, have both," he said.

As a journalist I was not asked to pay for the tour experience, but industry professionals, such as nursing home operators, are charged US$600, or more, for the basic tour.

We get down to the conversation. Van Hal talks. He has a lot of points that he wants to make clear, weary after years of distracting headlines.

He's not the only one.

When I visited San Diego's Glenner Town Square, Scott Tarde could not understand why so many news stories assumed he copied the Netherlands' famous "dementia village."

Far, far away from sunny southern California, Van Hal offers his unsolicited opinion. "I don't like the words *dementia village*."

To Van Hal, that term and the comparisons to a satirical Hollywood movie about Truman's unquestioning acceptance of a false reality distract from the goal: a normal life for people with dementia.

It all began in 1993, when two managers of a traditional nursing home called Hogewey realized they were providing meals and safety but little joy in an institution that looked too much like a hospital.

Yvonne van Amerongen and Jannette Spiering didn't like the traditional nursing home reality of 30 people forced into one ward, not living together but put together. The women decided to shake it up. Remember, these were the years when nursing homes were proudly institutional. When the doctors were not holding court during their rounds, the nurses ran the show. In a system focused on medicalized care, residents disappeared into the background, like living props.

Van Amerongen and Spiering had management roles but they were nursing home outsiders, coming from the hospitality business, trained to focus on the needs, desires and happiness of the customer.

Van Hal continues, "Yvonne and Janette said to each other, 'Let's change it.' They started a project — a normal life for people with dementia. That was the vision. They said, even if you are unable to stay at home with the right supports and care, if you have severe dementia, you are still a human being and you still want to continue your life. We must focus more on what you are still able to do and what you want to do.

"You are an individual. You are not your disease."

In the ensuing years, the women got rid of those wards of 30 people and created smaller groups, living in households with kitchens and washing machines that would, as Van Hal says, bring back the "normal lifestyle."

To create a natural home, they gathered people with similar interests, allowing them to live together.

"In many models, you are put together because you have the same disease, not because you have the same habits, personal preferences, music, meals and daily rhythm. No, you have the same disease. So, they started with lifestyles, matching people in their personal preferences."

All of this unfolded in the old building, the "ugly building," Van Hal calls it. In 2002, nine years after its inception, Van Hal arrived as the facility manager, ready to help with what ultimately became a plan to design and build a new home. Hogewey — the nursing home — would become de Hogeweyk, the neighborhood.

Together, Van Hal, Spiering and Van Amerongen created a new plan, this one to be realized through an architectural design that considered the basic desires of all people: freedom of movement, independence and community, even if it unfolded behind doors locked to the outside world. This was long before most advocates started promoting the idea that people with dementia should be part of the wider community, like anyone else.

"What do we need when we talk about a normal life?" he asks, posing the question before providing the answer.

"Where are people in the Netherlands living? In houses. So, you need houses. You need the human scale. We made groups of ten people instead of 30, but ten is still not the human scale. So people are living in a house with six people, where you can cook in every household and you can leave through a front door.

"Yes, that is normal."

But, he asks again, is it natural to live inside with the only daylight from airtight windows?

"We had to decide. Should it be covered? Or, are you also standing outside in the fresh air, wind, rain, sun? And we said, 'What is normal?'

"It is normal that you can leave your house and step outside."

De Hogeweyk's design included a long outdoor community square with a fountain and tables and chairs for café-style conversation. The courtyard had greenery, an entrance to a beauty parlor and an exercise club. Inside the doors to the main building, along with the public restaurant where I am meeting Van Hal, would be a pub, a grocery store and club rooms for baking or art.

It was built on the edge of Weesp, a city of 19,000 people, just 20 minutes from Amsterdam. From a North American perspective, that makes it a suburb, except our suburbs aren't 664 years old. Nor do they have winding cobblestone streets with cyclists of all ages, holding on to upright handlebars, zipping over the bumps in the roads. It's a small city of canals that flow beside narrow streets with tiny shops selling cheese, pastries and fresh, dark coffee. Even in the chill of March, its outdoor market sells bright tulips and dense breads so rich with flavor that the North American practice of carb counting becomes irrelevant.

After de Hogeweyk officially opened in 2008, Weesp expanded and revitalized around it. Today it is surrounded by townhomes, schools and offices. People visit the de Hogeweyk restaurant for lunch and businesses rent it for parties.

When I visited in 2019, de Hogeweyk had 27 homes, all attached, built inside the minimalist architecture that is part of the Netherland's modern design culture. Each is home to six or seven people and their caregivers, most built with three or four bedrooms on opposite sides of the household. "Three people on each side means you only have two people to annoy you at night," Van Hal says.

Perhaps the one connection between San Diego's Town Square and de Hogeweyk is the use of reminiscence techniques, creating calm in unique ways. Town Square used the storefronts of shops and diners from mid-century California to help people connect with vivid earlier memories. In de Hogeweyk, reminiscence is more subdued with a focus on familiar lifestyles that enable people with dementia to live in comfortable surroundings that can lessen confusion and anxiety. It is one of several approaches used, depending on the need. By understanding an individual's former life, their career, family and important events, caregivers can speak with them about those experiences, talk about their affinity for certain décor or discuss films that they liked to watch in earlier years.

"It gives many opportunities for good chats, laughs, pleasant moments and . . . and sometimes tears," Van Hal says. "It also explains the behavior of a resident or a resident's specific needs. They often need our help on their daily decision-making, and so we need to know that background very well."

Each home has décor, music and food reflecting four different styles, influenced by the socio-economic and cultural histories of the residents. A shared disease doesn't mean shared interests.

In the gooi, the term de Hogeweyk gives to a "formal home," residents drink fine wine at a beautifully set table. Classical music plays in the background. At the traditional home, residents eat simple Dutch staples — meat, potatoes and that delicious hearty bread. Folk songs play on the stereo, and residents lean toward local news, not CNN. The urban home has big, vivid paintings and residents who hang out at the outdoor sidewalk cafés. In the cosmopolitan home, residents and staff eat Italian or Spanish food and get their news from international stations.

There's always an exception to the art of house matching. Walking along the sidewalk, Van Hal points out a formal-style home and tells the story of a woman whose children wanted her to maintain her upper-class lifestyle, the way she had raised them. Except with dementia, her mind settled into her younger years growing up in Amsterdam, a busy city life spent outdoors surrounded by people. At de Hogeweyk, she left her formal home every morning and walked around the corner to the urban house, spending her days there.

"Your lifestyle preferences are more or less defined in your early 20s," Van Hal says, "so she could not act anymore as that formal lady. And of course, she moved to that [urban] house when there was a place available. In principle, you don't move anymore but of course, we made a mistake."

Each home has a door that opens to the courtyard or the narrow, winding lanes of gardens, much like the old section of Weesp, founded in the Middle Ages.

De Hogeweyk was designed with a focus on public spaces like those found in the old villages or town squares, the gathering place of the traditional European community. On a slightly warmer day, even in the winter, residents will sit here, faces upward, enjoying the warmth of the sun. Inside the main building is a grocery store, with meat, vegetables, cheese and bread, open for 90 minutes every weekday morning and two hours in the afternoon. Sometimes the caregivers order beef or pork in advance, and the butcher delivers it to the store wrapped in paper with a black ink number written on it, for house 19 or 27. Most days, except Sundays when the store is closed and the cashier is at home with her family, caregivers and residents walk over to buy food for the day's meals. It gets people outside, Van Hal says, "They can go back and talk about the weather."

Three shelves are devoted to wine and a selection of beer. Mostly Heineken and Amstel. It's not unusual to visit a home and see ladies in the living room, holding a glass of wine. Homes in Canada are starting to allow dietary options. "If Mrs. Jones is 94 years old and wants ice cream for dinner, then let her eat ice cream!" one administrator said. At de Hogeweyk, Van Hal says most people live for about two years after they arrive, so why not let them enjoy?

"Who is going to say in your last two years of your life, 'This is not healthy'? You're going to die in two years but in the last two years you will eat the best, well-balanced nutritious meals you ever had. You won't like it. You won't eat it. But this is what we will serve you.

"I always said we don't support alcohol abuse, but a glass of wine is typically Dutch."

In the atrium near the grocery store, a man from the outside community was tuning the piano, testing the pitch of the same key. *Ping. Ping. Ping.* Another man, a resident, stood alone, mesmerized by workers applying a non-slip coating to the outside walkway on the upper level. "He's always outside," Van Hal says of the curious man. "Lock him up and you're in trouble." Right now the man looks like any other guy who stops to watch construction workers at a job site.

It is all normal life, Van Hal says.

Normal appears to be a recurring theme. A day earlier, I had visited a seniors' home in Deventer, another ancient Dutch city, this time where university students get free rent in return for spending time around the home, interacting with the older residents. When a 29-year-old man chatted with a 94-year-old woman about an upcoming party, the manager of Humanitas Deventer told me, "Don't make this a big deal. This is just normal."

I ask Van Hal, "What is it with the Dutch and the desire to be . . . normal? Is that a thing here?"

He laughs, a bit.

"Very generally speaking, the Dutch will say, 'Just do normal.' We are not, generally speaking, like the Americans. But in this case, here, normalcy for people with brain damage means a recognizable environment. Normalcy helps you understand the world. If you don't understand the world anymore, then you become aggressive, agitated, stressed."

He smiles again, then offers to hold my tape recorder, speaking into it, while I take pictures of the grocery store wine collection. Van Hal continues the tour outside along the walkways of green brick where gardens will soon bloom. A man walks past us. Van

Hal says hello. The man keeps walking. "At first I thought he was the son," Van Hal says, "but he lives here."

We walk along the laneways where the many small gardens are planted. People going for a walk will encounter plants and flowers. We walk past urban homes, then formal homes. We do not go inside. I don't see the fakery alluded to by earlier news stories. The hair salon is not so unusual. Most nursing homes have a beauty parlor; it just opens into a hallway, rather than the outdoors. A few steps away is an exercise room with options for physiotherapy, also not uncommon in more traditional nursing homes. Van Hal says a lot of residents stay limber from their walking, and daily walks also diminish the use of antipsychotic drugs that many homes give to elders to keep them placid. The theater is across the way, a large room, often used for community events. It is more fabulous than some, but still, many homes have a big room, a gathering place, where sing-along performances are held.

De Hogeweyk seems . . . normal.

We arrive in the restaurant again for more coffee.

Van Hal shares his greatest regret.

He designed the restaurant without a door that opens to the street, without a direct connection to the outside community, so diners can come and go with ease. Opening the door to the outside world would be a risk. It would mean finding ways to keep a close watch on people with dementia, to make sure they stay inside and safe, following Dutch nursing-home regulations.

"I was a coward," he says. I mention this comment, months later, to Matthew Melchior, a nursing-home operator who has plans to build a new seniors' hub outside of Toronto. "A coward!" he said. "Hardly!"

For now diners enter through the main foyer, buzzed inside the locked doors by a receptionist sitting in a cubicle. The foyer is the first stop for schoolchildren on their weekly visits or new parents coming for the "baby talk" program, a support group for those first months when life feels overwhelming. Unlike the allusions to the constant surveillance of *The Truman Show*, Van Hal insisted that de Hogeweyk's only cameras are here in the foyer, so the receptionist can see who is arriving with deliveries.

It has been more than a decade since de Hogeweyk opened, and the ideas are always evolving. That's why nursing-home innovators back in North America say it's so important to get the designs for new homes right — they will last for at least 30 years. "It'll be us, living in those homes," they say. It's no surprise that Van Hal is pushing new design ideas, opening the doors to a community shared by people of all ages.

"We are working on the emancipation of the elderly with dementia, but it is step by step, because society is not always prepared," he says.

"Society looks at people with dementia in a different way. We look at nursing homes as those scary, stinky environments. So, with de Hogeweyk, it worked out better than we hoped even. Now, we can make the next step."

Interest from Australia, Canada and the United States led to the creation of a new department, called Be. It sends Van Hal around the world, speaking to long-term care groups, sometimes signing contracts to build an updated version of the village model. Hogewey (the nursing home), de Hogeweyk (the neighborhood) and Be are all part of the not-for-profit organization Vivium that runs the entire operation. "Too many names," he says.

The new villages, he hopes, will be more inclusive.

"In my future dream the school is incorporated in the neighborhood, the library is included. It is steps toward a *really* normal environment again for people with dementia."

As he leaves, I ask about a comment he made nearly three hours earlier about offering residents the freedom to be outside, in the wind, the sun and fresh air.

What does that mean to the people living here?

"It means, to feel alive."

Duncan McKercher is a rancher and real estate developer in Saskatoon.

His mother, Peggy Wilton McKercher, was the chancellor at the University of Saskatchewan. She received the Order of Canada. His father, Robert, graduated from Harvard law school and founded a law firm in town. There's a street named after Duncan's grandfather Stewart, a First World War fighter pilot and lawyer, in the city's College Park neighborhood. It's a north-south street, a few blocks from Suellen Beatty's Sherbrooke Community Centre, where Peggy McKercher once served as chair of the fund-raising committee.

Duncan is following his own path. He's working with Van Hal on the prairie version of de Hogeweyk. McKercher has already started building what he hopes will be an aging-in-place community of bungalows, ten minutes south of Saskatoon. Crossmount Village has a craft brewery, a café with lattes and a medical office. Young parents living nearby bring their kids here to skate in the winter or watch the pollywogs in the pond in the spring. For the next step — caring for people with memory loss — McKercher and his wife traveled across North America, making surprise visits to nursing homes to see what worked best.

Asked how he knew which homes were good, McKercher puts his hand over his heart. "You could feel it," he says. He decided on de Hogeweyk's village model. He's got the site picked out in a field beyond the bungalows. It's just long grass and trees for now, unlike the cold spring mud in the construction zone of the seniors' community, where green lawns don't yet exist. McKercher seems to have enough clout in Saskatchewan to have conversations with federal and provincial politicians, but so far the investment money hasn't flowed. Toronto bankers want a government commitment first, and each level of government wants to know what the next is doing.

"It's like herding cats," he said, in an email.

"It's very frustrating," he said, in another.

The struggle for funding is a recurring theme for others trying to build, like Kathy Gillespie in Pennsylvania's Clearwater County, who is still trying to get her village of Minka homes built. She's not giving up, and it appears that McKercher isn't either although he's decided to fund a smaller version of the project internally.

He has the vibe of a man accustomed to success and wants to open Canada's first officially sanctioned de Hogeweyk, transplanted from Weesp and adapted to the windswept Prairies.

"I'm still very confident we will pull this off."

Another "village" for people with dementia opened in Langley, British Columbia, in June of 2019. It's not the first to create a little community for itself, nor was it done with de Hogeweyk, which charges fees for its services. In the world of long-term care, a good idea is there for the taking, just like Dr. Bill Thomas did with Suellen Beatty's small households, incorporating it into his own concept. The Village Langley was inspired by de Hogeweyk and Dr. Thomas's Green House Project, but Elroy Jespersen spearheaded the plan independently. Jespersen has worked in Canadian seniors' care for decades. "I'm 70 years old now. I'm at the end of my career," he said in the months leading up to the opening. He spent years following the leaders who spoke at the Pioneer Network, which has a mandate to change the culture of long-term care, before he chose his model.

In southern British Columbia, the Village Langley is settled on seven acres secured by an eight-foot-high cedar fence that Jespersen promises will be disguised by greenery from landscaping and trees. Architects who designed the cluster of small homes were under explicit instructions to avoid anything that spoke of an institutional setting, anything they would not have included in their own home. When they first drew a community with big-box designs, he told them to start over. "Think about a little European village or think about walking through a little Newfoundland town, where you see these little houses and they are all unique," he told them. It worked. The homes are different heights and shapes and colors with zigzagging rooflines, even though most are connected inside.

It is going to be a mix of independent living, assisted living and higher care. In the Netherlands, the government pays de Hogeweyk's not-for-profit operator Vivium 75,000 euros a year for each resident. That's roughly US$85,000. It's not cheap. In return, each resident pays the government between 150 and 2,300 euros per month, depending on their income. In B.C., the Village Langley is owned by a private operator, so it will charge nearly $7,000 a month for assisted living and $8,700 for complex care. Jespersen acknowledges the cost is financially out of reach for many. But, he said, it's a start. Two more villages, both inspired by de Hogeweyk, are planned for Vancouver and Vancouver Island, built by the not-for-profit Catholic-based Providence Residential & Community Care Services Society, with local and provincial partnerships.

Jespersen has spent his career working in this field. He has been inspired by the work of Dr. Bill Thomas and Dr. Allen Power; Dr. Power has been a mentor to Suellen Beatty and Dr. Jennifer Carson, the academic who works with Dr. Thomas's Changing Aging organization.

Dr. Power has been speaking about the segregation of people with cognitive decline for years. "I remember the civil rights movement," he says. He mentions a conversation he had with Jespersen about his wish for a group of residents living together, with and without memory loss. "What if I'd like to live here too?" Dr. Power asked Jespersen, of his village. "I said to Elroy, 'You know, if I were a person without dementia, I'd want to live in a place like that too. Why do only people with dementia get to live there? Why can't I live in a place where I can get outdoors and go to the store?'"

The Village is a secure home, meaning residents won't be able to leave on their own. They have freedom within the grounds, however, and Jespersen says that is the one element that has excited most families.

"We've had people contacting us saying, 'My mother or father is living in a nursing home and they can't go outside and they are getting very frustrated,'" he says. "When you are dealing with dementia, most homes have taken away the freedom in the name of security. As Bill Thomas says, 'surplus safety.' That's what we have [in the industry]. We absolutely have surplus safety."

He talks about the regulators who looked at the outdoor design and raised alarms over plans for a pond, saying he'd have to put a grate over it, for safety purposes. "We can't do that, because once again, it will just look like another institution."

I tell him about a conversation I had with Laura Tamblyn Watts, the CanAge CEO who worried that early recommendations for change within the City of Toronto nursing homes were still focused on the avoidance of risk. Keep everyone safely tucked away.

"You have to have a certain level of risk in order for people to be able to move about," he says.

"We're going to have a firepit. What is more natural than sitting around on a summer evening, roasting marshmallows and telling stories? We will have a shutoff valve, staff will be there. There has to be risk. If none of us had any risk in our life, we'd be living in a . . . nursing home," he says with a laugh.

"If you want to have risk you try to manage it, you try to minimize it, but you don't take it so far that you take away the joy of living."

◎ ◎ ◎

"Did you know your father fell twice last week?"

My mother announced this over salad, and fish and chips. It had been weeks since their house went on the market, through a wild winter of snowfall and freezing rain. We'd go for lunch during every open house, which made my dad happy, although there were only a few restaurants that met my mother's standards and their menus were getting repetitive.

"He fell in the bank. He was waiting in line. The two tellers came out and picked him up. They told him next time they'll call the ambulance," she said, like the schoolteacher she once was.

"It happens so damn quickly," Dad explained. "You just go down before you know it."

Sitting across the table, watching my dad eat his fish and chips, I could tell he was feeling jaunty.

"Beverly!" he said, eyes twinkling, "Should I grow a mustache?" He turned to look at my mom full on.

"I have to have hair growing somewhere," he said.

She rolled her eyes. "You have enough growing out of your nose."

Thankfully for my father, their house sold that week.

As part of the admission to the retirement home, my father had a chest X-ray for tuberculosis. It didn't show any TB, but it did pick up spots across his lungs, a discovery that needed fast medical attention.

I was at work when my mom called. Newsrooms have very few private spaces for personal calls, especially when one is required to speak loudly to be heard. I walked to the couches near the old darkroom, where the photographs were once printed in trays of chemical solution.

"The doctor," my mother said, her voice cracking, "believes that your father has cancer throughout his lungs."

Oh no.

"He's having a CT scan on March 2, which is a Saturday, and we will get a driver to take us. We've already made the reservation, so don't drive out, and if that doesn't disprove it, then it is advanced cancer," she said, sighing deeply.

"Wait a minute," I said, having lived through previous health dramas. "Is it a likely diagnosis? Or speculation?"

She started quoting the terminology in the specialist's letter, written in a language neither of us spoke, although her knowledge was no doubt greater due to her dog-eared copy of *The Merck Manual of Medical Information*, the home health edition.

She read the section of the doctor's letter that, she said, noted the likelihood of cancer in all lobes of my father's lungs.

"The doctor mentioned the possibility of bleeding and a stroke, but that is all I can remember at the moment because I am upset about it," she said.

She continued reading.

"What he is saying is, if it ends up being cancer, it will be advanced. That is the nitty-gritty."

The alternative, she said, is that my dad is getting bits of food in his lungs because he's having trouble swallowing properly.

"Well, that's better than advanced cancer," I said.

"Oh, you wouldn't want bits of food in your lungs, that would hurt you badly," she scolded.

It was a bit remarkable that for all their medical appointments, it was a routine X-ray for admission to the retirement home, their chance for an easier life, that led to this discovery.

And so it began, the family discussion on whether my dad, a frail 88-year-old, should have chemotherapy and radiation to fight cancer to stay alive for his wife and children. It is unclear how my mom felt when I suggested that the cure might kill him first. Weeks passed with no answer on his condition. Eventually, I told my mom about a book that my *Toronto Star* colleague Kevin Donovan had lent me. It was called *Being Mortal: Medicine and What Matters in the End* by American surgeon Atul Gawande. It was a wildly popular book, and I admit to only reading bits of it, fearful of any details lodging in my brain since I was writing on a marginally similar topic. I told my mom about the chapter that discussed society's modern belief that science should keep us alive, and that we will fight death at any cost, even though the attempt at a cure often poisons our final months of life.

My mom ordered it from the local bookstore. I'm not sure if she ever picked up the *Merck Manual* again because *Being Mortal* became her new bible. A year earlier, when either parent went into the hospital, my mom was adamant that the staff knew they wanted every possible life-saving measure to be taken in case of an emergency. "Just keep my husband alive," she told the nurse who asked about their wishes when my dad went in for knee surgery. Now, at 91, after reading Dr. Gawande's book, she had a new perspective. She wanted resuscitation, yes, but not to the extreme, not to the point where she'd be left with chronic problems or dependency. I think she felt a bit of relief to discover a different perspective, that death is a natural part of our existence, after years spent terrified that it would come too soon.

"I told Dr. H. about *Being Mortal*," she said, of her family doctor. "I hope he reads it."

With the darkness of the cancer diagnosis hovering, my parents moved into their double room in the retirement home, unsure if they'd need quite so much space, or for how long.

As usual, my mother found the bright side.

"I laughed when I walked through the front doors," she said gaily. "I said out loud, 'I am walking toward my fate.'"

## CHAPTER SIX

# *Primacare and the Potential of Virtual Reality*

I T WAS CHRISTMAS 2017.
Armin St. George was packing for a visit with his mom in Cambridge, Massachusetts. He and a longtime family friend John Michael Adamo ran a digital media company in Buffalo, New York. Their company, Crosswater, developed spatial audio, and they worked mostly with an Edinburgh tech company called Two Big Ears, until it was bought by Facebook. Together, the tech and audio companies created the sounds that provide an immersive 360-degree virtual reality experience, such as a dog barking in the distance or the swoosh of a bat flying through the night sky. On his way out the door, Armin grabbed Crosswater's Samsung Gear virtual reality headset to show his family the latest technology.

Dr. Genevieve St. George was 85 that year. She lived in a first-floor condo of a renovated Federalist home near Harvard Square, the cobblestoned plaza lined with bookstores, coffee shops and restaurants. Genevieve had a doctorate in education and wrote poetry. She also had Alzheimer's disease, with a lingering depression. She still kept her own home with help from her daughters and home-care workers. "We are grateful to the Massachusetts health-care system," Armin likes to say.

Genevieve's five children arrived with their families. They squeezed into her condo, sharing a holiday meal. Tonight, like most nights, Genevieve was quiet.

During dinner, Armin's brother described a hike through the Muir Woods National Monument, a redwood forest just north of San Francisco. Genevieve perked up. "I'd like to hike there too," she said. The forest held special memories for her, having walked its trails years ago.

Her excitement got Armin thinking. He had brought the virtual reality headset to show his family the projects that he was working on with the University of Buffalo's medical school, but his mom gave him a new idea. After dinner, as Genevieve sat on her living room couch, Armin asked if he could show her a video of the forest. She said yes. When he put the headset on her, gently steadying it, Genevieve looked like a thoroughly modern grandmother, a double strand of white pearls around her neck and 3D goggles over her eyes. Crosswater didn't have a video of Muir Woods, so he downloaded one from a content provider called Oculus, bought by Facebook a few years before it acquired Two Big Ears, part of its plan to create a virtual reality platform with a spatial audio engine. The 360-degree video began playing, and from Genevieve's perspective inside the headset, it felt like she was there in person, going for a walk in the wooded terrain. If she looked up, way up, she could see the trees stretching high, their leaves a neon etching against the sun. If she looked down, Genevieve could see the trail pointing forward. Behind her, a black-and-white virtual dog ran up, tail wagging. Together she and the dog marveled at the wide old trees standing like ancient Ents from Tolkien's Middle-Earth.

From Armin's perspective, in the living room of a condo in Cambridge, Genevieve came back to life. Holding the goggles steady, she turned her head from side to side, taking in the surrounding visuals. He could not see the look in her eyes, but he could see her smile, laugh and talk to the dog. Twenty minutes later, when his mom was finished her hike, he removed the headset. For the rest of the evening she chatted about her adventure, entranced by the "little doggie" and the view of the beach. It felt good to see her happy again, even for a few hours.

The next day Armin played another video for his mom, taking her for a walk along the Great Wall of China, another happy memory from her traveling past. Genevieve laughed through her virtual experience, and after, she seemed content.

"That is when we realized," Armin says, "that this could be helpful to others."

◎ ◎ ◎

As Matthew Melchior says, it's a wonderful, wonderful time to grow old. What he means, specifically, is that technological innovators are now tapping into the needs of the biggest demographic in a confluence of tech, aging and the boomers' buying power.

Melchior and his family are longtime real estate developers and own Primacare Living Solutions, which has three nursing homes in Ontario, with a fourth in planning. Their business began in bricks and mortar, but Melchior is preparing for a much different future. It will combine hands-on care for elders that focuses on emotions, with architectural designs that mimic a home instead of an institution, and it will layer in the technology that allows people to virtually visit old Berlin, or just sit under a canopy of cherry tree blossoms.

He is creating a "campus of care" called Griffin Ridge Seniors Community near Hamilton, Ontario, for seniors of different ages and abilities. Some will live in apartments, for independent or assisted living. Others will live in long-term care and share social space in a community hub that is accessible to all.

The campus of care concept, much like the Atlanta development that Andy Isakson built in honor of his mother, allows people to move from independent living to the nursing home, as their needs change. In Melchior's plan, there will be trees, gardens and green outdoor spaces for walking, so that people can age on stronger legs. Residents will help one another, through peer-to-peer supports. It will be built on land that is close to stores and restaurants, so residents can go about their days with shopping or banking, much like they did in the past.

Right now, he says, the people starting to look at seniors' housing are from the same demographic that shook up society during their youth, and as their adult years advanced, they have embraced another revolution, this one in technology. Melchior believes this generation will make tech work for them, easing their elder years. "They did not accept the status quo," he says. "They sought change. Now that they are seniors, they will not accept the status quo. They will seek change through technology that allows greater choice to enjoy their senior years."

The opportunity to tweak the act of aging through the use of technological innovation is already a burgeoning field. AARP says it plays a growing role in what it calls the Longevity Economy. AARP commissioned Oxford Economics to examine the potential for American growth and business opportunities related to aging, and the report concluded that the Longevity Economy is responsible for US$7.1 trillion in annual economic activity (which AARP later updated to US$8.3 trillion). It's expected to top US$13.5 trillion by 2032. While these numbers reflect a massive array of services, products and actions by and for America's 50-plus crowd (including extra years in the workforce), technological advances factor heavily. As the report said, the Longevity Economy is "fueling a new wave of start-ups, along with expansion of established industries catering to people over age 50." Beyond the antiaging markets and regenerative medicine is the innovation that focuses on basic life choices such as the desire to live at home longer. The Oxford Economics report details the options that are already in play. Telemedicine allows physicians to monitor seniors at home, instead of requiring a hospital or nursing-home stay. A sensor-based system installed in the home transmits live data to doctors and family, tracking movement throughout the house, intake of medicine and even sleep activity and blood sugar levels. These changes are heralded as the progressive way forward, strategies to keep people out of expensive hospitals and nursing homes, even though it seems a bit invasive. Maybe privacy is just a state of mind, since CCTV cameras are in public spaces everywhere. Maybe it's better than the alternative. In any case, the "mobile health market," as the report said, was expected to account for more than US$20 billion a year in 2020.

There is talk of personal-service robots or, as some say, nurse-bots, using artificial intelligence to help with vacuuming and other chores, although no one has quite figured out how to use a machine as an emotional companion, since most of us still need a human touch. New devices can be used to keep people safe, such as wristbands in long-term care that unlock some doors but not others. Or in Langley, B.C., at the Village, similar technology gives people with dementia the freedom to walk outdoors in a large enclosed area, while allowing staff to track their whereabouts if they don't return. For those who prefer the dignity of discretion, GPS trackers can be hidden in the soles of shoes. Apple Watches can detect falls, with an option to call emergency services if needed.

Because we still like to read, ebooks give the freedom to increase type size — no reading glasses needed. Audiobooks allow us to disappear into a story in a different way. In San Diego's Glenner Town Square, Susie carried a GrandPad, tapping the photos on the screen to call her son or daughter. Skype and FaceTime allow visits with grandchildren. When my nephew made the Canadian relay team for the 2019 World Track and Field championships in the Middle East, my mother asked her iPad, "Where is Doha?" and Siri gave her its location.

In Canada, Michael Tamblyn is the chief entrepreneur of Age-Well, a technology and aging network based at Canada's University Health Network that mentors people with ideas for technology that can improve life for seniors. Despite the opportunities presented by a large demographic of older people, Tamblyn, president and CEO of e-reader and audiobook company Rakuten Kobo, believes Canadian markets are "still radically under-invested" when it comes to solutions for aging.

"One of the appeals that I find in my work with Age-Well is being able to be part of one of the few collections of companies and entrepreneurs who are focused in this area," Tamblyn says.

"I think it speaks to aging and older adults that this has been one of the overlooked markets for Canadian business and for entrepreneurs. Most people still don't know the sheer amount of buying power, of expenditure, in this demographic. There is a lot more that could be done."

What is emerging, he says, is a group of engineers, designers and entrepreneurs who are developing technologies that can help seniors, sometimes after seeing the struggles of their grandparents. Entrepreneurs are working on a device for nursing homes that, Tamblyn says, is a bit like a sheet that acts as a conveyor belt. It could replace the use of lifts, devices that move seniors from bed to chair — a perilous journey.

As the husband of seniors' advocate Laura Tamblyn Watts, he is attuned to biases against older people, however unintentional, particularly in the technology field staffed by people in their 20s and 30s. "They are very interested in building products that reflect their own experience in the world. They want to build things that their friends will like. They are not really thinking about building products that their grandparents will like.

"So it's an act of education and awareness building to take that group of people and make them realize that there is an additional set of requirements when working with older adults, but also there is a huge commercial opportunity if you do it well."

A few years ago, Matthew Melchior, president and co-founder of Primacare Living, and his chief operating officer, Jill Knowlton, started discussing the possibilities of virtual reality. They had heard about results that seemed promising in studies of VR on people with early cognitive decline, but they wondered if it would work for the people in their care living with serious or advanced dementia. Knowlton thought it might help with a big, strapping man who once drove long-haul trucks across North America and now, living in the limited space of a nursing home, had episodes of rage. She wondered what a video of a courtroom would do for a retired judge who spends his days presiding over the nursing station that looks a lot like his old courtroom bench, surveying the room, meting out justice. He now instructs the nurses, and woe to those who don't follow his orders. "You don't speak unless you are spoken to," Knowlton says. "He's running his life like his courtroom. If the nurse says something, well, you're probably going to get clobbered, because you're speaking and he didn't tell you that you could speak."

Knowlton began her career as a registered nurse, spending most of her time in privately operated long-term care, and is a leader with the Ontario Long-Term Care Association, the province's largest nursing home group. She is equal parts warm and professional. She is unafraid of risk, willing to take the unorthodox approach if there's a good chance it will improve lives. In one of my first interviews with Knowlton, she told me a story about long-term care that I've never forgotten. A man, a resident with serious dementia, was frustrated by a high libido. He was young, just in his early 60s. His dementia left him with few inhibitions and sometimes he would touch female residents in his home. His wife had a plan to fix that. She asked his nursing home for permission, and it was granted. Once a month, the wife hired a sex worker to visit her husband at the home. Staff reserved the private family "stay-over" suite. It was beautifully appointed, like a luxury hotel room, with a comfortable bed and soft lighting. They left the man and the sex worker alone. After, he seemed more relaxed, and for the next month, his behavior was under control. Everyone was happier.

Knowlton likes possibility thinking. So does Melchior. Together, they have pushed the rights of LGBTQ2S people. Understanding sexuality is an important piece of long-term care. They sought help from The 519, a City of Toronto agency that advocates for the LGBTQ2S community. It provided the mandatory training for staff and volunteer sessions for resident and family councils. Knowlton says the resident councils embraced the sessions. "We're all living here, together, so let's make everyone feel welcome." One resident, Knowlton says, identified as a woman, wearing feminine clothes, but when she was sick and couldn't put on her wig, she looked like a man. With The 519 training, Knowlton says staff always approached her as a female, no matter how she appeared.

With Melchior, Knowlton researched ways to improve the lives of people in their homes, choosing the Butterfly program because of the way it helped shift the culture from a medicalized model to one that allowed individuals to live with freedom, to follow their interests. They looked at technology for people with dementia, examining the possibility that it would help people stay calmer, happier and avoid the problematic antipsychotics that many use to keep people quiet. Or the physical restraints, to keep them still.

Knowlton approached the Centre for Aging + Brain Health Innovation associated with Baycrest in Toronto. She was interested in participating in its research projects, part of its Industry Innovation Partnership Program. CABHI, as it is called (pronounced *cabee*), describes its program as "an opportunity for companies around the world to accelerate their disruptive senior care innovations by testing them in a real-world opportunity."

Trial sites are found across North America, in long-term care homes, community care, hospitals, memory clinics and day programs. Before applying, CABHI connects the industry players with tech companies to see if they can make a match. "Like dating," Knowlton says.

Around the same time that Knowlton reached out to CABHI, Tara Kruse was at work as a server in a downtown Buffalo restaurant. Armin and his business partner, John Adamo, arrived on a March evening, holding court at their table for four hours, celebrating Adamo's 75th birthday, discussing life, aging, technology and Genevieve St. George's virtual reality experience. A few nights later, Kruse waited on a couple from Toronto, and after learning of their professional connection to CABHI, she mentioned the owners of a local company who were interested in virtual reality with spatial sound in research for the elderly. She described Armin's story about his mom and her happiness after visiting the virtual forest. The next time Armin and Adamo returned for dinner, it quickly became clear that Kruse shared a mutual interest in medical education. She was in school studying to become a physician's assistant. Armin called it serendipity. Armin and Adamo offered Kruse a job. It worked out well.

Adamo was a friend of Armin's mom; sometimes they wrote poetry together. The two men became business partners in the late 1970s, involved in arts, music, advertising jingles, marketing or the creation of fine food, as restaurateurs. But these days they focus on Crosswater, their company that produces virtual reality, including teaching videos for many of the University of Buffalo's medical instructors.

It was Kruse's fortuitous restaurant meeting with the CABHI people that ultimately led to the meeting with Knowlton and the discussion about Crosswater Digital Media playing the role of tech partner in Primacare's application for 2018 research funding. After an initial connection with a VR company didn't work out, CABHI sent Primacare three more options. Knowlton and her team spent an afternoon interviewing each of those potential matches. Crosswater was one of them.

Kruse, Crosswater's new medical content director, drove with Armin and Adamo to London, Ontario, for the interview with Knowlton and her team. It turned out to be a meeting of the like-minded. The group discussed the possibilities that virtual reality combined with Adamo's instrumental compositions and Crosswater's spatial audio sounds could take people with moderate to severe dementia to a peaceful place, tapping into memories, creating a relaxation that pharmaceuticals, with nasty side effects, could never match. Knowlton focused on the potential outcomes of their proposed study. Would it help residents relax, rather than grow angry, depressed or aggressive? Could it lessen the use of antipsychotic medication given to people with dementia? Would it help people calm down at the end of the day, enabling a deeper sleep? Could it lead to greater contentment? Make life easier for workers? Or create a fun, happier experience, enticing families to visit more often?

Knowlton didn't commit, not that day, although it felt as though the meeting would end with a swipe to the right, as the kids say, a match and an agreement to work together on Primacare's application. After the handshakes, Armin fired up his champagne-colored Equinox SUV for the three-hour drive back to Buffalo. As they pulled onto Highway 401, he and Kruse chatted about ideas, hopeful they would be chosen. Adamo sat alone in the back, wrapped in his own space. He is one of those people who absorbs others' feelings and watched Knowlton's excitement, imagining the possibilities, impressed at the kindness he felt in the nursing home. Now Adamo turned inward, constructing chords and melodies in his mind, creating a sense of peacefulness. It would be instrumental, otherwise the brain would have to work to interpret the words and their meaning. Music for the videos is meant to provide a support system for the visuals, not a distraction.

"It is very much in the tradition of Debussy," he says, referring to the French composer. "It's languid, it's beautiful, it's emotional, but it's not intense. One thing musically I am looking at is to under no circumstances create a huge curve of emotions, as opposed to gently moving and bringing people to a place and providing a support for what they are seeing."

Knowlton and Melchior picked Crosswater and applied for the grant. The Centre for Aging + Brain Health Innovation awarded them the grant, with additional funding from the federal and provincial governments. Knowlton organized her research team, a PhD researcher, an epidemiologist and a health economist from Western University. Adamo started composing the music to accompany all the videos. One of his songs was in the style of the Glenn Miller Band, another influenced by the Dorsey Brothers, a slow piece he called "I Want to Hold You Close." Other songs would be country, or soft rock, jazz, even early New Wave. It all depends on the region, the culture and the age of the personalities within the home.

Once the plans for the study were finalized, Armin and Adamo met Melchior, who told them about his father's experience with dementia. Albert was the larger-than-life patriarch of the Melchior family who had built a successful real estate development company. He had started as a teenager with two friends, Rudy and Angelo, building bungalows in the Bathurst and Wilson area of Toronto, close to the present-day CABHI office in the Baycrest Health Sciences Centre. The trio named their little company ARA Construction. The first *A* was for Albert, who went on to build houses, apartments, malls and commercial buildings across Toronto. The *R* was for Rudy Bratty, who became a lawyer and one of Canada's wealthiest real estate developers with Remington Group. The final *A* was for Angelo DelZotto, who, with his brothers, created the Tridel Group, building condos, subdivisions and commercial towers that transformed the Toronto region.

Albert started as a carpenter and a cabinetmaker. He learned how to build a house from the ground up, which helped him understand the building process as his projects grew bigger. He loved technology and was always interested in the next new thing. He was transfixed by the style of the automobiles of his era with their jet-age styling from bumper to tail fin. Albert was a Cadillac man. His first Caddy was white with a robin's-egg blue top. Albert and his bride, Valia, drove it to California on their honeymoon. Decades later, when he allowed his children to run the development company, Albert bought a Heritage Classic Harley-Davidson motorcycle that he drove alone because Valia told him there was not a chance she'd climb on the back of that machine. "You're crazy," she said. He took great pleasure in his long rides.

Albert never really retired. He always offered his advice, solicited or otherwise, in developments, including the construction of a nursing home just north of Toronto called Villa Leonardo Gambin. He still dressed beautifully but started having what Melchior called "seniors' moments." Those were the first signs, although it was hard to believe that they predicted something deeper. Soon enough it became clear: the man who spent his life as a leader could no longer lead. In his 70s Albert was diagnosed with dementia. His children and their families all cared for him until they could no longer manage on their own. They lived it, daily. "Dementia is very cruel because at one moment someone is so, so vibrant and the next they are so challenged," Melchior says. "In mathematical terms, it is not a bell curve, but a step graph. The floor falls out." Some days, Albert grew frustrated. At other times, he was withdrawn. And there came a time when Albert needed full-time care. He moved into Toronto's Villa Colombo and later, when construction was finished, he transferred to Villa Leonardo Gambin, the non-profit nursing home that had benefited from his instruction as it was being built. Melchior was the founding chair of the non-profit group that developed the home.

"He worked on the structure of the building he ultimately lived in and died in. A true builder's story."

Melchior is tall, like his father, another dominant presence. While his father succeeded with a high school diploma, Melchior went to graduate school at McGill University in Montreal, earning a degree in accounting, and then began to run the family development company with his older brother Randy.

Melchior speaks of his father with reverence. The man who had guided him through so many years eventually disappeared into his disease, although he always seemed sharper during lunches with friends when they'd talk about flashy cars and sports. Those were good times. Melchior laughs when describing his dad's joy at sitting around the restaurant table, one of the guys.

Given the prevalence of dementia, it is not difficult to find leaders in the long-term care industry with family who have lived it. His father's experience resonated with Melchior and his siblings. Primacare invested "family money" to improve care by adding Butterfly principles to all three of their nursing homes and designing the fourth to include tiny, homey living areas for eight people with dementia, instead of the traditional designs for cost-effective units of 32.

In October 2018, CABHI announced funding for 31 studies, including Primacare's The Albert Project. Adamo named his song, the one he wrote in the back seat of Armin's car, "For Albert." Primacare's goal was to use Crosswater's virtual reality visuals and spatial surround sounds along with Adamo's music to evaluate the viability of VR as a therapy for long-term care residents with moderate to severe dementia, examining potential benefits to the residents and the caregivers. The research would be conducted by Western University's Dr. Karen Campbell and her team, working out of Primacare's three Ontario nursing homes in London, Brampton and St. Catharines.

CABHI funded several projects that examined the use of virtual reality on people living with dementia, including one led by

York University's Lora Appel, who was working with Toronto's OpenLab, a "design and innovation shop" operated out of the University Health Network that focused on creative solutions in health care. Appel's research looked at people with limited mobility and cognitive impairment in hospitals, long-term care and the community. She focused on nature, the benefits of what the Japanese call "forest bathing," for people who do not get to spend time outside.

"Unfortunately, this group, because of their mobility issues, they can't get outside and they are increasingly confined indoors, supposedly for their own benefit," Appel says.

"They [the families] might not have the finances or social supports to come to their long-term care homes and take them outside, so they really are lacking exposure to naturally beneficial environments. The idea behind my research was not can technology replace these instances, but can it provide exposure to these helpful environments to people who otherwise can't get outside," she says.

It is not an exaggeration to say that in the current state of long-term care, a lot of people haven't felt a full breeze on their skin for years. That speaks to the fact that people are living in homes that were designed as institutions, to keep people inside and safe, creating as little trouble as possible for the staff. Most of those homes were built about 30 years ago. From now on, the most humane new designs will recognize the need we all have for freedom, to walk and be out in the trees or gardens, puttering, just like people do in their own homes. As Eloy van Hal from de Hogeweyk in the Netherlands said, people who get outside every day have better mobility, eat more and sleep better too. And while the goal should be to find ways to allow people to enjoy the freedom of the real outdoors, technology might be able to help fill the gap if that's not feasible. It could also serve another purpose, by calming people. Primacare's research showed the emotional benefits created by transporting the senses back in time to a familiar place, or exposing people once again to the beauty of the world, even if VR can't create the smell of fresh leaves on a forest trail. Although, there may be an app for that.

◎ ◎ ◎

Crosswater Digital Media offices inhabit the second floor of a dark brick building on Buffalo's Delaware Avenue, a few blocks from the University of Buffalo's new Jacobs School of Medicine and Biomedical Sciences. Here, staff created two types of videos for the Albert Project. The first are real scenes taken from a film shot on location, some created specifically for people living in Henley Place, in London. A video was shot from the cab of a big rig driving along a highway for the former long-haul truck driver with dementia. The hope is that the film will take him back to his years of freedom on the road. When he watches the video, it feels like he is sitting inside the cab, in the passenger seat, with the roof of the truck overhead, looking at the greenery outside all of the windows. The man doing the actual driving is a trucker friend of Armin's, with short gray hair and a no-nonsense face. He's focused, hands gripping the wheel, so the nursing-home trucker can relax and enjoy being on the road again. Some of the men were dairy farmers from the agricultural communities outside of London. Armin sent a filmmaker to a dairy farm in Batavia, New York, to shoot farmers bringing cows into the barn in the evening with the hope that the visuals and soft mooing of the animals would help the retired farmers settle into their new routine and get a good night's sleep.

Some videos, such as these prototypes, will be made from real images. Others will be animated, creating an alternate reality, like video games. Armin wonders whether people respond better to real film over animated images.

One of Crosswater's newest hires is Alex. He is 22 years old and went to school to study video game development. Now he is building a scene for people with dementia. It's on the Pacific coast, and features a cabin with a front porch below a hill, surrounded by trees, looking onto the ocean. He started with a basic structure for the cabin, the porch and a chair, and he layers images until he creates a scene so detailed it feels like the viewer can rub the grain of the wooden chair or see the soft crest of the waves in the ocean. Alex says the user can choose to hear Adamo's music or natural sounds of animal life indigenous to that area. "There's water, wind and all the different types of birds, and when it becomes nighttime, then the birds go to sleep, and the different animals will come out," he says.

As Kruse points out, Alex has designed a scene that creates a primal feeling of safety in most people. She cites the work of biologists, such as Harvard University's E.O. Wilson, who has said that human genes hold an instinctive bond with the natural world and contain deep intuitive connections to the water, the land and its creatures.

"This is inherently what people, throughout humanity, seek as a safe place," Kruse says. "Having water close by, having the hills close by, having visibility, having shelter — that is the art that tends to appeal to people throughout time because it has that feeling of safety, and that's what satisfies humans."

It is a fascinating theory, because social beings that we are, millions of us are living in large urban centers that are growing into powerful city states. We live amongst asphalt and concrete without understanding why we still crave a patch of grass, a forest or the sound of the waves. This is, in part, why seniors' communities like Carol Woods, in the North Carolina forest, start with the perfect backdrop for contentment. It must also be why some people who live in long-term care, with or without cognitive decline, feel lost or angry, because they never, ever, go outside or feel sun on skin. It is an unnatural existence.

Down the hall from Alex, past the studio where Adamo's compositions were previously recorded, is the room where Fred, the sound guy, creates Crosswater's specialty. Crosswater uses high-quality audio microphones with four capsules pointing in different directions to pick up all manner of sounds. Back in the studio, Fred will place those sounds in the video, where they need to appear as the film unfolds. It enables the viewer to hear a dog barking from the porch or birds singing high above in the trees. Those are the naturally recorded sounds. Next, Fred adds new sounds to enhance the experience. If the visual shows the ocean breaking on a rock, he will create the sound of the waves and add it to the rock location. He adds sounds throughout the video to give the full sensory experience.

When Genevieve St. George watched the video in her condo, Armin says the sound was still mono or stereo, propelling Crosswater to push for an immersive experience when they began to create videos for the study. Spatial audio changes with the viewing experience. "As you hear something coming from behind you, and when you turn to look in that direction, you also hear a change in the sound as your ears face the source," Armin says. "With spatial audio, the sound changes perspective, depending on where you're facing, similar to real life."

As the study began, it didn't take long for the lead researcher Dr. Karen Campbell to realize that people did not like wearing the VR headset. Unlike Genevieve, most fiddled with it, distracted. It also posed a problem for staff, who had to leave it in a cleaning machine for half an hour after each use to prevent the spread of communicable diseases, a time-consuming endeavor. Armin looked around for a solution. Enter Broomx, a Spanish start-up tech company that makes a 360-degree immersive device that can project video on three walls of a room and the ceiling. Broomx advertises its image projections for nightclubs, museums, restaurants, amusement parks, health care or a totally awesome bedroom. The Broomx machine is round and glossy white, and when placed in the white wheelbase that Armin commissioned so it could be rolled down long-term care hallways, it looks a bit like *Star Wars'* beloved R2-D2.

Crosswater has a Broomx room in its Buffalo office. With Adamo's instrumental compositions that match the resting heart rate of 72 beats per minute, the spring cherry blossom video shot in Buffalo's Delaware Park enables the viewer to relax with a view from a park bench, watching people wander below the canopy of soft, pink flowers. Another time, the Batavia dairy cows, noses raised with curiosity, march forward as if they were stepping off the wall and into the room. Watching their big, curious eyes as they amble closer feels a bit trippy, like a wholesome hallucinogenic.

As soon as the Broomx arrived, the research began with Dr. Campbell reminding everyone that data will show whatever it shows, including the possibility that VR doesn't work for advanced dementia. That is the objectivity of research. Whatever will be, will be. Dr. Campbell led two studies. The first looked at feasibility. Would people tolerate the headsets? That answer didn't take long: No, they would not. How long would they sit? Dr. Campbell wondered if people would last beyond one or two minutes but with Broomx, most stayed for 30. Most importantly, could the impacts be measured? It was too soon to say if their depression or agitation would lessen, but people sat and stared, mesmerized. One woman from England, whose personal history included a stint as a British spy, loved the videos of Berlin because she had been stationed there as an undercover agent in her 20s. Like many with cognitive decline, she spent her days reliving the most vivid period of her life. It doesn't get more dramatic than the years spent spying on the Germans during the Second World War. She would only eat German food and drink German wine. She didn't like eating in the dining room with 31 other residents. "That's pretty stressful if you were a spy," says Jill Knowlton. "Because every single person is a suspect." Knowlton's staff, following the Butterfly protocol, gave her the freedom to live in her most comfortable emotional space, but she was also nosing around in others' rooms, spying, perhaps, which didn't always go over well. With the virtual reality she returned to old Berlin every day. "She's happy, she's in her element. She talks in German. She's much more relaxed," Knowlton says.

Melchior, Primacare's CEO, watched the changes unfold and saw that virtual reality enhanced the Butterfly program, prompting workers to reach deeper into the emotional needs of each resident, seeking out the video that might connect them with a peaceful place. "It demonstrates a respect for the life of that individual before they came into our environment," he says. "We can create an environment that is safer, more welcoming and therefore less likely to have unsuccessful events, falls, aggression, emergency room transfers, all of which are expensive, all of which are disruptive, all of which take the limited amount of care that we have."

After Armin filmed the interior of a courtroom, the judge stopped hovering over the nurses' station. Staff at the nursing home brought in law books. His wife brought his gavel. When the video plays, the judge runs his courtroom. He is in control again. "He's in his space where he needs to be," Knowlton says. The videos are not meant to occupy an individual for an extended period. Instead, they are one of many "tools," as Knowlton calls them, available to help people over the course of a day or a week. If the videos are found to calm people, decrease agitation, then they would be a superior option to the typical response, which is medicating people with antipsychotic drugs and using physical restraints.

Knowlton and Dr. Campbell announced the results of the first study at the Global Ageing Conference in Toronto in September 2019. The study concluded that the impacts of virtual reality therapy can be measured and ultimately used in long-term care homes for older adults with moderate to severe dementia. The results of the feasibility study have been submitted for publication in *BMC Geriatrics*, an open access journal that publishes peer-reviewed research. The second study measured the actual changes that VR created in 120 residents. It was a randomized controlled study, which means it follows established methods to collect information, providing hard evidence. It found evidence that people slept better, which is restorative to health, emotionally and physically. It also pointed to a 33 percent decrease in clinical depression, and while Dr. Campbell says the numbers are not considered statistically relevant, she believes those results matter immensely to residents and staff.

Melchior plans to add this technology and others permanently to Primacare's homes, combining it with the Meaningful Care Matters focus on emotion and the new designs for smaller, living spaces within the hard structure of the building. It is a shift, an evolution, that combines the unlikely triumvirate of technology, emotions and bricks. What Melchior wants, what Knowlton wants, are new designs that allow free movement outside the residence, so that people with or without memory loss can meet for coffee or walk in the garden, all leading to an improved quality of life.

Technology, such as location sensors in wristbands or shoes, can enable freedom. But the relationships that will thrive in our later years still rely on human interaction.

The need for friendship among older people is undeniable. During the COVID-19 lockdown in seniors' homes, news coverage of the despair created by social isolation exposed the reality that emotional connections matter. Perhaps the frustration so many of us felt, hidden in our homes, allowed us to empathize with older people who withered from the loss of family and friends. If that shared experience taught us anything, it exposed the fact that elders are not "others."

Long before the pandemic, Melchior spoke of the way many look at older people, as if they are different, no longer needing the humanity the rest of us seek, because of their age. "Think about this," Melchior said. "It's always easier to say 'us' and 'them.' That's one of the biggest problems. You can talk about people saying, 'I don't like what you are doing — for them.' Which is really crazy, because them is *us*. Them is us.

"Think about that."

◎　◎　◎

As it turned out, my father did not have advanced lung cancer.

It was some kind of undetermined infection, but it cleared up quickly, and my dad moved on, ignoring the cancer scare as if it had never happened. He joined the exercise classes at the retirement home. My parents chatted with the couple at their table who own a well-known business in town.

"The husband is 97," Mom said. "He drives to work every morning. And his wife is 96. When he's at work, she goes to exercise classes. I was behind her the other day and I thought, *She walks just like a teenager!*"

Mom was starting to enjoy life here. Previously, she had insisted that she didn't need a retirement home, privately saying she was just here for her husband. My dad made the same comments in reverse when she wasn't around.

Every time I called their room in the retirement home, my mom answered the phone and I could hear her saying thank you to someone. I started to wonder: Who is this worker who is in their room so often? Who are you always thanking?

She said, "Oh, it's the woman who says 'You. Have. A. Phone. Call.'"

I paused. "You know that's an automated voice, right?"

"I know," my mom said, "but I thank her anyway. When I bump into a mannequin in the store, I always say sorry."

Mostly, she was amused by the habits of the people around her.

"I'm Nancy Drew," she announced one day. "I need a good mystery.

"I call it the case of the missing bananas."

The home put out bowls of fruit, and my mom watched as the bananas disappeared, eventually determining that a certain few were the likely suspects. One man appeared to have stuffed them in his pant pockets, she said, laughing as she described his profile as he walked by. Another resident, a woman, was more brazen. My mom decided to call her out subtly.

"I asked the lady who seems to get the most if she could bring me one. She said, 'Oh, you should get some exercise and walk over to them.' I said, 'Yes, but they do go so quickly.'"

A few nights later, my dad got up to use the washroom and fell. He beeped his wristband alert button for help from the nurse, and it wasn't long before the ambulance attendants arrived, loading him on a stretcher for a trip to the hospital.

"I'm feeling better now," my mom said over the phone the next morning. "But it would have been nice if my husband hadn't left me in the middle of the night. I got close to him when he was on the stretcher and I leaned over and told him that I loved him. He said he loved me. But he loves me because he needs me."

"Oh," I told her, "I'm sure he loves you."

"He does. In his own way."

If she only knew.

CHAPTER SEVEN

# Sherbrooke Community Centre and the Eden Alternative

I NSIDE, THE BIRDS ARE SINGING.
It's 7:30 a.m.

Most of the people who live in the Sherbrooke Community Centre are still in bed. They're definitely not in the halls, not yet, but the cockatiels, well, their morning routine begins with a crescendo. They sing with raucous abandon, then softly, before returning to peak bird. It sounds like the Nike commercial version of *Carmina Burana*.

Sherbrooke is a nursing home with celebrity status in the city of Saskatoon, Saskatchewan. I'm meeting Eric Anderson, communications director, wondering if he is as ebullient at this hour as he has been in his emails. Yup. Anderson is a young guy, a former journalist who left public radio for a career at Sherbrooke. He wears big glasses and is a huge Harry Potter fan. He thinks he's a Hufflepuff. But he's not.

Sherbrooke is the home of Suellen Beatty, who inspired Dr. Bill Thomas's Green House Project, a leader who keeps advancing the meaning of long-term care. In April 2018, Beatty spoke in Toronto at a conference organized by AdvantAge Ontario, the association for not-for-profit seniors' housing. Several hundred people listened as she described her realization that locked dementia units were akin to segregation and equated the need to open these doors, allowing people to live among residents of all abilities, to the American civil rights movement. Dr. Allen Power, Beatty's American peer and mentor, wrote about locked doors in his 2010 book, *Dementia Beyond Drugs*, and in the 2017 reprint, said the "persistent segregation of individuals who live with a diagnosis of dementia flies in the face of what our societies are trying to accomplish."

While no longer an entirely new idea, Beatty's opinion was still radical to many in the mainstream nursing-home industry. Beatty, industry folks said, is someone you need to meet.

Three days after leaving Amsterdam, I flew to Saskatoon, two cities that share the same latitude, although not much else. In Saskatoon, the words *coffee shop* are inextricably linked to Tim Hortons. In Amsterdam, coffee shop means marijuana café. Amsterdam is built around a busy shipping port near the North Sea Canal, sliced up and down with canals from the sea and the river Amstel. Saskatoon has a river too, but it is locked inside the Prairies, where sunsets over the flat horizon burnish clouds in yellow and red.

The Sherbrooke Community Centre sits in a residential neighborhood called College Park, a nice mix of middle-class houses. There's a high school up the street and a couple of elementary schools nearby. One of those schools, École College Park, coordinates a daily sixth grade class in Sherbrooke, mixing children with elders for shared learning and friendship. The class is called iGen, for intergenerational. During a graduation event in 2014, a woman who is a long-retired literacy professor and Sherbrooke resident said teaching the 12-year-olds brought her back to life. The iGen classes, the professor said, are about learning and fun, but also "about elders discovering that we still are of use, that we are valued."

Just off the main hallway, where the birds sing, is a day care with babies and children up to kindergarten age. Many are children of staff, others come from the community. Sometimes the toddlers march the hallways, waving to the elders, a gang of chunky legs and charm. Take a right turn at the bird entrance and a door leads to a full-sized swimming pool with a hot tub. Recovering from a stroke, Alice Cowell learned to swim here at the age of 91. "I was petrified," Cowell said. "But I said, 'Okay, let's try.' I bought the first bathing suit I've ever had in my life. I just love it now." Down the hallway, near the resident art studio, is the physiotherapy room that looks almost like a room in a GoodLife gym. As part of their job, the occupational therapists learn their way around the gadgets and spare parts that can quickly fix the broken footrest on a resident's wheelchair or the crunched eyeglasses that an exuberant young man, recovering from a long-ago accident, inadvertently sat on.

Sherbrooke feels like a meandering village. At one end is a collection of little households, the homes that inspired the Green House Project. At the opposite are four nursing-home floors with 20 people living in each area, a design that replaced the original 80-person units built in the 1960s. Sherbrooke has a population of 263 residents, 100 day-program visitors, 500 staff and another 500 volunteers, plus 20 birds, eight cats, one resident Chihuahua, five visiting dogs, three aquariums of fish and one gray guinea pig named Harrison Ford. Not to mention thousands of plants. It has just enough organized events and random interactions to make it seem like the outside world, even though it is not. The wine-making club, never short on volunteers, works on new blends, while taste-testing the fresh bouquet of their latest red or white. A chaplain writing a deadline report turns away from his computer to listen to a man yearning for stronger legs. The headliner of Happy Hour in Veterans' Village is a bar cart loaded with Canadian Club premium whisky, Johnnie Walker Red Label Scotch, Captain Morgan amber rum, spiced rum and original rum and Great Western pilsner, a local blend that lingers sweetly on the tongue. All of which means that oft-told stories sound new again.

Woven throughout is a philosophy that enables it all, called the Eden Alternative, created by Dr. Bill Thomas in the early 1990s, after he saw the loneliness of that New York State nursing-home resident who changed the trajectory of his life, the woman with white hair and blue eyes. Beatty embraced the Eden Alternative right away. It's a philosophy that could have meaning for any age, really, but in seniors' care, it acknowledges what Dr. Thomas has defined as the "three plagues of loneliness, helplessness and boredom," all of which conspire to create a miserable existence. Dr. Thomas spoke about ways to build a community focused on elders, rich with relationships between people of all ages and all abilities. He described a home abundant with plants and pets, like the four cockatiels that live at the front entrance and the three others in the big wooden aviary outside the art studio. It includes older dogs that have exchanged the car chasing of their youth for a ride with their human friend, perched on the arm of a motorized wheelchair. The Eden Alternative says these emotional connections — the caring for another living being, whether plant, pet or person — help alleviate loneliness and helplessness.

Of those three plagues, studies show that loneliness may be the most destructive. A research team led by Julianne Holt-Lunstad, a professor of psychology and neuroscience at Brigham Young University in Utah, analyzed data drawn from 308,000 people who were followed for roughly 7.5 years and concluded that those with decent social relationships had a 50 percent greater likelihood of survival than those with fewer connections. The impact of that isolation, Holt-Lunstad's team found, was similar to the negative effects of smoking and drinking, and it exceeded health problems created by obesity. Research like this is leading to a growing awareness of social isolation, prompting the British government to appoint a minister of loneliness to combat the epidemic harming the old and young.

Boredom brings its own curse. For some, it can open a space for creativity but that requires the freedom to explore. In traditional homes that leave people to sit and stare, except for the 2 p.m. beanbag toss, boredom deadens the spirit. It seems both heretic and sadly, quite normal, to believe that people lose the spark for life, their humanness, because they have lived to a certain age. It only makes sense that people need a purpose, a reason to live. Otherwise, what is the point of the medical advances that offer longevity?

My interview with Beatty is scheduled for later in the afternoon, so Eric Anderson is the Sherbrooke guide, although throughout the day, her philosophies are invoked by staff and the people living here.

Every weekday, Anderson, the former journalist, sends an Eden news flash to staff. It usually starts with an Eden Alternative principle, such as "Meaningless activity corrodes the human spirit. The opportunity to do things that we find meaningful is essential to the human spirit." Next comes the question that managers discuss with staff in group huddles. "How much planning does it take for staff to help an elder enjoy a meaningful activity? Why is that planning worth it?" Everyone has to jump in with an answer. The goal is to keep people talking about the Eden principles, the importance of friendship or sense of purpose among residents, all the time. Otherwise, even in the best homes, good intentions slip away.

It's also a way to foster leadership. Workers are taught that everything they do matters. In a good, or bad, way. Even something as simple as a facial expression matters, particularly to people with dementia. Beatty tells her staff that residents are looking for peace, joy and acceptance. Never anger or impatience. Definitely not judgment. People with dementia, she will say, already get strange looks, rude words or just plain negativity. So workers learn to manage the energy they bring into a room.

The news flash is a reminder. Workers here know that Beatty likes reminders. She believes they keep staff at their best, not slipping back into the old ways, like using words that label people, which is still common in homes. Every industry has its own language. Some homes label people with dementia. "Oh, he's a wanderer," they'll say about a man who walks up and down the hallway, not recognizing the fact that he is seeking something the home is not providing. "Shoppers" or "hoarders" are people who go into another person's room and take a hairbrush or clothes or pictures. As Beatty explains to her staff, a person who takes things has a need for stuff, so get them their own stuff. Otherwise, the label lets the home off the hook. Words have power.

In the Sherbrooke hallway leading to the little village homes, with their big, bright kitchens, Anderson points to the framed artwork hanging on the wall, all painted by residents. The pictures are hung at wheelchair eye level, a sign of respect that Beatty insists upon, he said, to make people feel comfortable in their space.

One of our first stops is the same stop made by a lot of new residents. Mark Trew is Sherbrooke's manager of spiritual care. He is 42 years old but was in his 30s when he applied for the job, wondering if his youth worked against him. It didn't.

Trew has an undergrad psychology degree and a master's of divinity. He moved to El Salvador to get married in his wife's home country and stayed, leading Mennonite churches that operated in local houses, while working with people who had intellectual disabilities. Back in Saskatchewan, his father forwarded him the job posting for Sherbrooke.

"I had never had any intention of going into long-term care," Trew says. "It held no interest for me, but when I looked into the Eden Alternative and what it was they wanted to do, it aligned very well with my beliefs, it aligned with my passion, what I had come to understand about people and how they need to be treated."

What captivated him was Eden's obsession with living.

"When I thought about long-term care, I thought about people waiting to die. And when I looked at overcoming the three plagues and I was thinking about the struggles that people go through, I saw the potential for so many great opportunities to bring life to people."

Sherbrooke is supported by five Christian churches, all of which provide religious services. All religions are recognized. Traditional church services offer people a sense of familiarity, which brings comfort, according to Trew, but some residents just want to come to his office to talk. What he has learned through the Eden Alternative is that no matter if there is a report to file or a sermon to write, the person standing in front of him is more important. If the goal of a home is to enrich lives, then the freedom to stop work and just be with people is fundamental. It is where the goodness begins.

"Relationships trump tasks," he says. "You might need to have a five- or ten- or 15-minute conversation with a person and, yes, you've got something that needs to get done but that can wait because these moments we have with a person, they'll get lost. The task will be there.

"In my role, I have a unique opportunity. There are people who will require an hour or an hour-and-a-half of my time. Because they are going through a major grief or a loss or memory of something that happened in their life. I've canceled worship services based on the fact that I really need to have a conversation with somebody."

Often, emotional pain starts with admission. No matter how lofty its reputation, Sherbrooke is still long-term care, and this new world means the loss of an old life. As Dr. Thomas said, nobody ever requested a move into a nursing home.

Sometimes, grief comes from the death of a brother or a sister. There is a time in life when friends and family start dying, naturally, of old age. I remember my maternal grandmother feeling sad because she had outlived all of her friends, going to their funerals, mourning her own shrinking world with each death. Even though it is expected that people have a life span of, say, 80 or 90 years, it doesn't mean that the loss of a lifelong girlfriend isn't painful. You can't rationalize grief.

Death is not the only path to Trew's door. A man comes in regularly just to shoot the breeze, but conversations always lead to his loss of mobility, the result of a progressive disease. Trew plays the guitar regularly throughout the home, and once people get to know him, they drop by his office to talk about the struggle of sharing space in a big home. Little interactions, maybe feeling left out over seating arrangements at dinner or annoyed by another resident's inability to recognize personal space, can build into something bigger. These are not feelings most of us have to deal with living in our own homes. In long-term care, nobody gets to choose their neighbor. If something goes wrong, odds are you'll run into the subject of annoyance again. Trew and his part-time colleague give people the space to vent, so they hopefully receive the emotional sustenance, the nourishing of the human spirit, that Eden Alternative says is one of its ten principles of living. Those principles all flow together, starting with the recognition of loneliness, helplessness and boredom; veering into companionship that combats loneliness; the ability to care for and be cared for; the need for trust; a life with meaning and growth; and a respect, not just for leadership, but also the wisdom of elders.

Trew sees his role as a builder of trust first. Then he becomes a listener.

"We step into places where other people might not want to go," he says. "I don't find it draining, I find it invigorating to help people. There are folks who come in with interpersonal conflicts, and we talk through what another person's understanding could be, helping them have empathy for what that person might be going through." He sees a mix of people, with and without cognitive decline.

It is a unique role, not the title of chaplain, because that position exists in many homes, but Trew's job is meant to create deeper connections that allow him to see the nuances of life in a nursing home that most of us miss. The mourning for one's old self, while struggling to find peace in a place that usually symbolizes finality, well, that's something most of us don't think about. Imagine how good it must feel, then, to find someone who understands, who is able to stop and listen.

Outside Trew's door, voices grow loud, people are waiting to see him. Eric Anderson arrives. It's time for the Java Club.

Several times a week, the Java Music Club meets, a hybrid of music and peer support created by Canadian PhD, Dr. Kristine Theurer to combat loneliness and depression. It is one of many programs that Beatty is always adding to Sherbrooke, as long as they fit into Eden's philosophy of well-being.

Three men sit at the table with Allison Sarauer, the group leader. They open with the Official Java Club Song, voices shy, but rising.

"OH YEAH!" One man sings out high and loud, as exuberant as the cockatiels at the front door. He speaks like he sings. The others are quiet. For now.

Today's topic is "letting go." Each person has a binder with talking points and songs about loss, accepting loss and moving forward. A brown "talking stick" gets passed around the table. No stick, no talk. That's the rule.

"We usually don't get through most of it because we talk quite a bit," Sarauer says.

"Especially me," says the burly man at the end of the table.

"We have a rule," Sarauer adds, "whatever happens in the Java Club stays in the Java Club."

The music selection begins with "Somewhere over the Rainbow," from *The Wizard of Oz*, which launches a conversation about the weather and skating on the Rideau Canal in Ottawa.

Anderson and I have an impromptu agreement. If he sings, I sing. "I don't have much of a voice," Anderson says. "We don't judge," jokes the enthused man, so we all begin trying to match Judy Garland's perfect pitch, although ours is considerably different.

"Amen," says the burly man. "Hallelujah," says the enthusiastic singer. They jump back in.

At a certain point Anderson's voice rises above the rest and for a moment it sounds like he might burst out of our diminutive chorus line, but he pulls back, letting the others shine. The song winds up, a vocal pedagogy of soprano, alto and bass.

"Sing it, Julie!" the enthusiastic man says, to the recording.

"Except that's not Julie," Sarauer says. It was Judy Garland, not Julie Andrews.

Everyone laughs.

Sarauer opens the conversation theme with a quote: "To let go is not to criticize and regulate anyone, / but to try to become what I dream I can be. / To let go is not to regret the past, / but to grow and live for the future."

As the brown stick makes its way around the table, the burly man spoke, at length, about letting go of his ex-wife who let go of him many years ago. The energetic singer worries about the mental health of a relative. A third man, quiet until now, describes his struggle to accept the death of his grandfather and the way he died, on a neighbor's property. Once he begins speaking, the words start flowing. He talks about an uncle's funeral, held on a bitterly cold winter day when the roads were closed and he couldn't go. Now, the man says, his aunt is trying to sell the family farm. "There are no takers yet."

Sarauer listens.

When he stops speaking, she plays the Beatles' "Let It Be."

Everyone sings.

◎ ◎ ◎

The dog named Motu with the gorgeous dark face sits at the front door of the art studio. He's part of a package deal, arriving every day with Alana Moore, Sherbrooke's artist-in-residence, wagging his thick plume of a tail, greeting the people who come to create. It's just down the hall from Trew's office. The floors are splattered with color, a patch of yellow here, a smear of green near the door, four small blue handprints under the table where Inez Moorcraft paints. Sometimes the vibe is all about energy, music blasting. Or it can be a quiet space, contemplative, where people disappear into their work. Natural light flows into the room. The walls are lined with shelves to hold the paintings of each artist. All are exploring their creativity, but some unexpectedly create legitimate works of art. Inez paints animals in a bright, folksy style that was so captivating Moore flew to Atlanta, Georgia, to show her work at the June 2019 conference of the Dementia Action Alliance, called Re-Imagining Dementia. Inez's style is reminiscent of Maud Lewis, the renowned Nova Scotia artist who was inspired by the people and animals around Yarmouth and Digby in the southern end of the province.

Some of the people living at Sherbrooke are professional artists, like Paul Sisetski, who has a master's degree in fine arts and created a wild series of acrylics called *Island of the Damned*. His application for a Saskatoon exhibit was entitled "What I Like about My Art," and in his list of ten examples, Sisetski wrote, "It's still a magic ride; it keeps me young; I'm not bored; I love the paradox, many times I experience such things as déjà vu, synchronicity, serendipity."

Inez spent decades as a caregiver, a nurse who also raised two boys, the children of a friend. Diagnosed with dementia later in life, Inez started coming to Sherbrooke's day program. The art studio felt comfortable, but it was her first time with a paintbrush.

"The entry point for her was her joy for animals," Moore says. "So, she started. Just with an image of a dog and images of these other animals that she loved. She started doing rough tracings of animals and then painting them. And now she has this incredible portfolio.

"She said, 'I can't believe I didn't do this my whole life. I could do this all day. It is so peaceful and relaxing.' It gave her a space away from all the noise," Moore says.

For a long time, Inez was prolific. As her dementia advanced, she moved from the day program into Sherbrooke, but for a few weeks, her art studio sessions dropped off. When she returned today, Inez sat with Moore, staring at a blank paper. She made a few scratches. Moore stayed with her. They talked about dogs and drawing.

"The biggest thing for me is not giving up," Moore says after Inez left. "Because the work changes, I feel like I had to even challenge my own ideas of how somebody changes with dementia and how their art will obviously change.

"At first, I could have had the tendency to give her the same materials and the same methods that she was working with before, but there have been so many changes that it has shifted, so giving her something different has helped. She has been working on a much smaller scale, kind of narrowing down."

Sherbrooke has another artist who takes a mobile art supply cart into the old side of the building, the floors that were built in the traditional nursing-home style. Moore and her colleague have seen how big works created by people with dementia change as they do, often growing smaller.

"They feel more intimate," she says. "With Inez, there was so much storytelling while she was working. I really love that feeling, like it is part of the art-making process. A shape will turn into a conversation about an eyeball and a dog. Or she will talk about a whisker and talk about a feeling. I try to listen to what she is saying. Even just having that space to share, to still have that intimacy and connection. It's so important."

◎　◎　◎

John, Buddy, Baby and Julio are the front-door songbirds, a choral choir of cockatiels. They live just outside the door to the greenhouse. The flowers and plants throughout Sherbrooke have their origins here. So do the seedlings, growing in dozens of reused Tim Hortons coffee cups. Sour cherry trees began this way, now growing outside, tended by the residents. One woman prefers crassulaceae, the succulents with exotic shapes. She visits the greenhouse every morning, checking on their low-maintenance needs. Maybe a touch of water but not too much. Their thick waxy leaves feel good to touch. Later, the plants will find homes throughout Sherbrooke, their care entrusted to the hands of another. Sherbrooke used to have a master gardener named Ramsay, but he retired a few years ago. The woman who replaced him, Joy, laughs at the green thumb cliché. She's an occupational therapy assistant who did a lot of reading to understand the needs of each horticultural species. Instead of fixing broken wheelchairs, she helps elders care for plants. Sometimes they learn together. Sometimes the elders teach her.

In the summer, Sherbrooke brings out the garden boxes. Residents design their own miniature garden, with flowers or vegetables. The boxes go outside near an open courtyard, the same place where the sensory gardens are planted for people with cognitive decline. They respond to the smelling boxes, with aromatic herbs, and the touching box, with a soft ornamental flower called stachys byzantina, otherwise known as lamb's ear.

The outdoor courtyard is near the front entrance, wide open to the neighborhood. In most homes, designed decades ago, the courtyard is in the center of the building, an outdoor space surrounded by four walls. It might be filled with pretty flowers, but it still isolates people from the sights and sounds of the real world. Jill Knowlton, of Primacare Living in Toronto, calls those courtyards "prisons with walls." They're either full of snow in the winter or insufferably hot in the summer, Knowlton says. "You need to see the schoolchildren coming home. You need to hear the church bell. You need to see the buses going by. That's how you lived."

At Sherbrooke the front yard courtyard has an awning for shade. People gather here for a coffee, barbecues, for conversation. It is open to all residents, with or without cognitive decline, and is home to the outdoor music scene, where the members of Sherbrooke's Young Country Rebels band meet every Thursday afternoon, weather permitting, to jam. The 15 or so musicians range in age from their late 20s to their early 90s. A lot of Johnny Cash is played.

That outdoor courtyard offers a not-so-subtle hint on Beatty's next move.

Beatty and her team are rolling out plans to open Sherbrooke's dementia households, enabling people from the greater community to spend their days alongside those who are frail or living with disabilities. This idea, living without the limits of their diagnoses, is still controversial. Beatty has made speeches on this, watching from the podium as the people who nodded and smiled throughout her speech suddenly disengage when she talks about opening the doors of memory care units. Not everyone believes.

Dr. Power cites two large-scale literature reviews, including one from Cochrane, an international network of researchers, that found no compelling evidence the actual separation of people with dementia led to better care.

"I think you can find excellent examples of care in both separated and integrated environments," he says.

"You can find horrible examples too. But the actual separation of people per se is not the determining factor, and the conclusion was that perhaps it is better to work on better care practices than to put our efforts into separating people," says Dr. Power, who is an associate professor at the University of Rochester and the Schlegel chair in aging and dementia innovation at the Schlegel–University of Waterloo Research Institute for Aging.

There is no blame, he says, just a realization that over time our understanding evolves, leading to a new awareness that will hopefully create change.

"Many of us had the experience of actually designing and opening separate, segregated memory care areas," Dr. Power says. "I did that right before I left my first long-term care job. I was quite proud of it and thought it was state of the art at the time."

There are natural shifts in thinking, waves of awareness, that shake up traditional values. Decades ago, people with intellectual disabilities were sent to institutions to live away from their parents, who were often told that was the best approach. People with mental health issues were locked away, sometimes in the same places as those with Down syndrome or physical disabilities. My great Aunt Isabel, who married the auto executive in Detroit, had, decades earlier, given birth to a daughter whose brain was starved of oxygen during the delivery. Or that was the family story. Gloria, who lived well into her 80s, spent years in one of those Ontario institutions that was shut down not so long ago, with class-action lawsuits launched for abuses committed there. There are similarities between those outdated beliefs and the current mainstream philosophy which says people with dementia should be kept separate from the rest. According to AdvantAge Ontario, which represents municipal and not-for-profit homes, 80 percent of long-term care residents have some kind of cognitive decline. So, really, what is the point of separation?

Some people fear the behaviors that have been associated with cognitive decline, although many advocates, from Beatty to Dr. Power or Dr. Thomas, believe those are connected to unnatural lives spent sitting, doing nothing. Or, as Beatty says, 90 percent of the time we miss the cues that people give us, causing them to react, often in fear. She believes there is a small percentage, mostly men, who will remain physically aggressive and who she believes need to live separately. Perhaps it has nothing to do with dementia, it's just who they are, just like it is in the greater world. That is the everlasting challenge of placing large groups of people in one space.

There may be some good news about the incidence rate of dementia. Some studies show the number of people with cognitive decline is not increasing as rapidly as originally predicted, possibly due to a growing focus on health and as a result of medical advances. The bad news comes in the form of the massive demographic of boomer-aged seniors, meaning the overall number of people diagnosed will increase. "It's just math," as Laura Tamblyn Watts says.

All of which means that we, as a society, had better adapt. Right now, most of us are afraid of what we don't know, so we accept the idea of locking people away to keep them safe and out of view.

Dr. Power approaches the separation discussion with benevolence. "I think we have a lot of preconceptions about what dementia is and what's the best place for people." Dr. Power says he discusses this idea constantly with Dr. Jennifer Carson, the researcher from the University of Nevada, Reno. "The idea of memory care 30 or 40 years ago didn't come from a bad place, it came from a place where the care for people with dementia was pretty horrible, and people were trying to create better environments," he says.

"We've learned a lot from that. But I think in doing so we've also created a system that does impose on people's rights to live in an inclusive community."

Beatty's awareness began in the 2000s after her mother was diagnosed with cognitive decline, reaching the point where she would be found walking along the freeway near her home. She moved into Sherbrooke and quite vocally expressed her dismay at living in a household full of people with dementia. Beatty realized that her mother was right. Why shouldn't she be free to interact with others? Why shouldn't she be inspired by conversations with people in the hallways or the greenhouse? But Beatty didn't know how to fix it. Thousands of miles away, in New York State, her friend and mentor, Dr. Power, was working on a plan.

After Dr. Power tried and failed to bring the Eden Alternative to his employer in a traditional nursing home, he went to work for a more receptive organization, the not-for-profit St. John's in Rochester, New York. It was a big multistory nursing home with three locked areas for 75 people with dementia. Of the 350 remaining residents living in unlocked areas, 70 percent also had dementia. He began to wonder why some people with dementia lived among those who did not have it and why the others were locked away.

Dr. Power went to a management meeting with a one-page summary detailing why he thought the home should stop separating people. St. John's was already talking about adding alarms to the outer doors of the whole complex, so people could walk freely inside. "Once we did that and made it safe to be anywhere in this complex and not just get out where the road was, it really took away the reason for people to be in those locked areas," he said.

When Dr. Power wrote *Dementia Beyond Drugs* more than a decade ago, he included a small section called "A Modest Proposal," in which he called separation a civil rights issue. It was updated slightly, for the book's 2017 reprint. "The basic idea of the dementia-specific living area stems from an institutional mindset that places people into an environment largely defined by a nonspecific syndrome, not by who they are," he wrote. "Herein lies what may be the greatest misconception in aged care: There are probably more than 100 different forms of dementia, with widely different causes. Within those different forms, there are individual levels of ability, patterns of difficulties, rates of progression, individual personalities, cultures, coping styles . . . and just *one approach to life and care??*"

He is, in part, talking about the unerring ability of each person to respond to cognitive changes in a different way, the same uniqueness that altered the perspective of Dr. Susan Vandermorris, the clinical neuropsychologist at Toronto's Baycrest Centre. Over the years, she too began to see the individual response to the disease as more profound than a brain scan or even diagnosis.

"I get to work with lots of people who, in theory, have the same kind of signature findings on a brain scan, but in reality, in their day-to-day life, they may look very different," Dr. Vandermorris said. "Their unique needs and concerns — what makes them human and stresses them out and what they need help with — is never predicted by the brain scan or not always by the diagnosis."

In other words, our individuality remains unchanged by the disease.

COVID-19 restrictions delayed it, but the doors on Sherbrooke's four dementia households will no longer require a secret code and keypad, although some people will wear wristband technology that monitors their location, allowing them to walk through some doors but automatically locking others. People weren't necessarily moving out of their longtime living areas into new parts of the building, just getting freedom to mingle, although changes were put on hold during the pandemic.

Alice Cowell could be Sherbrooke's poster-elder for inclusion.

She arrived in spring 2018 after suffering the physical effects of a stroke that slowed the movement in her left leg. When the physiotherapists told her to talk to her leg, to cheer it on, Alice told them, "If I'm going to talk to it then I might as well give it a name." She called it Charlie, which is more appealing than my mother's version of The Leg. "It helps!" she says. At 92, Alice's mind is sharp. She lives in one of Sherbrooke's dementia homes and wouldn't have it any other way.

"I didn't choose it," she admits. "I wanted to come to Sherbrooke for their physiotherapy because they have a really good program here. My husband had had a stroke, and he was here for six years. I was really pleased with his care."

At first, Sherbrooke was full so she spent six weeks in another nursing home before an offer came. Sherbrooke had a room — except it was in the dementia unit.

"I asked them, if I move in there and a new room comes available, can I move into it?" The answer was yes, so Alice moved in.

Alice has a sturdiness, one of those people who takes life as it happens. She and her husband raised six children on their farm about three hours northeast of Saskatoon. They grew fields of grain and raised cattle on 700 acres. "Just a small farm," she says.

In Alice's bedroom at Sherbrooke is a photograph of her family, taken in the 1980s. They stand outside, in a thicket of trees. The hot camera flash flattens the white dress shirts of her two sons, but Alice's high-waisted blue dress is rich in color. Her husband stands beside her, and her four daughters wore matching tailored outfits, two in beige and two in green.

"Six kids," she says, "but we lost two. We lost our daughter to cancer. And the day after her funeral, our son was killed in a farming accident." She offers this detail in a matter-of-fact way, much like the rest of her conversation, calm and steady.

"You know, I was never with people with dementia," she says, shifting to talk about her new life. "I knew nothing about it and it frightened me a little bit. When I moved in, I was greeted by a lady who accused me of taking her husband. Oh, she went up one side of me and down the other. She was angry. And I didn't know what to make of this. But anyway, she settled down after a while. We never did become real good friends." Alice soon moved to the household next door, where she said people have milder dementia.

"Since I've been here, I've been asked several times if I want to move to a different floor, and I said no. I made friends here. I got to know a little bit more about dementia and found out that, you know, they cannot help being like they are. It's a sickness, and we have to accept that.

"If I was struggling and needed help, I would feel really badly if everybody would just disappear and put me in a place where everybody is the same as me. So, I thought, *No, I can't leave them.*"

Alice's experience is unique. She didn't intend her living arrangements to be an altruistic experiment, but she realized that she could, despite a few early mishaps, form deep connections with the people living there. She became close to several women. She eats breakfast with one, discussing childhood and the complicated relationships between daughters and mothers. "She always said she wished her mother had made her pretty dresses when she was little, but she never did," Alice says. "Of course, I don't really know if she's telling me the truth." Alice says another friend tells stories about her long-ago adventures, driving a semitruck.

"I don't view them as having dementia," she says. "They're just ordinary people. They have a sickness that they cannot control, and I think we have to show them love and try and understand them. I think Suellen is right, I think it is good to mix with other residents. But sometimes it's hard on the other residents too. I used to get very upset, but I got over it. It's not their fault. I think I say that a dozen times a day, it's not their fault."

She loves watching her friends' reactions to music. Each afternoon Sherbrooke's recreation workers come by and play an instrument for a sing-along. "I don't sing well, but I sing anyway," Alice says. And every Tuesday one of Sherbrooke's employee-musicians arrives with his guitar. Sometimes he comes with the Young Country Rebels. Sherbrooke is home to some young people who have brain injuries or other disabilities. "He sings and plays. Everybody dances. You can't stay still, his music is so happy," she says. "You Are My Sunshine" is a big hit.

"Everybody just comes alive. It's just like watering a plant that is in need of water, and you give it a drink and it perks up. I look around at all these people. If they're not dancing, they're tapping their feet. And I, myself, I come alive."

In Alice's mind the others, those living on the outside, just need a bit of education to understand the benefits: friends with a sharp recall of history and an infectious, dancing joy of music; the good feeling from helping a friend through a rough moment; and, at least for Alice, the gratitude she feels that the arthritis in her weak leg is the worst of her complaints. In her plainspoken way, she talks about the challenges too, because they are real and no altruistic words will change that. While it is true that good homes create calm, flare-ups can still happen. And it is human to sometimes get annoyed, upset or even angry, with or without dementia.

"Most of the time people are good. They have these . . . outbreaks every once in a while. They are angry. They're angry with you. They are angry with the whole world," she says. "So, I talk to them. I take their hand, and we go for a walk. People come in and out of one another's rooms quite frequently. If somebody comes through my door, I don't kick them out. I let them sit. We chat. By the time they are ready to go, they are fine. It passes."

So, here is a bit of unvarnished advice on inclusion from a 92-year-old with a left leg named Charlie who is thriving inside a Saskatoon dementia home: "Be kind. Don't let your tempers fly. Don't swear at them. Or yell at them. They're not deaf. And don't be afraid to hold their hand — they won't let go. It's a connection."

◎   ◎   ◎

Suellen Beatty is in her office, the late-winter light flowing through the window. It has a thin blue cast, but still sheds a bit of warmth, a brightness needed after the long winter. We sit at a round table. Beatty seems relaxed, in control, which makes sense since Sherbrooke is, as the saying goes, her house and has been for more than 30 years. Like the others who have devoted their careers to seniors, Beatty considers it a calling. Every industry has its own anthropology, its hierarchy, and in the world of geriatrics, star power exists. "There's a bit of a cult following around her," someone said.

At some point during our three-hour conversation, Beatty and I talk about her hair, which is gray, streaked with silver. It looks good, like the women on Instagram who get thousands of followers because they've gone gray in a glamorous way. Beatty described her decision as both a convenience and a way to champion longevity.

"We've got to embrace growing older, or what does that say about old people, right? And we're all going to be old people."

She quotes Dr. Thomas on the natural changes that come with aging, like waking up several times in the middle of the night. That's just normal aging, he likes to say, not a reason for sleeping pills.

You can see the way these leaders influence one another by the way they share credit. When I interviewed him in Montclair, New Jersey, Dr. Thomas spoke about Beatty's influence on his career and Beatty shares that reciprocity with Dr. Allen Power, who speaks the same way about University of Nevada, Reno, academic Dr. Jennifer Carson, part of Dr. Thomas's Changing Aging tour.

Beatty quotes another Dr. Thomas observation on the aging brain that will make a lot of us feel good. People worry about remembering (or forgetting) little details but, over time, our brains have filed away so much information it can take longer to retrieve it.

"What happens to you is that you've lived so long and have so much in your head. A 20-year-old has five files to go through and you've got 500," Beatty says. "You can't retrieve something as quickly as you did before because the file folder is too full. But you have something that a younger person doesn't have — you immediately understand the *gist* of something. Would you give that up? That understanding? That knowing? In order to retrieve a name more quickly? Not in a million years."

She laughs, describing an older man who became a friend after his wife moved to Sherbrooke.

"When you asked him something, he'd say, 'Well, how soon do you need to know?' I adopted that. 'Let me get back to you.'"

In long-term care, culture change is one of those industry buzzwords. In 2011, the *Toronto Star* published an investigation into nursing-home abuses, including sexual assault, that I wrote with my colleague Jesse McLean, and the end result was a government-initiated task force that wrote a good report on leadership and culture change. Yet nothing truly transformational happened. The problem is that without a massive effort, good intentions cannot override the medicalized system that controls nursing homes, with its slavish adherence to rules.

There are a lot of different theories on how to create change and make it stick. From what I've seen, it starts with leaders who are brave enough to buck the system. Instead of operating a workplace designed to create efficiencies for medical staff, those leaders need to empower frontline workers to step away from the task-driven schedule and help each resident find a way to engage. Dr. Power introduced me to an Australian consultant named Daniella Greenwood, who has adopted a hard-core pragmatism in her work. Forget about the big personalities at the top, Greenwood says. Better to focus on the frontline staff. First, spend a few days working alongside them to see what they are up against. Then, teach them ways to relate to the people living in the home that put the residents' needs first. Even if the administrators aren't willing to go for flat-out change, educated staff can make a difference in the daily experience. It could be something as simple as recognizing that a mother's interests have changed, allowing her new pursuits to take precedence over family expectations. Greenwood's idea is so practical that it seems a bit subversive. Not all homes are willing to go through a massive transformation, but every little bit helps the people living there — and the staff.

Ideally, the desire for change emerges from a group of leaders within the home not just one charismatic person. Beatty may be the face of Sherbrooke, but she is adamant that its success relies on a team approach.

"I never did anything by myself. I don't think anybody does. Fortunately, we've done some things right — a very certain type of leadership style. It has to be a leadership style that is warm and inviting. That can inspire people, and you have to have a really compelling *why*. Why are we doing this?

"When we have a staff meeting, I always remind the staff about our mission, our vision and our values. I always tell them how proud I am of them. And I specifically talk about the things I've seen to reinforce them."

Sometimes she is blunt. "There was one staff meeting, with about 150 people, where I said, 'I don't want any cranky people working here.' There was dead silence in the room," she says. "'This is not a place where we can be cranky, because we are building quality of life for people, and you can't do that if you are cranky. So, if you need help, tell somebody. I'm not saying deny your feelings, but you can't be cranky here.'

"Pretty soon everyone was laughing," she says. "But we are really serious about those things. We talk about love and kindness. We have taken pretty much everything we've done and used it over and over again in a new way."

An interesting point that people raise about Eden, as they call it casually, is the need to constantly reevaluate the way they work. Does it fit with new beliefs or research? In doing so, Beatty and her staff keep changing, recognizing when planned changes do not achieve their goals. There's a certain freedom in that kind of fearlessness, the ability to say that I was wrong or we can do this better, that ultimately improves the lives of people living in the homes.

As Sherbrooke prepared to open its locked doors, Beatty created an education program for residents and their families, just as Alice Cowell had hoped. Much like the "persistent dissatisfaction" that propelled Dr. Thomas to new ideas, Beatty is working on a project for an empty pie-shaped piece of land in front of Sherbrooke. She wants to create an "aging-in-place" community of apartments and life lease condos for people of all ages to live together. It's a do-over, if you will, the way Eloy van Hal in the Netherlands wished he could remake de Hogeweyk, built and designed with ideas that are now nearly a few decades old. Beatty has the space to create that community in her front yard, and she's designing it with inspiration from Dr. Thomas's MAGIC communities, which advocate for a place where people of all ages and abilities live.

There is no hard funding commitment yet, but apparently Beatty does not find that intimidating. The way she described her plans, you could almost see the community rising, with kids riding bikes on sidewalks and elders working in gardens around the high-rise tower.

"This is going to be an aging-in-place community that I have never seen anywhere," she says.

"People talk about aging in place, but they make you move. So, you have to move from one building to another, from assisted living to a care home.

"We are going to have affordable housing for families, affordable accommodations for university students. They will live in there and have reduced rent for their volunteer hours. And the families who live in the townhouses that are affordable, they can actually rent out parts of their home as well. They are going to be built that way, so you can section off a place."

There could be life leases, a way to purchase a condo without technically owning it, getting back most if not all of the money at the end. Those units would be more expensive, possibly for seniors who want to downsize. She plans to go to the school board to get permission for another iGen class operating out of the new building with, if approved, a stronger focus on Indigenous studies and spots for Indigenous children. She envisions a large preschool with a focus on painting and drama, and maybe language, integrating those kids into the Sherbrooke community, where they can work with the artist in residence. She wants a bakery or a pub. "I don't know if you have ever been to a coffeehouse, where someone was singing and playing the guitar. I'd like one of those, so people from the community can come. And an event space for bands. Eventually, there will be a walking exercise track on the second floor. And then, it will be attached to Sherbrooke and part of our larger community."

Dr. Thomas was an inspiration, but Beatty says the vision began because of her own interest in housing, as she reaches an age when she and her husband are starting to talk about travel, which comes more easily with a condo than a single-family home with grass to cut or a driveway to shovel. From her perspective, the current housing options are limited.

"So, where do I want to live? Well, if I had to live in a seniors' place, I couldn't do it. I think those are ghettos. Where else do you put people together by age, other than a university dorm, and we know those are supposed to be short term. But the idea of putting seniors together is crazy to me because it is not healthy.

"It never happened before in the face of history, until this last period of time. They don't work. I've been to a lot of seniors' places. The seniors are competing to see who is the sickest. Or if you come with a walker one day, everyone turns on you. It's not age-friendly. If somebody gets dementia, everybody gossips about them. It is very interesting what I've watched happen in so many of these places. People are afraid to lose their abilities. They hide their losses."

The horror. My parents just moved into a retirement home in their little town, the only legitimate option available. A wave of guilt quietly hits, knowing that I supported their plans. The truth is, we'd all rather hold onto our independent lives, when we were busy, needed by family or work, with freedom to live as we wished. I once met a woman in a Rochester nursing home who said she misses the days when she was driving her car, running errands for family. Some of us complain about the exhaustion of those busy years, and here she was, yearning to be needed again. For people like Beatty, in the home that she and her team created, there can be purpose and independence. It is different, but it still exists.

The morning music session, where the man sang with the same joy as the birds in the front hall, makes me think of Dorothy, when she was over the rainbow. She realized there is no place like home and spent the entire movie trying to get back to the house where she felt safe and loved. That is our natural instinct, to find our place, even if we sometimes have to begin anew. Beatty is creating that feeling here, opening the doors, allowing people to follow their road.

◎ ◎ ◎

After my trip to Saskatoon I asked my mom if she was happy to be living in the retirement home, worried that we had all helped them move along to a fate they did not want. Her voice had a sharpness when she told me, dear child, that moving there was her choice because she was tired of cooking three meals a day. We did not speak of it again.

She insisted that I call her after every visit to a different nursing or retirement home, first to determine that I returned safely, and once that was confirmed, she wanted to know the latest about each of the places I visited for my book research.

In a way, she interviewed me. I told her stories about local innovators, like Peel Region's Mary Connell, the Butterfly project manager whose father, once a Latin teacher, now has Alzheimer's disease and who inspired her to make life a pleasure again for those in her care. Connell understood the disease, the little things that make such a difference in the lives of people living with cognitive decline, even the architectural design of nursing-home bedrooms, so people with dementia could easily see their washroom, instead of searching, confused.

Mom loved the stories from Malton Village, but she was especially excited about international visits, like de Hogeweyk in the Netherlands. We spoke about the value of walking outside, in all that fresh air, enabling a better appetite and sleep. Plus, it just feels good to have the sun on your face. "Your father and I walk every day," she said. When I described the gardens within the forest at Carol Woods in North Carolina, she told me about the flowers in the backyard of her retirement home. It was a sensitive subject for a woman who had created beautiful English gardens over her lifetime, but some of the other ladies at her home seemed in charge, and she hadn't found her place in the gardening hierarchy just yet. "I miss pulling out weeds," she said.

It wasn't long before my mother started informing me, with her schoolteacher authority, about ways to improve the lives of seniors. Her advice happened to be precisely what I had just told her, but she articulated it so well it seemed like she was teaching me. Not content with our new knowledge, she decided to put it into action, describing the improvements she was creating in the lives of seniors at her new home, showing them friend-ship, connection. She described a wee lady who walked with a stoop and seemed withdrawn until my mom stopped her in the hallway. She'd reach out to touch the woman's hand, saying hello and smiling, beginning a conversation. "She lifted her head and smiled at me," my mom said.

After describing several such interventions, all successful, it occurred to me that my mom might be playing to the crowd, so to speak, providing good copy for her presence in my book, which she insisted on reading first, for accuracy.

A few weeks later she told me that one of the tiny ladies, and there were a few, well, one of them had passed away. I was starting to get the feeling that mom was keeping track of who goes first, happy to avoid the inevitable. The home didn't share many details, she said, but the people living there were aware when a fellow resident died. With everyone in their late 80s or 90s, it seems possible that they might all be looking at one another, wondering who was next.

After sharing this information about the tiny lady, my mom told me that a girlfriend who lives in a retirement home a few hours away said her home never confirms a resident's death.

"She told me they can't give out information, for privacy purposes," Mom said.

Well, that's not necessarily true, I told her. When I spent a year in Malton Village, the staff performed what they called the honor guard after a death, standing in two rows, facing one another, as the funeral home workers rolled the resident's body up the middle on a covered stretcher. The nurses and personal support workers in those two rows sang "Amazing Grace" as the resident left through the front door.

I told this to my mother, expecting to share a moment of emotion. Instead she said, "Do you remember that nurse who killed all those people in southern Ontario nursing homes? Well, would she have stood there and sung when their bodies were taken out?"

It was a question that left me speechless, but my mother expected an answer for the serial-killer nurse.

"Yes, Mom, I guess of all people, she would have sung with aplomb."

My mother laughed in her gallows way. Then she said goodbye.

## CHAPTER EIGHT

# Carol Woods and the Importance of Freedom

P AT SPRIGG GRADUATED FROM COLLEGE with a degree in therapeutic recreation, hoping to help youth at risk. The bonus, she'd joke, was getting paid to play. The real reason was simple. Sprigg wanted to help kids who were struggling, and she loved the analytical side of recreation therapy that broke games into little pieces, matching strengths to activities so kids could lock in success.

It was the mid-1970s, when young people, the boomers, began their long domination of America's culture. They were entering adulthood and ready to change the world. For Sprigg, the possibility of helping those who didn't catch the wave of early success offered a career of altruism and fun.

Except she couldn't find a job. So when new federal government-funding rules mandated the presence of a certified-activity specialist in long-term care, Sprigg followed the pragmatic path to employment.

She got a job interview at a county nursing home with beds for 700 people in southern Pennsylvania, her home state. It was

1975. A decade or so earlier, that facility would have been called a home for the indigent or the poorhouse.

The administrator took her for a tour down white-tunnel hallways and through long residential wards, as they were called, with row after row of elders in metal beds, many tied down.

As the job tour ended, Sprigg excused herself and quickly found a washroom.

"I threw up, cried, got myself together, went back to the administrator's office and said I'll take it."

Instead of improving the lives of young people, Sprigg changed her trajectory when she was exposed to the warehousing of the old. "What I saw and what I experienced showed the degradation of elders: the way we treated them, the way we annihilated them, the way we objectified them. No matter what they did, it was because they were senile. I told myself that there had to be a better way. That we had to, as a society, deal with our aging population in a more humane way.

"It called to me," she says. "It called to me."

In those cold, white wards, Sprigg found her profession.

After a few years on the job, she concluded that no one was going to listen to the transformational ideas of a recreation worker, so she went back to university and got a master's degree in gerontology. She found work in a Philadelphia retirement community and, before long, was promoted to director of health services.

She told workers to stop tying down people, in chairs or beds. There wasn't any empirical evidence that said locking people in their chairs made for a better life. Instead, the practice was based on the notion that old people had to be kept safe, and therefore the best way to do that was to stop them from walking on their own. Also, it made life easier for staff. It was just the way things were done then, with few people questioning the rights of humans who, Sprigg thought, were essentially held as prisoners because of their age and, sometimes, cognitive abilities.

The use of restraints, as they are called, was a common practice, one that is sometimes still used. The industry calls them physical restraints or, in a tidier version of the truth, belts. They hold people into beds and chairs. Other devices like bed rails can do the same. Portable tabletops, ostensibly used to hold meals, can also serve the unspoken purpose of keeping people locked in place. Of course, medication offers a less visible form of restraint. Many homes use antipsychotic drugs to keep people still and quiet.

In the quest for efficiency, traditional homes view good care as keeping people safe, fed and clean. No one over the course of the interviews for this book ever suggested that a fragile person be placed in danger. But no matter the age, there's no end to the human desire for independent movement. Even if it is slow and excessively cautious, it is still personal freedom. And with freedom comes some risk, which a great many advocates are starting to believe is preferable to the alternative.

One of the saddest stories I've ever heard as a reporter came from a nursing aide who told me that ladies who walked into her nursing home, upright and jaunty, were restrained in chairs with a belt and so quickly lost their strength that they soon became immobile. In old age, it does not take long to lose the muscle strength needed to stay upright.

Years later, I wrote about a woman who wanted out of her chair so badly she slid down in her wheelchair, trying to wiggle under the belt. She asphyxiated herself in the process. The industry explained it as an unfortunate accident, but the health minister of the day, the same man who once promised a revolution, took a harsher view. Over time new guidelines have emerged across North America, with groups like the Registered Nurses' Association of Ontario calling for limits on the use of restraints.

Back in the 1970s and '80s, homes held training sessions to show staff how to properly tie down residents. I recently met a lovely woman in the U.S., a seniors' advocate, who started her career as a nursing aide. As part of her job, she put people in restraints. "It was just what we did at that time," she says. "Now I have to live with that."

In the early 1980s, after Sprigg finished graduate school, she wanted to get rid of those restraints, at least in the Philadelphia retirement home that had hired her. In those days, nurses ran the shop, in starched uniforms and white hats emblazoned with the name of their nursing school. Sprigg decided to use the power of her job as health director.

"And therein lies the challenge," she says.

"When you want to do transformational change, not only is it challenging, but the individuals who have based their life work on work that supports the tradition, the status quo, they find it very difficult to open their mind to something different.

"[They believe], in a way, you're negating what they have done. You are poking holes in what they have done. You are saying what they have done is not right.

"What I am saying is, we do the best that we can with the information and education that we have at the time."

Which brings us to 2019 in a North Carolina forest just outside of Chapel Hill, where 500 elders live among the trees.

The Carol Woods Retirement Community was founded decades earlier by local residents who chose to spend their later years living independently, but still close to the vibrant college town where the 100-year-old Carolina Coffee Shop serves roasted coffee or espresso martinis, depending on the time of day.

Chapel Hill was founded in the late 1700s, taking its name from a church called the New Hope Chapel, built, unsurprisingly, on a hill. It is home to the University of North Carolina (UNC) at Chapel Hill, the oldest public college in America, its colonial campus an elegant presence in the center of town. The main thoroughfare, Franklin Street, named after Benjamin, rolls under an awning of oak trees, past the massive columns on the

UNC president's house and the smaller manses, one with a sign that reads *Sigma Sigma Sigma*.

Beyond the university alumni that includes Democrat James Polk, America's 11th president, and the legendary Tar Heels NCAA Division 1 athletics program, it's the trees that make the impression. Chapel Hill grew inside a forest and pays homage to its oaks, pines and cedars with tax dollars devoted to their care the way Canadian towns maintain their hockey arenas.

It is in the forest, five minutes outside of town, on 120 acres, that Carol Woods grew.

This is a non-profit retirement community that thrives with the founding philosophy of social connection, independence and freedom. Residents are expected to stay involved in the outside world and, most importantly, to one another.

One woman arrived after a thriving career with the North Carolina state government. "I was afraid there would be the usual moat around this community," she says. "That's not the case. There was no moat around Carol Woods. I was encouraged to keep doing what I felt joy in doing, what I felt productive in doing."

People put their names on the waiting list a decade before they're ready, with the hope of spending two or three decades living here after the age of 65. When it is time, if ever, for a higher level of care, Carol Woods has apartments in assisted living and skilled nursing.

Arrive young enough and you can live in a duplex or town-house on a tiny shaded court and walk to the main building for dinner at night. On the way home in summer, fireflies sparkle in the darkened woods and the night birds sing.

Long glass walkways with wooden ceilings connect to the outer buildings, creating easy walking in the winter when North Carolina gets its share of snow. In the main building, those wooden ceilings lead into a family room with clusters of couches, coffee tables and comfy chairs near a ski-chalet fireplace.

The dining room serves buffet-style meals, with support, for breakfast and lunch. At dinner, people can opt for table service or the buffet. They sit where they wish, in the open section or smaller rooms with ceiling buffers for sound enhancement. As I've experienced during restaurant lunches with my parents, there's nothing worse than trying to converse with people wearing hearing aids in a room with bad acoustics.

I learned of Carol Woods when I first met Dr. Jennifer Carson, the director of dementia engagement, education and research program at the University of Nevada, Reno, Dr. Carson got her PhD at the University of Waterloo and has close connections to the Schlegel–University of Waterloo Research Institute for Aging. Canadian academics recognize her name. "She's amazing," one academic told me early in my research. "You need to talk to her."

Unexpectedly, we met in Montclair, New Jersey, while she was performing with Dr. Bill Thomas's Changing Aging. In bare feet, she stood on the Montclair stage, telling the audience about her life growing up in an Arizona nursing home, the child of a nurse who worked in long-term care. "They called my mom the Doris Day of the dementia unit because she had a smile that just beamed, like the sun," she told the audience.

That day, just before the show began, Dr. Carson described her research at a place in North Carolina. "I get to stay there for a few days every month," she said, her eyes crinkling, smile wide. "It's a really special place. Try to go. You'll feel it when you get there."

Pat Sprigg arrived in the forest in 1992 and never left. Like a lot of the people I've met who are immersed in advocacy work with seniors, she seems youthful. Sprigg is president and CEO of Carol Woods Retirement Community, but the people who live here have a strong voice in the community's operations. They serve on the not-for-profit's board of directors and its finance committee, along with another 80 other resident-created groups that oversee home operations, activities and emotional sustenance.

There are committees for folk music, classical music concerts, flower arranging, dance, painting and art exhibits. Committees oversee recycling and rose gardens. There's a dog park committee. At least 30 dogs are registered residents of Carol Woods, although rumor has it that the number is underreported. There are socially conscious groups such as the emergency-room committee, so no one goes to the hospital alone, the companion corps, so people don't spend their days alone, and the vigil corps, so no one dies alone.

Beth Schultz leads the companion and vigil committees. "It touches me every time I put out a call," she says, "and have so many responses from people who are willing to come and sit at the bedside of someone they may not know at all. That is not easy for the companion or the resident who is dying."

Schultz describes a call for a companion that she put out a few days earlier, on a Friday night, for a woman who is well into her 90s and still in independent living. "She loves to write notes but cannot write anymore because of her arthritis. So I put out a call and asked who would be willing [to write] and I can't sort through the number of people who have responded. I have to say, 'Okay you can do this, and you can go on a waiting list and be backup.'

"And that, to me, is what makes Carol Woods. It's the fact that people are there for each other. And I would second that in terms of staff and the subtle ways that they are aware of residents who need something extra. It was staff who said, 'We try to make sure that someone is always there at the bedside of someone who is dying. But we can't guarantee that — can you help us? Can you train a group that will always be backup for staff?' That, to me, is incredibly special."

When I visited Carol Woods in spring 2019, Schultz had lived there for about three years. She had received early acceptance, meaning she had joined the community and was able to participate in events before actually moving there. Schultz had spent her career as an occupational therapist and didn't necessarily love the idea of retiring to a seniors' residence, even if it was a good one.

"We chose this because it is a resident-driven community. Knowing myself, I was not going to walk easily into retirement. I wanted a place where I could find meaning and purpose, and feel like I was contributing to the community I was in.

"The move for me represented a loss of control. And I did not want to be in a community where residents have no control. So being part of a community where residents do have a voice was very important to me."

The traditional role of recreation director does not exist here. There is no predetermined schedule, with beanbag toss at 2 p.m., bingo at 7 p.m. and if you miss the daily events, too bad. That is still the normal recreation schedule in many nursing or retirement homes.

Here, residents create activities. They organize events and cajole one another into taking on leadership roles. "It was like I was fresh meat!" jokes Joe Clontz, a retired Baptist campus minister at UNC. An economics professor, Dr. Jim Wilde, created the folk music committee in 2014 to work through his grief over the sudden death of Pete Seeger. Another woman, Jeanette Pfaff, who owned a toy store, surprised herself by leading the residents' association.

There's a joke here that people self-select before they fill out the residency application. It's a progressive community. "We get a lot of professors and nurses and social workers," says Sprigg.

From its inception, Carol Woods has been inclusive. That word is increasingly used by people in the aging field as a way of describing homes or communities that accept those with cognitive decline or other disabilities from strokes to the physical struggles of an aging body.

As awareness of dementia expands, along with the number of people living with some form of the disease, there is a growing conversation about inclusive communities. The key word is *conversation.* Many homes still lock away people in secure units because they have memory loss.

Some homes, such as the Sherbrooke Community Centre in Saskatoon, made sweeping changes decades ago, with its intimate household model that allowed a handful of residents to share an open-concept kitchen where meals are cooked from scratch. Still, in 2019, it was just starting plans to unlock its dementia units. In Ontario, most nursing homes still have locked units, although the concept of inclusivity is gaining traction. Dr. Samir Sinha talks about the need for a new attitude toward people living with cognitive decline, for friendlier communities, as part of Canada's new dementia strategy. Dr. Bill Thomas, in the U.S., is talking about inclusive communities built around tiny homes that people can manage in their later years.

Carol Woods is that rare example of inclusivity, showing how seniors of all abilities can coexist.

It offers everyone the freedom to come and go. If a lady with dementia joins the others in the dining room, the workers or residents will discreetly observe and, subtly, help her to a table, or point out the buffet, with fresh corn bread and ribs. If a man needs help finding his way home, he'll start his walk and, along the way, one resident will pass him to the next until he is safely at his room. That is just how it's done here. It's casual, accepted and copied by new residents as they settle in.

It wasn't until Joe Clontz, the Baptist minister, became chair of the dining services committee that he discovered the ways staff interacted with residents who were confused.

"I became aware of the way staff were being trained, to look out for us in a very subtle, quiet and observing way," he says. "As I saw residents coming, particularly in the dining area, who didn't quite know what was going on, the staff just gently went over and helped them get into the line to serve the food and later to find their way home.

"What amazed me even more is that it was actually happening through the whole staffing community. Everybody had been taught to know who we are and what our needs are. So, if somebody on staff spotted one of us wandering around, without being frightening, someone was there to walk with them.

"I've also watched my friends age into dementia. And that has been interesting. It is one thing to watch people you don't know go into this state, but to watch your friends, your peer group, people you've known for years, decades, begin to slip into that, you begin to realize how caring staff and residents, for the most part, are with helping each other do these things that we want to do."

His awareness, the understanding that little acts of kindness can keep everyone moving forward, is exactly what Sprigg wants to hear. She believes the residents watch, act and ultimately, teach one another.

"Once you drink the Kool-Aid, you share it."

At the same time, the Carol Woods experience proves that these practices must be nurtured and protected. No matter how altruistic its philosophy may appear, there are periods when Sprigg has had to fight to retain freedom for all residents.

When she arrived at Carol Woods in the early '90s, "memory support" units for people living with dementia were growing popular across the United States. Homes promoted them as a way to keep people with dementia safe, offering specialized care, while at the same time keeping people with cognitive decline away from the others, who didn't always appreciate the visitors wandering into rooms or pacing the hallways.

"Everyone was building memory care," Sprigg says. "And the pressure was on. Residents actually believed that we needed to have one.

"It has been an over two-decade dialogue with residents in terms of the importance of really understanding, appreciating, honoring and taking pride in being inclusive. I know that sounds pretty flowery, but I really believe there is something to that."

The conversation takes Sprigg back to the 1970s, when people were held down with restraints.

"We do it [use locked units] because we do not have a capacity for risk. So just like we tied them up, with no evidence behind that, we now lock them up with no evidence. We are trying to prove that inclusiveness is a civil rights liberty. And that inclusiveness is really what human beings want.

"The only people we lock up are criminals. And we don't do that real well. Why would we lock up someone who has a diagnosis? So, I am trying to do the same thing we did in the 70s. Because locked units are a physical restraint.

"More importantly, even if you take the locks off, what approach do you put into place?"

The answer to that question lies with the work Dr. Jennifer Carson is doing at Carol Woods. She is one of those people who immediately puts the elders at ease. She also likes a dry martini after work.

When she was a student at the Murray Alzheimer Research & Education Program at the University of Waterloo, about an hour west of Toronto, Dr. Carson worked on a study that looked at the "domains of well-being." What gives people with cognitive decline a good life? While the research relied on the answers supplied by people living with dementia, its findings could apply to any of us.

Led by Dr. Sherry Dupuis, the conclusions narrowed those domains to seeking freedom, being with (other people), being me (not losing the sense of who you are), finding balance, growing and developing, making a difference and, finally, having fun. Who doesn't want a life like that?

At Carol Woods, Dr. Carson's work is called The Quest Upstream. It is "participatory action research" based on critical social theory, which focuses on social justice and creating change. With Sprigg, Dr. Carson seeks ways to help people with dementia live fulfilling lives alongside the other residents who might have their own physical or emotional struggles, just not with cognitive decline. The word upstream is used to denote the place where the problems — and solutions — begin. If a person with memory loss lives with purpose and freedom from the outset, then some of those other so-called behavioral problems likely won't exist in a significant way.

In May 2019, Dr. Carson's research, in part, is unfolding in shift-change huddles. When the afternoon workers start their shift, they meet with the day workers who are going home. For Dr. Carson's study, they discuss a resident who is struggling, usually with cognitive decline or emotional needs. Each worker rates that person's well-being and talks about ways to improve happiness, purpose or peacefulness. It's a proactive approach ultimately designed to meet an individual's needs before distress begins.

Sprigg says workers now hold huddles regularly. Sometimes, if there is a problem in the middle of a shift, staff will stop, come together and discuss solutions. That's the goal of participatory action research, Dr. Carson says, inspiring ongoing reflection and change.

Now that the Quest Upstream study is finished, Dr. Carson and Sprigg are sharing their findings so other homes can build on their work. Dr. Carson says the data showed positive change, including improvement in culture, teamwork and the well-being of elders and staff. Some homes, she says, learned of the Quest Upstream findings and cancelled plans for locked memory units, moving instead toward a campus that is open to all residents.

While I am at Carol Woods, during a Dr. Carson-led huddle, a young woman, traditionally called a nurse's aide but here a "resident life specialist," stays behind to talk about a lady in her care who has grown unhappy as her abilities decline. The worker is close to this woman. She sits, shoulders slouched, sad to see her friend struggle. "I really love her," she says.

As the woman speaks, it becomes clear that she is looking for comradery, the support she needs to help with a job that can be both fulfilling and draining. Dr. Carson listens. So does Jen Wilson, Carol Woods's vice-president of well-being, a title chosen with purpose. Job titles here are designed to make people think about the meaning of their role. Nursing aides are called resident life specialists because, as Sprigg said, their job is to help residents live well.

For Sprigg, these huddles and even the conversations afterwards empower the workers as much as the people who live here. "It's like being an investigative reporter," she says. "If we keep unearthing perspectives on how we might look at this, we are going to find the one that works."

For some residents, it is the freedom and the forest that give peace. It would be difficult to design a more relaxing location than a retirement home ensconced in acres and acres of trees. Like many people, I've always gone hiking. I grew up outside the city, and my friends and I spent hours in a huge swath of forest, creeks and fields without hovering parents. It's that nature fix, the time spent among trees that somehow revitalizes us.

The concept of nature as an antidote arose during conversation at a Friday night pizza and champagne party, a monthly event at the west Toronto home of Laura Tamblyn Watts. She is a connector. You never know who you'll meet over a slice of pepperoni and Veuve Cliquot. Near an outdoor firepit, I chatted with Dr. Cyndi Gilbert, a naturopathic doctor and environmentalist who wrote a book called *Forest Bathing*.

As we were serenaded by a backyard musician, Dr. Gilbert explained the Japanese practice of shinrin-yoku, or forest bathing, the simple act of being in nature, not rushing, just absorbing the rustle of the leaves, watching tadpoles in a pond or sitting on an old log while the sun filters through the leaves.

In her book, Dr. Gilbert wrote, "Spending more time in the green and blue spaces of the natural world can help to normalize blood pressure and blood sugar, build resilience to stress, increase vitamin D stores, encourage healthy aging, ameliorate mood, and enhance cognitive functions." That sounds a whole lot better than antipsychotic meds.

As soon as I arrived at Carol Woods, I understood what Dr. Carson meant when she called it a special place. Part of that is the forest. Another is the freedom residents have to step into those woods, or the gardens, and enjoy being part of the natural world. This is a long way from the white wards and metal beds where Sprigg started her career.

A few days after meeting Dr. Gilbert, I emailed Sprigg to ask if she has seen the calming effect of nature on people living at Carol Woods, especially those with memory loss.

She wrote back, "I do believe in the therapeutic value of nature and the outdoors. . . . That is why we strive to maintain a beautiful campus with buildings that have views of gardens, woods and the pond. You saw it when you were here as group of persons living with dementia were outside engaged in gardening (nurturing a sense of purpose) or just enjoying the beauty.

"As one resident told me, her daily meditation is walking from her building to the main one and soaking in the beauty of the trees. On nice days you will see me having 'walking meetings.' It simply takes conversation to a very relaxed level," she wrote.

Imagine the difference all of this makes in the lives of people, to be offered the freedom to sit in the fresh air, near a garden, in the sunshine.

Consider the retired CIA agent, a resident with memory loss. He got up early every morning. Workers had his coffee ready. "And then," Sprigg says, "he would go out on patrol."

He'd march through the forest or along miles of connecting sidewalks around the circular road that runs through the Carol Woods community. Sometimes he walked so long that he grew dehydrated, veering off course. To counter this, residents volunteered to walk with him, usually several paces behind, carrying bottles of water in case he needed a drink.

"We knew we couldn't take away that freedom, because he was on patrol in his mind," Sprigg says. "After his walks, he would come into my office and tell me that cities were not safe. He would tell me about the snipers. He would tell me about the children that were getting killed. He would tell me that it is safe now, he took them out, everything is clear, I am okay to leave.

"Now, what would have happened to him if we locked him in a segregated unit?"

For the longest time, people have talked about the so-called responsive behaviors of dementia, as if the disease forces people to act out, sometimes with violence. Now leaders like Sprigg, Dr. Bill Thomas or Suellen Beatty are pushing back against these stereotypes. In the many cases, they say it is not the people or the disease but the institutions that lead to this behavior.

Imagine if we were locked inside our homes every day. Now imagine what it feels like to be a person with dementia who is frustrated, maybe because you don't get to go outside or you spend your day sitting, staring at the floor. Is your frustration a result of your disease? Or the fact that your life has no activity, no purpose, no joy, no connection to the outside world?

Much like the studies that showed restraints were harmful, Sprigg expects research on locked units will reach the same inevitable conclusion. "I think that in time, the same information is going to be coming out: what detriment did we cause people by locking them up?"

At Carol Woods, I meet retired doctors, medical professionals, professors and federal government officials, some of whom are living with cognitive decline. I join two ladies at the fellowship table in the dining room for a cup of morning coffee. At this table, all are welcome.

"Well, you're new here," says one. "Where are you from?"

I introduce myself. We talk.

"I love living here," says the dark-haired woman.

"They don't tell us what to say," laughs her friend.

We talk about dogs. One of the ladies, wearing a soft pink cardigan, says her dog disappeared. "He barked a lot," she says. "One day he was outside barking and then — nothing. I always wondered what happened to him. Maybe somebody didn't have a sense of humor."

The dark-haired woman talks about her childhood. She was always afraid to dive, so her father told her if she dove into a pond, he'd get her a dog. "I climbed up on his shoulders and went down into the water. The next day we got a Scottish terrier. We named him Diver."

The women say they've become good friends and sit together for meals. "But not always," says the lady in the cardigan.

"We like to be able to sit with new people too," says the dark-haired lady. "Where are you from?"

People here say Carol Woods is like moving to a university campus, living in a sorority or fraternity house again.

The main building makes me think of a Frank Lloyd Wright home. It is built with clean lines and a purposeful design, in this case creating a visual connection between the indoors and the forest, while at the same time making it easy for people to move from their living quarters to the dining room.

As Sprigg and I walk, we stop every few minutes to chat with workers or the people who live here. Sprigg greets her staff by name. She says the happiness of workers is equal to the well-being of residents. Just outside the staff room, where the housekeepers are having a coffee break, a waterfall tumbles down boulders, while half a dozen residents work at the top of the hill.

A few minutes later, we are standing on the hill with the women who have been working there. They are wearing wide-brimmed hats and gloves, planting a new garden they designed themselves with the grounds crew. Sprigg credits Eva, a woman in a wheelchair who is overseeing the proceedings, for spearheading the plans for the garden and the waterfall. "Pat helped too," Eva says, of her friend.

Robin, the groundskeeper, asks Sprigg her thoughts on the wording of the sign that will be posted near the garden. The residents will design it.

"Anything that is artistic," Sprigg says. "I just don't want a big old sign that says *Do Not Pick the Flowers.*"

The ladies laugh. "We want a sign that says *PICK the Flowers,*" says Eva.

"Or *Eat the Flowers,*" jokes another.

They're still laughing as we walk away.

◎　◎　◎

Six women sit at the table.

One worked at the U.S. Department of State in Washington, D.C. Another is a retired bureaucrat from North Carolina's state department, in Raleigh. A third ran a medical department. All are accomplished.

Every month they meet as members of the official Memory Loss Committee.

While I can guess the answer, I ask Sprigg why the committee name breaks from the norm — why not call it the dementia committee?

"No one would come if we did," she says.

It's a good point. The more people I meet here living with neurological disorders, the more I wonder why we, as a society, keep using the word dementia. Canada's new dementia strategy says it wants society to stop stigmatizing people with cognitive decline, in which case, there has to be a better way to describe it.

When Sprigg asks the women to share their experience with cognitive changes, the lady beside her, with gray hair and a kind face, begins to speak.

"I have severe memory loss," she says. "It affects so many parts of life. Every day, all day long, I'm struggling with memory loss. Little things. Like, where are my things to blow my nose with? Where are my shoes? What am I supposed to do next?

"At the same time, it's part of my life. You can't just say, 'I can't do,' or 'I won't do.' Or stop doing. I will reach out and do what I can as well as I can, and find ways to get around it and find people who will help me and accept it. So, my life is a very rich life."

Across the table, a tall, attractive woman speaks. "I have some memory loss, and I've just decided that I don't have to call everyone by name. It used to be, 'Hi Kay, Hi Pat, Hi Judy.' Now, I can just say, 'Hi!'"

Everyone laughs.

"The name will come — when I'm in the next building. So forget it. Just say, 'Hi.' What drives me just absolutely crazy is word finding. That has made more of an impact because I can't conduct a meeting and get up there and in the middle of a sentence you can't continue.

"Of course, everybody is very helpful. It's like playing . . ." She pauses. Another woman says, "Charades!" They all laugh.

"I love it," says Sprigg.

"We-eell," the woman says, in an affected southern drawl, "you wouldn't love it if it happened to you."

The conversation shifts. Sprigg looks to the woman with the kind face and says, "When you realized you were losing your memory, you said that I can either be upset or I can accept the fact that it makes me learn differently. And I thought, *Those are pretty good words of wisdom. That's pretty wise. That's a challenge.*"

Another woman speaks. "Here's a challenge I didn't expect. I thought I would raise my children. They would find themselves a place in the world in terms of their work and other things that are joys to them. What I didn't expect is that they would grow old too. And that they would be dealing with adult development changes at the same time that I was dealing with adult develop-ment changes. Now I'm worried about my child's retirement."

"Oh — we're all worried about that," says another.

"And the joys," says the tall woman, "you reach out to the joys. I have two granddaughters. Both of them sing and dance. I stay involved in their lives and invite them into mine."

They start talking about the choice between a retirement community or toughing it out at home. The tall woman describes her experience years earlier, before she moved here, volunteering with Meals on Wheels. "I got a real window into what it was like being old if you stay in your own home," she says. "All your friends die. Your world becomes very small, and you are eagerly waiting for that person you know is bringing you your lunch. But it's not because you want your lunch, it's because you want human contact."

She describes a friend, an academic, who was popular and charming. "I realized she was coming down with dementia. She lived independently for a while but . . ." the woman stops speaking.

"I lost my . . . I lost my train of thought," she says to the memory loss committee.

A worker at the table jumps in. He asks a prompting question. "Did she have support staff?"

"Oh. Okay," the woman says. "She was a very engaging person. People always liked her. When things got very bad, I found a place for her, and a lot of her friends were furious. They said she did not need to be in a place for people with dementia. So they came up with a plan for her to stay at home. They said, 'You can get a person to do this. And a person to do that. And a person to do something else.' I said, 'Are you going to arrange for that?' They said, 'Oh, sure, sure, no problem.' I said, 'What happens when those people can't come? Are you going to do it?' They said, 'Noooo, I couldn't do that.'

"So, having somebody come in, if the person is not in excel-lent shape, it's a disaster."

The woman did move into a nursing home where, her friend says, staff recognized her interest in academic evaluations, so they would sit down and give her reports. They also discovered she liked ice cream sandwiches. She died a short time later.

The point of her story, of all the stories they shared that morning, is that sometimes tough decisions are necessary. There is no point in pretending that cognitive decline does not exist, or that life can continue exactly as it once did.

Every home I've visited has offered a new insight, sometimes in unexpected ways.

The overwhelming sentiment from the women at the memory loss table, and the others living at Carol Woods, is that time passes. Find a way to laugh with friends and always say hello, even if you no longer remember names.

◎　◎　◎

On Friday, September 13, at 8:15 p.m., I sent my son a text saying, "Grandma is in the hospital with her stomach problems. She didn't pay for a phone in her room, so I can't talk to her and I miss her."

My mom seemed to spend several days each month in her local hospital. Sometimes we joked that it was her spa escape. The week before I sent that text, she went in because she had fallen after tripping over her shoes. She stayed overnight and checked out the next day. A few weeks earlier, she had the same stomach trouble, a hernia, which might have been caused by food she should not be eating but ate anyway. It was never clear. She always stayed for a few days and came home feeling better, wearing perfectly ironed linen dresses in periwinkle blue. This was how she rolled. We all grew accustomed to it.

Fifteen minutes after I sent my son that text, my dad called my cell. I was in my living room, writing.

It was the call I had always dreaded.

"How am I going to live without her?" he said.

I phoned my sister. She was at work in a California hospital but picked up on the second ring. She sent her husband, back home, to spend the night with Dad in his double retirement home room. Dad woke him at 6 a.m., asking how he slept, because he didn't sleep at all.

Funeral planning kept us numb. Family flew in from across the continent. The electronic photo show of my mother's life was compiled with her 1940s portraits in beautifully constructed dresses and a tiny cinched waist. She always posed, her high heels positioned with lady-like etiquette.

An obituary was written. In my haze, I mistakenly called her a showgirl instead of a chorus girl when describing her dance career with the Windsor Light Opera, a distinction that refers to the amount of clothing one wears. I believe my mother would have found that amusing. A funeral reception playlist was downloaded with songs from the Broadway musicals *Kiss Me, Kate*, *South Pacific* and *Hello, Dolly!* and singles from Louis Armstrong, Edith Piaf, Billie Holiday, Julie Andrews and the inevitable Monty Python's "Always Look on the Bright Side of Life."

Flower and sympathy notes arrived. I had no idea that my girlfriends' memories of her voice, her laughter, would bring such solace. So did the sight of her four grandsons, all young men now, with her two sons-in-law carrying her pretty blue casket to the hearse. It's a moment that defines the passage of life, captured with a click of the eye and stored in the memory forever.

The loss of a mother. It felt like the Earth was spinning in one direction while I was moving in another. We were all spoiled by her presence, her ability to bounce back. Her toughness. She terrified me often.

I still think of the meeting with the hospital doctor the day after she died, held in a little beige waiting room that mostly had space for chairs. The doctor, a young man with tousled hair, squeezed in with my dad, my eldest son and my brother-in-law, while my sister listened on speakerphone. We were all trying to understand what had happened. She was only there for a few days and was preparing to leave. She was 91, but we all believed she would be here for another decade. When I had called the hospital the night before, a nurse told me that she found her, dead, after starting her rounds on the night shift. I was surprised by the bluntness of that word, *dead*. It felt so harsh, but euphemisms can't change the facts. My mom was dead. Officially, at 8:11 p.m.

The room was stuffy with the door closed, but the doctor seemed in no hurry to leave. He told us that Mom had recovered from her stomach issues. She had been up, walking and was most definitely talking. No one expected her to die, he said. We asked how, and he couldn't give a definite answer, saying it was likely a heart attack or a stroke.

"We had good conversations," said the doctor. "She told me about a book she had read because its ideas were important to her. It was about dying. I just can't remember the name of the book . . ."

I smiled. "Was it called *Being Mortal*?"

"Yes," he said. "That's it. She wanted me to read it."

That was my mom, educating the doctors to the end.

CHAPTER NINE

## *Other Ways of Living Well*

NOT EVERYONE GROWS OLD WITH COGNITIVE DECLINE, but it keeps appearing, in the backdrop of aging, in our fathers, spouses or sometimes within ourselves. Live long enough and you might even see it in your children, as a woman in that North Carolina retirement community observed.

Ever so slowly, dementia is being acknowledged as a part of our existence. I've encountered activists who describe it as a creative phase of life, rebranding it from something to be feared to a condition that leaves us in tune with our emotions. I mentioned this theory to Pat Sprigg, and her response was immediate: life with cognitive decline is difficult and she would never suggest otherwise. Opinions about the disease are as diverse as the people living with it.

Still, we are speaking more openly now about the experience. Paul Lea has vascular dementia brought on by a stroke in his late 50s. Now in his mid-60s, he is on the Alzheimer Society of Toronto speaking circuit. "We are still human beings," he says, "still members of the community, still capable of doing things, maybe not with the same ability, but we can contribute, not the same way in the past but we are alive. And we're not alone." He doesn't gloss over the challenges, calling them "terrible, debilitating," but he is also proud of overcoming. He talks about dementia hacks, like using Google Street View to familiarize himself with houses and shops in advance of a visit to avoid getting anxious or losing his way. And he takes pleasure in staying fit by walking 30 minutes or an hour in good weather, often to the Black Bull on Toronto's Queen Street West, where he has a laugh with his favorite server and, yes, she knows he has dementia. "She treats me like anybody else."

By talking about memory loss instead of isolating ourselves, we can stop viewing people with dementia as "others." They can be any of us, including the most charismatic.

For years, the Alzheimer Society of Toronto raised money for its music program by holding a concert in downtown Toronto, performed by the Canadian band Spirit of the West. For most of us of a certain age in Canada, actually any age that appreciates a good bar anthem, the songs from that band are ingrained. I can't imagine nursing-home dance parties of the future without "And If Venice Is Sinking" or "Home for a Rest," a mix of folk, rock and Celtic joy. The band's lead singer, John Mann, was diagnosed with early onset Alzheimer's disease on the cusp of 50. Instead of hiding it, John and his wife, Jill Daum, announced his diagnosis in 2014, choosing to elevate awareness of cognitive decline. Jill went on to write a play called *Forget About Tomorrow* about a wife learning to accept a new reality.

In 2015, the band played at Toronto's Mod Club to help the Alzheimer Society of Toronto buy iPods for its music project, so it could load them with clients' favorite songs. The concert grew into an annual event. For the first few years, John, a man of considerable presence, sang while reading lyrics displayed on an iPad that his bandmate advanced remotely, verse by verse. When his words faltered, the crowd sang with him.

In 2017, John did not sing. Onstage, he danced with abandon, snapping his fingers, twirling to the music he created, the songs of his life. As the crowds grew, the venue moved from the Mod Club to the Horseshoe Tavern and later to Toronto's east-end Phoenix Concert Theatre, the big stage that once held Bob Dylan and Patti Smith. In 2019, John did not come. He was by this time in serious decline and he would die before the year was out. Instead, Canadian artists such as Tom Cochrane, Jim Cuddy, Andrew Cash, Damhnait Doyle and the Skydiggers sang with John's bandmates, raising money and awareness for Toronto's Alzheimer Society.

Scott Russell, the society's CEO, said the 2019 concert raised $100,000 for the music project. Volunteers from high school and university come to the society's downtown Toronto offices once or twice a week to build a playlist for each client, adding favorite songs to the SanDisk MP3 players the society now uses instead of iPods. Sometimes the volunteers spend hours researching music from a specific time and country to make sure the songs connect with the individual. The society hands out about 1,000 players a year to Torontonians. The music project was inspired by the 2014 documentary *Alive Inside: A Story of Music and Memory*, and, in particular, a man in the film named Henry. He lived in a U.S. nursing home, spending his days with head down, unresponsive. When his caregiver placed the headphones over Henry's ears, playing the songs of his youth, his eyes opened wide and he sat upright, singing along. Later, interviewed on camera, Henry spoke in full sentences, describing his admiration for the 1930s and '40s jazz musician Cab Calloway. The interviewer asked simple, direct questions. Henry answered. "Music gives me the feeling of love," he said. When he listened to his songs, Henry became himself again.

Music has that hold over us. It makes many different connections within our brain, perhaps even tapping into regions that are resilient to cognitive decline, explains Dr. Claude Alain, a senior scientist with the Baycrest Centre in Toronto. "The sound of music reaches the part of the brain that processes sound and that part is also connected with other parts — the motor system, the part that allows us to move," Dr. Alain says. "When music reaches the part of the brain that allows us to remember, there is a sense of familiarity. We recognize those sounds and that seems to facilitate activity in other brain areas. Suddenly, you start moving to the beat of the music.

"You play music from the 1980s, let's say. Memories might come back from high school. And that music was associated with a bunch of things, because in high school it was very emotional," he says.

When people have dementia, music is able to activate or trigger memories, Dr. Alain says. People may not be able to verbalize what they are feeling, but they can engage with memories from decades earlier, particularly if they listen to the music of their youth. Some studies show that the areas in the brain that hold emotion may be more resilient. They will get activated. They will respond to music.

"It is so strong and so clear, it is one of those rare things we find that somehow makes a difference."

Recent brain imaging technology, such as MRIs, is showing that the brain connections are far more complex than earlier understood, and Dr. Alain is most excited about the research it's aiding into the neuroplasticity of the older brain.

"There is flexibility that we thought was not there," he says.

Previously, scientists believed that our brain peaked in our early 20s, and after that, the neurons began a long decline. While there is some loss with age, Dr. Alain says scientists now believe that older gray matter retains more plasticity than previously understood, which means it is still possible to improve our mind.

"You can teach old dogs new tricks."

The ability to engage through music unifies us, which is one of the reasons the Spirit of John performances are dedicated to the Alzheimer Society's music project. Nobody is suggesting that early onset dementia in a Canadian rock star will make memory loss cool, but the band's willingness to speak about it helps lessen the isolation that many families feel.

The music and the message resonated with Laura Tamblyn Watts in January 2019 when she pushed her way to the front of the Phoenix stage, as if she were at a punk show from her youth. "Every Canadian rock star you could imagine was up onstage, and they were playing like it was a kitchen party in honor of their friend," Tamblyn Watts says. "The energy was roof-shattering. Everyone was dancing, everyone was singing, because everyone knows every lyric to every song, even the ones that had nothing to do with Spirit of the West." In the front row, she sang and danced, hugging friends. When she turned back to look across the crowd, Tamblyn Watts saw parents dancing with their children. How fitting, she thought, that a night of rock honoring people with dementia drew all ages, from boomers to Gen Z, achieving the blend of ages that advocates say will keep us engaged in life.

"It's kind of like Canada's Elton John for AIDS," she says. "The concert brought it forward; it normalized dementia, destigmatized it. The number one greatest fear, study after study after study will tell you, is not the physical body aging. The number one fear is dementia. It's the sense of losing our current understanding of who we are."

Good news has emerged from research that concluded the incidence of dementia is declining. Research published in *JAMA Neurology* in 2015 found stroke and dementia incidence rates in Ontario decreased by more than 30 percent between 2002 and 2013. The challenge is the fact that the odds of dementia increase with age, and the demographic bulge of older boomers means there's still a big pool of people to come. Statistics reveal that the odds of getting dementia double every five years after the age of 65. So until the boomers fade away, society will have to deal with memory loss and, since it is a numbers game, there are as many millennials.

There is more good news. Researchers are working to develop tests that show a predisposition to conditions leading to dementia years before symptoms appear. If they succeed, we could try to delay the arrival of the disease. Eating food that is good for the heart, for example, is now considered good for the brain. And getting your ears checked. Canadian geriatrician Dr. Samir Sinha says hearing loss has been linked to dementia, possibly because the brain doesn't exercise all of its functions when it is focused solely on the act of hearing. Loss of hearing could also lead to isolation, which initiates decline. Dr. Sinha warns his patients away from expensive supplements advertised to promote brain health, saying it breaks his heart to see people waste money. "I tell them you'd be better off to put that $200 toward a vaccination against shingles, and then you'll have a 90 percent chance of not getting it," he says. There is evidence that suggests exercise and creative endeavors through art, learning new languages or playing musical instruments can challenge the brain, possibly keeping it sharper. As Scott Russell said, if we can delay the onset, a person who might have developed dementia at 85 can push it back long enough that they will die of old age before it ever appears.

There are no cures yet. With roughly 100 different forms of dementia brought on by various conditions such as strokes, Alzheimer's or Parkinson's disease, Canada's dementia strategy is investing money in research. The federal strategy, released in 2019, is focused on the creation of dementia-friendly communities, where police and people working in coffee shops, museums or art galleries are trained to understand and communicate. It's like learning a new language, one that speaks with emotional intelligence.

Police need it, Dr. Sinha says, because people with dementia often get lost, and if officers appear with flashing lights and aggressive voices, they could lash out in fear. "People get tasered," he says. Dr. Sinha cites the San Francisco Police Department, where officers get training in a program called Aging America to recognize the signs of memory loss and build empathy. Peel Region, just west of Toronto, is training its paramedics in the Butterfly program. When I wrote about Butterfly in 2018, one of the Peel Region councillors spoke of his wife, who had Alzheimer's disease and once called police to report a strange man in her home. That man was her husband, the councillor. He told his colleagues that he wished the police had a better understanding of people with dementia, so he wasn't forced to defend his presence.

As the boomers age, governments are trying to find ways to help seniors to stay in the community and out of expensive nursing homes. The Ontario government spent $4.28 billion on long-term care in 2018. Individual residents can easily end up paying their nursing home $2,700 a month or more on a private room. It's not cheap, although it is a lot less expensive than a privately paid retirement home, which can run from $3,500 a month to $10,000, depending on the home and the services required. Some of us will outlast our money.

The push to keep people in the community does not excuse governments from making investments in long-term care homes, nor does it mean they can avoid nursing home improvements that will allow people to live happier lives. Still, most of us want to stay out of an institution, even if it doesn't feel like one. Some want to move to a smaller house or condo in order to stay in their community. As long as there are enough programs and supports to enable people to get groceries or rides to appointments and, equally important, to avoid caregiver burnout, this could be a good option. The key to success, to a healthier future in the community, is to ensure that we don't simply cut costs by downloading care onto families who are already struggling to manage. Day programs like San Diego's Glenner Town Square or Toronto's Dotsa Bitove Wellness Academy, an arts-based program that was operated by the University Health Network and York University, are a few examples of respite that have helped caregivers reclaim some much-needed time for themselves. We need more options like these.

Seattle has a grassroots movement called Momentia, inspired by the words *moment*, *momentum* and *dementia*. The movement seeks to create community networks for friendship so people remain engaged. The goal of any happy existence is to feel welcome in the greater world, not ostracized. To have friends. Laugh. Exercise. And engage in lifelong learning, always developing one's sense of self, learning new skills, exploring talents like music or art in a deeper, different way. There are Momentia meetups in coffee shops, museums and art galleries, where workers have all been trained to connect with people who communicate a bit differently.

Movements like Momentia are growing. The Alzheimer Society of Toronto trains workers at the Art Gallery of Ontario, the Royal Ontario Museum, the Agha Khan Museum and the City of Toronto's frontline staff, including workers on subways, buses and streetcars.

"We want to emphasize that everyone is still worthy of living with dignity and obviously they are still a person despite their illness," the society's Romina Oliverio says. "We want the facilitators and volunteers to make that personal connection with someone with dementia."

City workers are taught to recognize potential signs of cognitive decline, such as confusion or someone standing at the city hall counter to make property tax payments who has forgotten the reason for being there. Staff learn to ask specific yes or no questions instead of open-ended queries. In museum tours, workers are asked to speak clearly and succinctly. Instead of turning to face a piece of art, Oliverio asks museum guides to make eye contact, to speak to the people in the tour, so they can easily hear and follow her other guidance. Keep discussions focused, on point, instead of digressing into nuances of 17th-century art history. Watch for visual clues: if people are fidgeting, move on to the next piece. Speak to the individual, not just the caregiver. Ask questions and encourage memories, so it is a conversation, not a lecture: if looking at a Monet, ask, 'Has anyone been to Paris?' As Oliverio says, it could inspire a moment.

"We've had some real gems that were not planned," she says. "We have a plan when we go in, but the best moments happen in the unplanned. We've had people who all of a sudden start telling us stories from 40 or 50 years ago, just because they saw something in a painting that sparked a memory."

Once, at the Royal Ontario Museum, Oliverio's group was discussing the portrait of a family. Everyone was seated, looking at the piece of art. A man in his 70s, spoke up, saying that the woman in the painting reminded him of his wife.

"This gentleman had dementia. His wife was right beside him, and he started recalling how he had met her and the first few times they had gone out, the dates and everything. She was completely taken aback because none of that had surfaced, because of his illness. But it sparked something in him and took him back 50 years ago," she says.

"It was pretty moving, to be honest with you, because you could tell she had longed to hear those details but they hadn't been forthcoming. To watch her watch him, it was pretty powerful."

◎　◎　◎

Built in the Dark Ages, the Dutch city of Deventer was destroyed by fire several times over the centuries, arson initiated by those pesky Saxons or Vikings, but always rebuilt. Today, it is a city of beauty, like a museum painting, with tall, medieval buildings reflected in the River IJssel and cobblestone streets winding their way to the community square. Here are the modern shops, selling skinny jeans and Euro scarves, and the flashy clubs like Formidable, frequented by Dutch professionals and students attending local universities.

All those young people in one small city inspired creative ideas for affordable student housing. At Humanitas Deventer, a seniors' residence in a bright, modern building with soft window light, six students live rent-free in return for their community spirit. The students can come and go as they please, as long as they don't disturb sleeping seniors late at night. In return for a small room with a washroom and space for a guitar or a TV, they agree to spend 30 hours a month being a "good neighbor" to the seniors. That could mean going for rides into town on a double-seated bicycle, the kind that rides low to the ground. It might involve card games, conversations or what seems to be a popular past time among students and elders, beer pong. This game requires a long table with cups of beer at each end. The goal is to toss a ping-pong ball and land it in a cup of beer. For each successful shot, your opponent must take a drink. At least those are the Canadian rules. It's a bit messy. Sometimes, depending on the elder, beer is substituted with wine. Sometimes, the ping-pong ball is tossed from a wheelchair or walker seat, which in theory could make it harder, although the elders apparently have good aim.

Peter Daniels, a Humanitas Deventer manager, philosopher and humorist, explains the Dutch system, saying the seniors' care is covered by government funds that citizens have paid into for most of their working lives. In recent years, the government has limited spending by increasing the age of admission from 80 to 85. Like most homes, some people living here are cognitively sharp, while others are frail or have varying degrees of memory loss. Each household decorates its common area with chosen paint colors, furniture and flowers. One group hung a toy reindeer head with enormous antlers above the elevators, like a plush hunting trophy. Dutch humor.

The six students live in the section with the active elders. Most attend the applied sciences universities in the Deventer area. Sores Duman has a room on the first floor. In winter 2019, he was 29 years old, graduating from a communications program at a nearby school. Duman learned about the home from his good friend Jurriën Mentink, the first Humanitas live-in student. Mentink has since moved out, but in 2016, the urban-design student recorded a TEDx talk about intergenerational living. In his video, Mentink said people his age (he was 22) were incredulous about his living arrangements. "'Why the heck would you live among elderly people? Aren't they very boring to talk to?'" Mentink quoted his friends, laughing. "To be truly, truly honest about those questions, no! Elderly people aren't boring at all to talk to." Humanitas students spend their time with the seniors, often explaining the latest technology, discussing travel and even the 2016 terrorist attack in Brussels. Elders, Mentink said, might offer guitar lessons or long discussions about life during wartime, sharing details that no history book could match. Sometimes, his older friends die. Through all of these shared experiences, Mentink said his perspective on life has shifted, widened.

Still living at Humanitas, Duman has a similar view. "You build a connection with the residents," he says. "That connection feels warm. It is also financially attractive for a student, because you don't have to pay rent. You just have to be yourself — open, spontaneous — and connect. That is something that has to fit your personality."

At first, the home picked the students. "Then the students took over," Peter Daniels tells me.

"We have three basic questions," says Duman. "Who are you? How do you want to spend your time? How will you enrich the lives of the elderly here?"

Yes, he gets free rent but the experience itself has been special. "They taught me two things," Duman says. "They have so much experience in life, from the things that went on back in the day.

They also teach us about the little things. Before, maybe ten or 15 minutes with someone didn't mean that much, but living here, you know, it gives more meaning to those moments. They appreciate those moments a lot. They pass that on to me and then I feel appreciated. That is one of the reasons why I don't want to leave here, because I feel appreciated," Duman says.

He looks side-eyed at Peter Daniels, who can't help himself. "In the outside world," says Daniels, "he is easily overlooked." Duman laughs. Dutch humor.

Duman's closest Humanitas friend is a 94-year-old woman named Marty. They met when staff asked Duman to help Marty with her iPad. She wanted to send her daughter emails of funny pictures. Duman taught her how to connect electronically with her family.

"Marty is a very special person," he says. "She likes to buy broken things and fix them. For example, baby carriages or dolls or other things. That is one of her hobbies. Mentally she is fine. Physically, well, it is decreasing. But I would say for 94-years-old, she is pretty good."

Duman helps Marty buy items on the Dutch version of eBay, called Marktplaats. Sometimes, when Marty wants to go to an out-of-town museum, she drives her car and Duman rides shotgun. Usually, he helps her get organized when her online purchases arrive. "We bought a baby carriage. She changed the wheels and painted it olive green and white."

Perhaps to prove the point, Duman knocks on the door to her room. She calls him inside, still sitting, due to an injured foot. Duman is right. Her room is full of what Butterfly would call "the stuff of life." The walls are covered with knickknacks. A doll in a red dress with a white lace collar leans beside her radio. Above the doll hangs a decorative plate lined with rhinestones. Beside the pink plate hangs a figurine of a bucking bronco. Next to the bronco are framed pictures of a dog, a landscape and an elegant woman pushing a baby carriage. A potted palm tree stands a few feet away amid a collection of old baby carriages, each holding a doll in a frilly white dress. An orange, red and green felt parrot looks down on a freestanding doll in a satin wedding dress. Two giraffe figurines stand on the dresser. Humanitas allows Marty to indulge in her love of *stuff*. I've never seen an Ontario home that allows such freedom of expression, but here, it's her room, her choice.

Duman sits on a velvet chair. His jeans are ripped. He wears a leather necklace with a gold medallion. Marty is dressed in a yellow cardigan over a frilly white shirt with silver rings on all ten fingers. Duman says something under his breath, something about beer pong, and Marty throws her head back, laughing.

Daniels looks at me taking notes. "Don't make this a big deal," he says. "This is just normal. Normal life. Two people talking."

◎　◎　◎

In Toronto, seniors and their houses are getting Uber-ized.

"It's a disruption thing," says Dr. Raza Mirza, a University of Toronto academic, part of a group of Gen Xers who are fast-tracking changes for seniors, impatient with the slow pace forward, intent on transformation that shakes up old ideas.

"If you look at the Uber approach, it is basically saying you have an empty seat in your car, why aren't you monetizing it?" says Dr. Mirza. "We're saying the same sort of thing. We have a report that says there are two million empty bedrooms [in the Toronto region] and 40 percent of them are in homes owned by older adults. We have another report that says we have a 1 percent vacancy rate."

What to do? Help students stuck with a $2,000 monthly rent on a one-bedroom apartment by connecting them with seniors who live alone in big, empty homes. The benefits are plentiful. Students can rent a room for about $500 or $600 a month, plus several hours each week helping with chores, a bit like a built-in job, just at home.

The benefits are obvious for students and for seniors, the extra money is usually enough to do long-needed repairs or pay for exercise classes. Just enough to make life easier. Most older people have their assets locked in the value of the home. As one man told Dr. Mirza, "I can't eat my kitchen." Many struggle to pay for daily life or property taxes and upkeep, but they don't want to leave their community, nor are they ready to move into a home. And besides, they probably aren't sick enough to apply to long-term care, and the other traditional setting, retirement homes, can cost $3,000 to $10,000 a month.

The Toronto HomeShare Program emerged from a brain-storming session of the City of Toronto Seniors Strategy group, which holds regular meetings with 100 or more community attendees of all ages, including leaders like Dr. Samir Sinha, Andrea Austen, seniors' strategy lead, Josh Matlow, Toronto councillor, and Dr. Mirza, who is also the network manager at the non-profit National Initiative for the Care of the Elderly. HomeShare began as a pilot project in 2018 and now has funding from the city with the potential to expand to across Canada and internationally.

Before the pilot began, Dr. Mirza says researchers examined existing home-share programs and concluded that the key to a successful relationship between the homeowner and the student are social workers who screen applicants, suggest a match, arrange the initial visit and, later, if the homeowner agrees to the roommate, they are there to mediate in case any problems arise.

When Kim Nguyen's son moved out of her townhouse in the Christie Pits neighborhood of Toronto, she heard about HomeShare and decided to apply. At 68, Nguyen missed the presence of another person in her home. Twenty-four-year-old Yuval Dinary became Nguyen's new roommate. Dinary is a fourth-year social work student at Ryerson University in down-town Toronto. He pays Nguyen $600 a month for a room in her home and helps with garbage and other chores. Dinary considers this a very good deal, for many reasons.

"I'm seeing more and more that people are paying double my rent and are living in one room with two or three other people," he says. "Whenever anyone asks me about my living situation and I tell them, they love it. It's so intuitive. Especially for my generation. We are so isolated from older generations, especially considering that we have more people living alone than ever before. We're all so disconnected. So, joining someone in your city and getting to know them and helping each other out, it's a real blessing. It's also very functional."

While Dr. Mirza has spoken with students who view the age difference as impassable, Dinary's embrace of intergenerational living seemed closer to the norm. For some, it takes time, Dr. Mirza says, but the realization does arrive. "The interesting piece from this study is that people said, 'We had so much more in common than I thought.' So age is not a factor that should be used to separate generations or individuals in society."

None of this comes as a surprise. Dr. Mirza's parents and their siblings all bought homes on the same street, just north of Toronto, in the early 1990s. "To age-proof their lives," he says. "They said, 'We are all going to go through a lot of good and bad things and we want this sort of communal living,' so all my uncles and aunts and cousins, we all live on the same street."

Like my grandparents did when they moved to Windsor in the early 1900s, Dr. Mirza's family created a built-in plan to support one another, and in doing so they will likely avoid the social isolation that has been shown to be so harmful. The new goal for many governments is to keep people out of expensive hospitals and care homes and help people live healthier, connected lives in the community.

"In some sense," Dr. Mirza says, "we are also future-proofing our own lives. For our parents and our grandparents, because we've seen some of the frustrations from our own experiences, we've seen our loved ones really suffer as a result of our outdated thinking and outdated systems that no longer match the demographics and the needs of the older population."

For many, the traditional housing trajectory for aging, down-sizing from a big home to a small condo or retirement home before the inevitable admission to a nursing home, no longer holds interest. In Toronto, studies suggest that many seniors will not leave their family homes until well into their 80s, refusing to follow the old norms. In America, the majority of people surveyed in AARP's Home and Community Preferences survey said they'd like to remain in their current home, in familiar surroundings. Still, given the huge numbers of boomers, there remains a healthy market for active seniors communities like Florida's Jimmy Buffet–inspired Margaritaville locations where, as the marketing slogan says, residents can "Live Life Like a Song." With the exception of Parrothead references, the Margaritaville communities are much like other Florida real-estate developments for seniors, with a focus on fitness, friendship and easy access to retail. Living is good for those who can sell the family home, buy a new place in a warmer location near the ocean, never mind the hurricanes, and pocket the rest in cash or investments. It's a bit like moving back to college and meeting new friends, except you live in separate houses and eat better pizza.

Not everyone can live that way, or wants to move south.

The *Toronto Star* published the story of the Golden Girls, four women in their late 60s or early 70s who live in a renovated house in Port Perry, Ontario, sharing a kitchen, dining room and living room, their name inspired by the 1980s sitcom. They all paid an equal share for the house, $275,000, with a legal agree-ment for protections around departures, decline or death. At first, the concept of co-living ran into a wall of confusion within the local government. It tried to block the plans to renovate the downtown heritage home. The women and a local contractor who understood what they were trying to achieve persevered. Ultimately, the Ontario Human Rights Commission ruled against the municipal government, calling its actions age discrimination. As reporter Tess Kalinowski wrote, the Golden Girls Act has since been introduced in the provincial legislature, an attempt to embrace innovation in seniors living.

Louise Bardswich is one of the women who live in the home. At 68, she is a retired dean of information technology and accounting at Ontario's Humber College and had lived on her own since her husband died years earlier.

"I was surprised at how well it works," Bardswich says. "I knew intellectually that up until the point that I moved in it was my best retirement option, other than living with my kids, which I wouldn't do to them. The very first week when I woke up, I could hear voices downstairs and I thought, *I wonder what is going on?* And it was just so lovely to go downstairs and have a cup of coffee and chat about the news."

So far, Bardswich says her roommates get along fine. If someone is annoyed about a coffee cup left on the counter, they express their annoyance and, voilà, problem fixed. "We don't let things fester." They each cook a meal once a week but otherwise live independent lives. "We didn't sign on to be each other's best friends. We signed on to live together. We are all nice to each other, polite."

The idea that she is living among people who will recognize her absence if she does not get out of bed is a bonus. After living alone for years, Bardswich says her family is constantly worried about her well-being, saying, "Someone better call to make sure the cat isn't eating her face." Bardswich laughs. It's a reference to a *Sex and the City* episode when Miranda is moving into a new apartment, and a neighbor greets her in the hallway, telling her the previous tenant was an older, single lady who died in the apartment. Miranda blanches. "Oh yes," the neighbor says, "it was a week before anyone realized she passed. Rumor has it, the cat ate half her face. So . . . just you?"

Humor aside, Bardswich no longer worries about isolation. "We've all had things that have happened to us. You can shout or send a text. We text each other a lot in this house."

The idea of co-living is gaining traction among millennials too. Housing prices are so unaffordable in many big cities that most will be shut out for years unless the real estate market takes a dramatic hit. Not everyone can get their head around the idea of shared living or find ways to bring people together. A beautifully renovated co-housing development near Guelph, Ontario, sat on the market without any buyers for months, each bedroom listed at $265,000.

In her Port Perry home, Bardswich loves the idea of being in control. She's happy that she is not going to end up in a seniors' residence, where she has to choose between two offerings on the menu at every meal. When it's her turn to cook, Bardswich chooses the menu.

"We're baby boomers. We want a sense of control. Living here, we are in control of our environment. We're in control of aging."

Bardswich has no plans to leave. "I'm hoping to die here, yes, I mean really," she says, and laughs. "There's a funeral parlor 100 feet away. And [my grandchildren and I] walked by it one day. I said, 'Hey, guys, when Grandma dies, all you need to do is get a wheelbarrow.' Really though, I am hoping to die here."

◎　◎　◎

Jennifer Recknagel leads Toronto's OpenLab research-through-storytelling project called Aging Well: An Exploration of Senior Social Living. By way of introducing its case studies, the Senior Social Living project says older people are casting an eye on the current options for supported housing and asking, "Are we really going to end up like this?" It is the question of our times.

Recknagel stresses that the research is anecdotal but found four general categories for newer ways of living. Home sharing, in return for support; cohousing, when seniors blend resources to buy a property and build a community that embraces older people; virtual villages that allow seniors to live in their homes and connect by telephone or email to a network of volunteers; and finally, the NORCs: Naturally Occurring Retirement Communities. Recknagel says New York City is the epicenter for NORCs, in apartments where tenants have aged in place, well into their senior years. Many of these buildings now offer built-in services such as housekeeping, meals and regular social activities suggested by the seniors.

"I think seniors themselves, and the cohort that is coming in now, they absolutely do not want to go into institutions," she says. "That is the option of last resort, and people are terrified of it. There is a strong desire to think of new ways." While many seniors are staying in their homes, those who are not are often moving to urban areas, into condos or apartments that are easier to manage, she says.

One of the easiest ways for governments to help seniors succeed at aging in place is to expand the options they allow under home care. In Ontario, for example, home care covers personal care like baths or showers, but many seniors don't need those services and are desperate for others. "If you go and talk to seniors about what can really help them, they want someone to get the groceries. Fix my TV. Take my dog out for walk in the winter. It is all so integral to feeling vital. So, a lot of it is falling to family, but families are overstretched. People are having children later in life; they are just not as available."

In her travels, Recknagel saw seniors who were creating support networks with neighbors who were often other seniors. She also heard a prevailing theme: don't underestimate the desire to spend time among people within their own general age group, people who understand.

"I know that intergenerational support is a hot topic, but what I saw was more seniors interested in connecting with other seniors, maybe younger seniors, who would almost see it as a paying forward situation. And people who are more similar to their age, who understand cultural references.

"I know seniors say they want to see kids, life. But in terms of having someone to help you out or be a network of support, I found that seniors are more willing to talk to a peer, rather than somebody who is much, much younger and doesn't necessarily relate."

She realized that elders want society to see them as individuals, not just old folks who are sweet or cantankerous, pick a cliché.

"For teenagers, we have all these different tropes for the different kind of teenagers there are. The nerd, the jock, the popular girl, the science kid. You understand there is a huge diversity. And with seniors, we tend to paint them all with one brushstroke."

The point is that seniors are just like people in any other generation, with unique personalities and interests. Perhaps they are shaped by the historical or cultural events of their time, but those born with comedic timing don't lose that just because they happen to live past the age of 75. The same individuality goes for the way they choose to live later in life. Some will love programs like Toronto's HomeShare. Some will gravitate to condos or NORCs, buying units on the same floor as their friends so they can help one another and even share the cost of a personal support worker, if that day of need arrives. Like any age, people have different interests. Some don't want to hear kids running around or the sound of balls bouncing against a wall. Others love the energy created by living amongst multiple generations.

If there is a generalization, perhaps it is found in the need for social connections and purpose in our day-to-day lives. The "junior seniors," as Recknagel calls them, the 65- to 75-year-olds, are in the midst of redefining their lives after leaving careers, looking for something to do with their energy and skills.

"The younger seniors, in my experience, they want to be part of something because they have left the thing they were doing," she says. "Most of us get our identity through our work. People spend so many hours doing that and then retire and . . . boom!"

◎ ◎ ◎

*Pop* goes the pickleball, which is really a Wiffle ball, which, for the uninitiated, is a small plastic ball with holes in it.

The game of pickleball is a bit like tennis on a smaller court. Sort of like badminton, except the ball is hit with a paddle, like table tennis, instead of a racquet with strings. If you want to get your daily steps in, play the singles game. Most play doubles and get hooked. One woman admitted her obsession on Facebook by half joking, "My name is Pat and I have a pickleball problem."

Considered one of the fastest-growing sports in the U.S., pickleball is wildly popular with people of a certain age, although the game is catching on with the young crowd too. In parts of the United States and Canada, tennis courts are being replaced with the slightly smaller pickleball version. Another example of supply and demand.

Tom Brett is a 72-year-old player who is so fit from his time on the court that he intimidates people 15 years younger. He has got a fast, hard swing and an engineer's brain that embraces strategy, so he envisions tricky landing spots, winning points for his team. Brett grew up in England around the corner from a kid named Reginald Dwight, whose mother, Brett says, introduced them and for years they rode their bikes to Pinner County Grammar School, with Reggie tapping the handlebars to the beat of the songs in his head. "He'd just invent songs and sing all the way," Brett says. "He went to the Royal Academy of Music, so he was trained very well. Sometimes I'd go around after we left school to have a game of tennis. His mom would say, 'Go sit in there because he has to finish practicing.' I'd have to sit and watch him play piano before his mom would let us out to play tennis." Reginald went on to have a wildly brilliant career under a new name, and Brett eventually moved to Canada as an engineer who worked on the end effector, the complicated handpiece of the Canadarm, for NASA.

The most important part of this story is the fact that Brett kept playing tennis. He played for decades. While he took a break after emergency quadruple bypass surgery in 2004 at age 57, Brett started playing again and was back up to three hours each morning when he tore his rotator cuff and could no longer launch an overhead serve.

"It was my tennis partner who said, 'Well, it's pickleball day, why don't we try to do some pickleball?' He introduced me to that. So, I fairly spontaneously went over to pickleball, which has an underarm serve. Same skill sets required. Fast thinking, fast moving. You've got to be mentally active, to have the reflexes of a cat. I can tell you for sure that my reflexes have diminished year by year, with every year I get older. I'm 72 now. I'll be 73 in January. And I've looked at graphs online as to how your reaction time fades away the older you get. And it fades away pretty quickly. But when I did a test, I was able to determine that I was younger in terms of reaction time. I was not my 72, but actually coming up at a 61 equivalent."

He credits those reflexes to pickleball. In fact, Brett credits pickleball with most of his emotional, social and physical well-being. His wife, Sue, has had stage four breast cancer for 18 months, and instead of resigning her to the hospital's palliative care unit, Brett brought her home. He is devoted to her.

"My life is caring for her and pickleball. There is nothing else. I have become totally dependent on it for my social outlet and getting my frustrations out on the court. It has actually been a savior, I would say.

"People have told me that if I'm going to take this on, the 24-7 caring business for my wife, that I'll have to watch it because my health can go downhill quickly. I could easily see getting into a complete rut. My wife encourages me to get out of the house.

We know what to do now. I can set up the meals. I can set up the drinks. I've set her up with Alexa, who can turn on the fan and the lights.

"I would have been in a state of depression . . . if I hadn't had all these people around me who know my situation. It is a great support, people are willing to chat, discuss it, offer me help in some way even though there is not much they can do other than play me a hard game of pickleball. That's the best thing anyone can do for me," Brett says, chuckling.

I ask Brett if his peers, the first wave of the boomers, talk about how they will live as time moves along. Do they discuss nursing homes or retirement homes? Or are they obsessively staying fit to avoid them?

He laughs.

"It's treated as a joke. We say, 'When I get to 90, I hope I'm still playing.' No one ever talks about going into a home. They don't consider it. I don't see why I won't still be playing at the age of 90. I talk to people when we sit and wait for our games, and they have the same attitude as me. I've always said I want to die on the court, but I want to make sure that when I'm carried off, that I did win the last point."

◎    ◎    ◎

Exactly one month after my mother died, we celebrated Thanksgiving. It was our first big family event without her. We were so accustomed to seeing her moving through that dining room, checking on kitchen preparedness and her husband who inherited the Scottish impatience for dinner. She should have been in the center of the room, laughing at a story she found ridiculous. She gave good dialogue, my mom.

When my brother-in-law led a prayer before the meal, asking us all to take a minute to think of her, my sister and I did not close our eyes. Instead, we watched our dad. His head was down.

I wondered if he would cry. He did not. A few hours later, after turkey, potatoes and pecan pie, my son and I took him back to his retirement home room. He looked so fragile when he hugged us goodbye, insisting on a call to report our safe arrival in Toronto. When we spoke on the phone the next morning, I asked how he felt after our first Thanksgiving without Mom.

"I kept looking for her. I was waiting for her to walk around the corner," he said.

"Me too," I told him.

"It's going to take a long time," he said. And then he told me he had to go because his exercise class was starting.

I don't know if it is due to the unexpected plasticity of the older brain, but my dad seems sharper. Maybe Mom ran the show, and he didn't need to speak, but he's got a lot to say. It's still about sports. And numbers. He recites every recent monetary trans-action, right down to the cents, to the point that it feels like I'm with Raymond, Dustin Hoffman's character in *Rain Man*. He also read the life insurance documents that my mother controlled and uncovered the fact that she had only bought policies on his life and her children's, not herself. I guess she planned to outlast us all. For some reason, after a lifetime of her humor, I love this detail. My dear, funny, invincible mom.

# Epilogue

"If you're going to kick authority in the teeth,
you might as well use two feet."

— KEITH RICHARDS

L ET'S BE BLUNT.
If the boomers and those who will follow want to change
the way they live in their elder years, we'd all better start agitating
for change right away. It takes time to enact real change, and we
don't want to get to our older, frailer, quieter stage without those
improvements in place.

When I presented this notion to friends, most grew somber.
"I hadn't thought of that," said a colleague during a newsroom
discussion. It's a bit unnerving. As they marched through life,
boomers reshaped much of society but now, they're getting on.
After reaching 80, in 2025, they can no longer identify as the
junior seniors, no matter how much pickleball they play.

Another way of pressing the need for government action is
to highlight the statistics. Dr. Samir Sinha says current analysis
shows that if we reach the age of 65, most of us will have another
20 years of life expectancy, of which 17 will be pretty good.

"I imagine that if I make it to 65 pretty healthy, I probably
have ten really robust years ahead of me where I'm going to
be pretty fit, I can travel all around and do a whole bunch of

different things," Dr. Sinha says. "The next five after that, I may not have the same vigor and energy that I used to, but I'm still not out for the count. Those last few years may be a bit of a struggle, and this is where I want to make sure that I've made preparations appropriately, so I'm not living with regrets."

However well prepared, our longer lives present a powerful case for policy change.

Here is another analysis that is so chilling it bears repeating. The National Institute on Ageing at Toronto's Ryerson University released a report called *The Future Cost of Long-Term Care in Canada*. The authors used the Statistics Canada population micro-simulation model, considered the gold standard of projection models, to provide a conservative estimate that the cost of long-term care in institutions and community will triple from $22 billion in 2019 to $71 billion in 2050.

Dr. Bonnie-Jeanne MacDonald is the actuary who worked on the study. "Baby boomers are strongly advised to take a long hard look at their own personal circumstances and plan ahead, to the extent that they have the health and means to better protect their future and possibly more vulnerable selves," says Dr. MacDonald, director of financial research at the National Institute on Ageing. "At the public policy level, the availability and sustainability of long-term care in Canada should be an immediate and national priority."

Translation: we've almost run out of time.

"Boomers need to have hard but illuminating conversations with family," she says.

Unless you have a whole lot of money, there is nothing good in this message other than the fact that it should, no, it *must*, push government leaders forward, taking progressive action that will give us real choices in how we live as we grow older.

Even more worrisome is the conclusion that shows our current reliance on unpaid caregivers, family or friends, is going to decline by 30 percent because fewer people will be available to help. If those unpaid hours of care, mostly provided by women, were paid by the public purse it would add another $27 billion in costs by 2050.

As my mother would have said, all of this makes the proverbial ending on an ice floe an attractive option. She'd also point out that warming sea temperatures are melting that ice so we might be stuck with the choices on hand. In other words, carry on.

The good news, and there is a lot to go around, is found in the abundance of ideas, programs and philosophies.

Let's acknowledge for a moment that we are now starting to focus on the needs of a society with a great many elders. If we push for it, we'll see a greater acceptance of seniors' rights and, according to Australia's Daniella Greenwood, "the rights of people to *live* with dementia. Because dementia is out there, in the world."

Even with no cure yet for diseases that lead to cognitive decline, scientists are making exciting discoveries. And the rest of us are learning too. Not just the ways to prevent dementia, but the ways that our brains respond to emotion, stimulation or, so important, the inestimable joys of music. Nothing we know of yet has such a profoundly positive impact on our brain.

Some of the ideas for housing and communities are still in experimental stages, but there is progress. As Dr. Bill Thomas said, "Things are not possible until they are possible."

Let's not wait. Why not adjust government policies and make it easier to build intergenerational communities of smaller homes or allow more cities to add laneway housing? That will give seniors options for independence. Why not support people living and thriving in Naturally Occurring Retirement Communities, home-sharing programs or co-housing like the Golden Girls?

There is a new focus on home care so that fewer people need to end up in expensive institutions, but there must be many different options for support. Some seniors don't need help with bathing but would benefit immensely if someone could pick up groceries or offer a ride to the bank.

The point now is to push governments to support these ideas, creating an energy for a different way of living. Demand the right to a life in which seniors have value, purpose and the contentment that Laura Tamblyn Watts calls bientraitment.

The open-village concept behind the Netherlands' de Hogeweyk was entirely novel when it was designed and built in the mid-2000s. Our ideas about inclusion and community have evolved since, as have those of de Hogeweyk's founders, who would have opened the doors for free-flowing community connections had their complex been designed today. The homes that we build now will last another 30 years, and many of us will live in them.

Let's get this right. Erase the old institutional standards and design homes with small living spaces, so we can live as comfortably as possible. Try to find locations near shops, restaurants or fitness studios, so people can walk to the bank or meet friends for lunch. Create the opportunity for freedom, instead of locking people away.

It is a time of innovation. When I look at the communities or programs I visited over the past year, it seems clear that all offer an inspirational blueprint. Most people I met have very strong ideas for or against certain approaches, which is fine. This is an industry of caring people with powerful opinions, not surprising among people who've spent years fighting the establishment.

There is a sort of eternal hope among those who run the warm, creative homes. Whenever the government promises a seniors' announcement, advocates message one another, hoping that this time the politicians will be bold.

In Ontario, at least, bravery is happening at a local level, as individual homes are starting to choose sweeping transformation. The big changes, the government policies that create systemic change, well, that hasn't happened yet. When so-called big announcements turn out to be quite small, I think of the people I've met along the way, who've worked for decades, sometimes flouting government rules, to make lives better for the people in their care.

Suellen Beatty, in Saskatoon's Sherbrooke Community Centre, built a career on risk. She is now focused on the design of an entirely new community, merging housing for families, elders and university students with an intergenerational school for Indigenous elementary students, focused on music and art.

Scott Tarde, from San Diego's George G. Glenner Alzheimer's Family Centers, believes high-quality day programs act as a balm for caregivers and can help keep our fathers, uncles or mothers out of long-term care, or at least delay it. Pat Sprigg, of North Carolina's Carol Woods Retirement Community, leads a dementia-friendly community that inspires seniors to organize their own groups and committees, all while living inside a forest.

It was Dr. Thomas who told me to find the positive stories, the ones that create the most danger for companies or governments that pretend it's too difficult to change, preferring the old rigid ways.

Mary Connell, the project manager in Peel Region's homes, has offered dozens of tours to the curious or inspired, helping advocates with pep talks and providing interested parties detailed information on improvements Peel has seen among its residents and, equally important, its staff.

Like Jill Knowlton, Connell had hoped the Ontario government would embrace long-term care that focuses on individual needs. It is clear that the traditional task-focused system with a few nice programs will not create lasting improvement.

When it seems like systemic change will never happen, Connell focuses on the people around her, residents like Maxwell and Tony who are still hanging on with gusto. The bigger changes will evolve, she believes, even if it happens one home at a time.

On her desk, at Peel Regional headquarters, Connell keeps a photograph of Peter, the man who spoke Polish to Inga Cherry until he remembered enough English to flirt with ladies on tours of his home. In the picture Peter is sitting in a comfy chair, glasses perched on the end of his nose, looking wise, like the nuclear researcher he once was. His hand is raised, in greeting. It was taken a few weeks before he died, but he did not look like a man in decline. He looked like himself.

Not all of us will have dementia. Many of us will not play competitive sports into our 90s, hoping for a flamboyant ending on the pickleball court, but we can improve the odds if we see a long and productive life as normal. Start now. Travel well. Learn a new language.

Tell the dangerous stories.

# Acknowledgments

FROM OUR FIRST CONVERSATION, I knew that Jack David, of ECW Press, was the right publisher for this book. He immediately understood the *gist* of it, as Suellen Beatty or Dr. Bill Thomas would say, and I am grateful that he took a chance on a new author. Thank you to literary agent Samantha Haywood of Transatlantic Agency, for making it all happen so smoothly. Susan Renouf was my editor. She amazed with her insight and wise, wise words. I can't imagine this book without her support, from New Jersey to the Netherlands. And a special note of gratitude to copy editor Jen Knoch, for her detailed eye, and to Samantha Chin, who co-ordinated this book's passage with an expert calm. I appreciate all of the support from ECW Press, including David Caron, Emily Ferko, Susannah Ames, Elham Ali, Jennifer Gallinger, Debby de Groot, and Jennifer D. Foster, who did the final, word-by-word proofread. It's amazing to watch a book come to life.

At the *Toronto Star*, I'd like to thank my editors, past and present, who've had an enduring interest in long-term care investigations: Irene Gentle, David Bruser, Lynn McAuley, Michael Cooke, Bert Bruser (the lawyer), Andrew Phillips, Catherine Wallace, Julie Carl and especially Kevin Donovan, who has been there since the beginning in 2003 and later gave excellent book advice.

Every person interviewed for this book has my gratitude. Sometimes wary, always helpful, the people who work with elders have much to say and were willing to share their ideas.

Mary Connell and Jill Knowlton shared so much knowledge, always fearless, pushing new ideas. Laura Tamblyn Watts was generous with her time, champagne and connections. Thank you for every coffee, telephone call and text, even when we were in opposite time zones. I'm also grateful to Dr. Jennifer Carson, who was right when she told me that a retirement community called Carol Woods was a special place. Dr. Allen Power was kind and generous with his insight. Eric Anderson, from Sherbrooke Community Centre, sent detailed updates during the COVID-19 lockdown, along with photos of his dog, Fred. Closer to home, in Toronto, I'd like to thank Dr. Samir Sinha, for always being available to answer questions and speaking so openly. I appreciate the time that San Diego's Joey Tennison gave, so thoughtfully telling the story of his mother, Susie, sharing the struggles and triumphs of family caregivers.

Thank you to John Cameron, for his patience. To my sons: Daniel, for listening, and David, who cooked fine French cuisine while I wrote, his creativity inspiring.

Finally, I'm deeply grateful for all the people living in long-term care, or a new variation, who shared their stories. They have much to teach us.

# Notes

INTRODUCTION

XIV  "I was about to publish a *Toronto Star* newspaper inves-
     tigation": Welsh, Moira, and Randy Risling. (2018, June
     20). The Fix. *Toronto Star*. https://projects.thestar.com/
     dementia-program/.

XV   "My first investigation included the story of a woman
     named Natalie Babineau": Welsh, Moira. (2003,
     December 3). Natalie's Story. *Toronto Star*, A1.

XVI  "City of Toronto wanted to improve care in its nursing
     homes": Armstrong, Pat, Albert Banerjee, Hugh
     Armstrong, Susan Braedley, Jacqueline Choiniere, Ruth
     Lowndes, and James Struthers. (2019). *Models for Long-
     Term Residential Care*. City of Toronto.

XVIII "Old and young lived together in poorhouses": Ruby,
     Norma. (1987). *For Such a Time as This: L. Earl Ludlow*

*and a History of Homes for the Aged in Ontario 1837–1961*. Toronto: Ontario Association of Homes for the Aged.

xix    "The suburbs were the place to be": Concordia University, St. Paul. (2015, June 23). The Evolution of American Family Structure. https://online.csp.edu/blog/family-science/the-evolution-of-american-family-structure.

xix    "The suburbs were the place to be, so families scattered away from the city core": Nicolaides, Becky, and Andrew Wiese. (2017, April 26). Suburbanization in the United States after 1945. *Oxford Research Encyclopedia of American History.*

xix    "Some nursing homes improved": Ruby, Norma. (1987). *For Such a Time as This: L. Earl Ludlow and a History of Homes for the Aged in Ontario 1837–1961*. Toronto: Ontario Association of Homes for the Aged.

xx    "America's culture-change movement": National Citizens' Coalition for Nursing Home Reform. (1985). *A Consumer Perspective on Quality Care.*

xxii    "research shows that every five years after the age of 65": Alzheimer Society of Canada. (2020, January 21). *About Dementia: Risk Factors.* https://alzheimer.ca/en/Home/About-dementia/Alzheimer-s-disease/Risk-factors; Canadian Institute for Health Information. (2018). *Dementia in Canada*; Corrada, Maria M., Ron Brookmeyer, Annlia Paganini-Hill, Daniel Berlau, Claudia H. Kawas. (2010). Dementia Incidence Continues to Increase with Age in the Oldest Old: The 90+ Study. *Annals of Neurology* 67 (1): 114–121.

XXII    "In the U.S., nearly six million people have Alzheimer's disease or other types of dementia": Bunis, Dena. (2019, January 2). Federal Government Spends $100 Million to Combat Alzheimer's. AARP.

XXII    "In Canada, with a population one-tenth the size of America's, there are 564,000 people with some form of cognitive decline": Alzheimer Society of Canada. (2019, March 7). About Dementia: Dementia Numbers in Canada. https://alzheimer.ca/en/Home/About-dementia/ What-is-dementia/Dementia-numbers.

XXII    "In the U.S., in 2018, the direct costs of caring for people with Alzheimer's and other conditions that cause dementia was $277 billion." Alzheimer's Association. (2018). 2018 Alzheimer's Disease Facts and Figures. https://alz.org/media/HomeOffice/Facts%20and%20 Figures/facts-and-figures.pdf.

XXII    "In Canada, it was $10.4 billion": Alzheimer Society of Canada. (2018, June 29). Canada's National Dementia Strategy: Latest Information and Statistics.

XXII    "Globally, the number has reached $1 trillion": Wimo, Anders, Maelenn Guerchet, Gemma-Claire Ali, Yu-Tzu Wu, A. Matthew Prina, Bengt Winblad, Linus Jonsson, Zhaorui Liu, and Martin Prince. 2017. The Worldwide Costs of Dementia 2015 and Comparisons with 2010. *Alzheimer's & Dementia* 13(1): 1–7.

XXII    "Dementia is the umbrella term for disorders that can lead to neurological decline, including Alzheimer's disease, Lewy body dementia and Parkinson's disease": Alzheimer Society of Canada. (2017, August 11). About

Dementia: Other Dementias. https://alzheimer.ca/en/
Home/About-dementia/Dementias.

XXIII    "Women typically live longer than men": Alzheimer
         Society of Canada. (2020, January 21). About Dementia:
         Risk Factors. https://alzheimer.ca/en/Home/About-
         dementia/Alzheimer-s-disease/Risk-factors; Einstein,
         Gillian. (2018, May 9). *Women & Dementia: Estrogens,
         Memory & Alzheimer's Disease.* Performed by Gillian
         Einstein.

XXIV     "These projections come from a report by the National
         Institute on Ageing": National Institute on Ageing. (2019,
         October 8). Long-Term Care Costs in Canada Projected
         to Triple to $71B in Only 30 Years. https://nia-ryerson.
         ca/commentary-posts/10/7/long-term-care-costs-in-
         canada-projected-to-triple-in-only-30-years.

CHAPTER ONE

2        "BBC2 documentary show *Can Gerry Robinson Fix
         Dementia Care Homes?"*: Robinson, Gerry. (2009,
         December 8). *Can Gerry Robinson Fix Dementia Care
         Homes?* https://bbc.co.uk/programmes/b00pf0s2.

22       "John Tory, the mayor of Toronto": Welsh, Moira.
         (2018, June 29). Mayor Tory Wants 'The Fix' in Toronto
         Nursing Homes. *Toronto Star.* https://thestar.com/news/
         investigations/2018/06/29/mayor-tory-wants-the-fix-in-
         toronto-nursing-homes.html.

22       "Josh Matlow wrote a motion": Welsh, Moira. (2018,
         July 23). Toronto City Council to Look at New Butterfly
         Nursing Home Care Program That Is a Success in

Peel Region. *Toronto Star*. https://thestar.com/news/
canada/2018/07/23/council-to-look-at-new-nursing-
home-care-model-that-is-already-a-success-in-peel.html.

22    "Both won unanimous votes": Welsh, Moira. (2019,
      April 24). After Unanimous Vote, Toronto Council
      to Plan for Emotion-Focused Care in all City-Run
      Nursing Homes. *Toronto Star*. https://thestar.com/news/
      investigations/2019/04/24/after-unanimous-vote-toronto-
      council-to-plan-for-emotion-focused-care-in-all-city-run-
      nursing-homes.html.

CHAPTER TWO

25    "in a nation that spends $16 billion a year to stay young-
      ish": American Society of Plastic Surgeons. (2017, April
      12). More Than $16 Billion Spent on Cosmetic Plastic
      Surgery.

28    "Thomas went home that night and pulled out his
      medical books to investigate loneliness": Holt-Lunstad,
      Julianne, Theodore Robles, and David A. Sbarra.
      (2017). Advancing Social Connection as a Public Health
      Priority in the United States. *The American Psychologist*
      72 (6): 517–530; Holt-Lunstad, Julianne. (2018). The
      Potential Public Health Relevance of Social Isolation and
      Loneliness: Prevalence, Epidemiology, and Risk Factors.
      *Public Policy & Aging Report* 27 (4): 127–130.

33    "although the city later chose a made-in-Toronto model":
      Welsh, Moira. (2019, November 27). Toronto Unveils Plans
      to Revamp Long Term Care Homes. *Toronto Star*. https://
      thestar.com/news/gta/2019/11/27/city-unveils-plans-
      to-revamp-long-term-care-homes.html.

34     "A foundation-supported study by THRIVE Research
Collaborative": Zimmerman, Sheryl, Barbara J. Bowers,
Lauren W. Cohen, David C. Grabowski, Susan D.
Horn, and Peter Kemper. (2015). New Evidence on the
Green House Model of Nursing Home Care: Synthesis
of Findings and Implications for Policy, Practice, and
Research. *Health Services Research* 51 (S1): 475–496.

36     "*Alive Inside*": Rossato-Bennett, Michael (Director).
(2014). *Alive Inside*. Performed by Dan Cohen, Louise
Dueno and Nell Hardie.

CHAPTER THREE

57     "Miss Patricia smiles": Pinka, Patricia. (1982). *This
Dialogue of One: The Songs and Sonnets of John Donne*.
Tuscaloosa: University of Alabama Press.

CHAPTER FOUR

68     "The headline on his 1995 obituary": Saxon, Wolfgang.
(1995, July 14). Dr. George G. Glenner, 67, Dies;
Researched Alzheimer's Disease. *New York Times*, A22.

70     "President Ronald Reagan, who was reportedly diagnosed with Alzheimer's six years later": Ronald Reagan
Presidential Library & Museum. (1994, November 5).
Reagan's Letter Announcing His Alzheimer's Diagnosis.
https://reaganlibrary.gov/sreference/reagan-s-letter-
announcing-his-alzheimer-s-diagnosis.

72     "In a systemic review published in the Cochrane Library
in 2018": Woods, Bob, Laura O'Philbin, Emma M.
Farrell, Aimee E. Spector, and Martin Orrell. (2018).

Reminiscence Therapy for Dementia. *Cochrane Systematic Review* (3).

72    "Still, Britain's National Institute for Health and Care Excellence recommends": National Institute for Health and Care Excellence. (2019, June 28). People with Dementia Should be Offered Activities That Can Help Promote Wellbeing.

73    "It was an important interview for Town Square in no small part because Tarde knew that Shriver would understand": Powell, Robert, and A. Pawlowski. (2018, April 10). Innovative Day Care Recreates 1950s to Trigger Memories for People with Dementia. https://today.com/health/dementia-day-care-looks-1950s-stimulate-patients-brains-t126727.

73    "Almost two-thirds of those diagnosed with Alzheimer's are women": The Women's Alzheimer's Movement. (2020, May 31). https://thewomensalzheimersmovement.org/; Public Health Agency of Canada. (2019). *A Dementia Strategy for Canada: Together We Aspire.* Government of Canada.

74    "Jacqueline Cochran whose 1964 Starfighter flight reached a record 1,429 miles per hour": San Diego Air & Space Museum. (n.d.) Jacqueline Cochran: Record Breaker. https://sandiegoairandspace.org/exhibits/online-exhibit-page/jacqueline-cochran.

80    "Senior Helpers was acquired by Altaris Capital Partners": Altaris. (2016, October 27). Investment in Senior Helpers. https://altariscap.com/investment-in-senior-helpers/.

81    "In the *Journal of Continuing Education in the Health Professions*": Ehlman, Mary C., Nimkar Swateja, Beth Nolan, Pamela Thomas, Carlos Caballero, and Teepa Snow. (2018). Health Workers' Knowledge and Perceptions on Dementia in Skilled Nursing Homes: A Pilot Implementation of Teepa Snow's Positive Approach to Care Certification Course. *Journal of Continuing Education in the Health Professions* 38 (3): 190–197.

82    "A study published in the British peer-reviewed journal": Day, Anna M., Ian A. James, Thomas D. Meyer, and David R. Lee. (2011). Do People with Dementia Find Lies and Deception in Dementia Care Acceptable. *Aging & Mental Health* 15 (7): 822–829.

CHAPTER FIVE

95    "In 2013, CNN declared it a 'dementia village'": Tinker, Ben. (2013, December 27). Dementia Village Inspires New Care. https://cnn.com/2013/07/11/world/europe/wus-holland-dementia-village/.

95    "*The Atlantic* likened it to a benevolent version of *The Truman Show*": Planos, Josh. (2014, November 14). The Dutch Village Where Everyone Has Dementia. *The Atlantic.* https://theatlantic.com/health/archive/2014/11/the-dutch-village-where-everyone-has-dementia/382195/.

CHAPTER SIX

112   "Their company Crosswater developed spatial audio": Matney, Lucas. (2016, May 23). Facebook Just Bought VR Audio Company Two Big Ears

and is Making their Tech Free to Developers. *TechCrunch*. https://techcrunch.com/2016/05/23/facebook-just-bought-vr-audio-company-two-big-ears-and-is-making-their-tech-free-to-developers/.

115     "AARP commissioned Oxford Economics": Oxford Economics. (2013). *The Longevity Economy: Generating Economic Growth and New Opportunities for Business.*

115     "which AARP later updated to US$8.3 trillion": AARP, The Economist Intelligence Unit. (2019). *The Longevity Economy Outlook.*

124     "In October 2018, CABHI announced funding for 31 studies": Townsend, Arielle. (2019, November 28). Picture This: How Virtual Reality Is Shaping the Future of Dementia Care. Centre for Aging + Brain Health Innovation. CABHI.

CHAPTER SEVEN

135     *"Dementia Beyond Drugs"*: Power, G. Allen. (2010, rev. 2017). *Dementia Beyond Drugs: Changing the Culture of Care.* Baltimore: Health Professions Press.

137     "Of those three plagues, studies show that loneliness may be the most destructive": Holt-Lunstad, Julianne, Theodore Robles, and David A. Sbarra. (2017). Advancing Social Connection as a Public Health Priority in the United States. *The American Psychologist* 72 (6): 517–530.; Holt-Lunstad, Julianne. (2018). The Potential Public Health Relevance of Social Isolation and Loneliness: Prevalence, Epidemiology, and Risk Factors. *Public Policy & Aging Report* 27 (4): 127–130.

147    "Dr. Power cites two large-scale literature reviews, including one from Cochrane": Lai, Claudia K.Y., Jonas H.M. Yeung, Vincent Mok, and Iris Chi. (2009). Special Care Units for Dementia Individuals with Behavioural Problems. *Cochrane Database of Systematic Reviews* (4).

156    "In long-term care, culture change is one of those industry buzzwords": Welsh, Moira, and Jesse McLean. (2011, November 17). Nursing Home Residents Abused. *Toronto Star*.

CHAPTER EIGHT

165    "Over time new guidelines have emerged across North America": Registered Nurses' Association of Ontario. (2012). *Promoting Safety: Alternative Approaches to the Use of Restraints.*

173    "Led by Dr. Sherry Dupuis, the conclusions narrowed those domains": Dupuis, Sherry L., Colleen Whyte, Jennifer Carson, Rebecca Genoe, Lisa Meshino, and Leah Sadler. (2012). Just Dance with Me: An Authentic Partnership Approach to Understanding Leisure in the Dementia Context. *World Leisure Journal* 54 (3): 240–254.

CHAPTER NINE

189    "Good news has emerged from research that concluded the incidence of dementia is declining": Sposato, Luciano A., Moira K. Kapral, and Jiming Fang. (2015). Declining Incidence of Stroke and Dementia: Coincidence or Prevention Opportunitiy. *JAMA Neurology* 72 (12): 1529–1531.

190    "Statistics reveal that the odds of getting dementia":
       Canadian Institute for Health Information. (2020).
       *Dementia in Canada.* https://cihi.ca/en/dementia-in-
       canada/dementia-in-canada-summary; Corrada, Maria
       M., Ron Brookmeyer, Annlia Paganini-Hill, Daniel
       Berlau, Claudia H. Kawas. (2010). Dementia Incidence
       Continues to Increase with Age in the Oldest Old:
       The 90+ Study. *Annals of Neurology* 67 (1): 114–121;
       Alzheimer Society of Canada. (2020, January 21). About
       Dementia: Risk Factors.

190    "So until the boomers fade away": Fry, Richard. (2020,
       April 28). Millenials Overtake Baby Boomers as America's
       Largest Generation. *Fact Tank.*

190    "Eating food that is good for the heart, for example,
       is now considered good for the brain": National
       Institutes of Health. (2017, August 15). Risk Factors
       for Heart Disease Linked to Dementia. https://nih.gov/
       news-events/nih-research-matters/risk-factors-heart-
       disease-linked-dementia; Johns Hopkins Medicine. (n.d.)
       Dementia and Heart Health: Are They Related? *Johns
       Hopkins Medicine.* https://hopkinsmedicine.org/health/
       conditions-and-diseases/dementia/dementia-and-heart-
       health-are-they-related.

190    "hearing loss has been linked to dementia": Griffin,
       Katherine, and Katherine Bouton. (n.d.) Hearing Loss
       Linked to Dementia. AARP. https://aarp.org/health/
       brain-health/info-07-2013/hearing-loss-linked-to-
       dementia.html.

190    "Canada's dementia strategy is investing money in
       research": Public Health Agency of Canada. (2019). *A*

*Dementia Strategy for Canada: Together We Aspire.*
Government of Canada.

190   "With roughly 100 different forms of dementia": Power,
      G. Allen. (2010, rev. 2017). *Dementia Beyond Drugs:
      Changing the Culture of Care.* Baltimore: Health
      Professions Press.

191   "Dr. Sinha cites the San Francisco Police Department":
      Brown, Rebecca T., Cyrus Ahalt, Josette Rivera, Irena
      Stijacic Cenzer, Angela Wilhelm, and Brie A. Williams.
      (2017). Good Cop, Better Cop: Evaluation of a Geriatrics
      Training Program for Police. *Journal of the American
      Geriatrics Society 65* (8): 1842–1847.

191   "The Ontario government spent $4.28 billion on long-
      term care in 2018": Ontario Ministry of Health; Ontario
      Ministry of Long-Term Care. (2018, April 13). Ontario
      Launches New Performance Tool on Long-Term Care
      Homes.

195   "Mentink has since moved out, but in 2016, the
      urban-design student recorded a TEDx talk about
      intergenerational living": Mentink, Jurriën. (2016).
      *Intergenerational Learning: Exchanges Between Young
      and Old.* Performed by Jurriën Mentink. Amsterdam.

198   "The Toronto HomeShare Program emerged from a
      brainstorming session of the City of Toronto Seniors
      Strategy group": Toronto HomeShare Program. (n.d.).
      Program. https://torontohomeshare.com/.

200   "The *Toronto Star* published the story of the Golden
      Girls, four women in their late 60s or early 70s":

Hanes, Tracy. (2017, January 23). Thank You for Being a Friend . . . I Can Buy a House With: Meet a New Generation of Golden Girls. *Toronto Star*.

201    "As reporter Tess Kalinowski wrote, the Golden Girls Act has since been introduced in the provincial legislature, an attempt to embrace innovation in seniors living": Kalinowski, Tess. (2019, February 27). Golden Girls Act Would Pave Way for Ontario Seniors to Co-Live. *Toronto Star*.

205    "Brett grew up in England around the corner from a kid named Reginald Dwight": IMDB. (n.d.) Elton John: Biography. IMDB. https://imdb.com/name/nm0005056/bio.

EPILOGUE

209    "Another way of pressing the need for government action is to highlight the statistics": Brown, Richard. (2016). A Deeper Look at Longevity Risk. Association of Canadian Pension Management. https://acpm. com/ACPM/Archive/The-Observer/Spring-2016/ Industry-Insider/ISSUES-ANSWERS/A-deeper-look-at- longevity-risk.aspx.

211    "If those unpaid hours of care, mostly provided by women, were paid by the public purse it would add another $27 billion in costs by 2050": MacDonald, Bonnie-Jeanne, Michael Wolfson, and John P Hirdes. (2019). *The Future Cost of Long-Term Care in Canada*. National Institute on Ageing.

# Index

JOHN CAMERON

M OIRA WELSH, an investigative journalist with the *Toronto Star*, has co-authored investigations that have won three National Newspaper Awards and a Michener Award for Public Service Journalism. She was a finalist for the Justicia Award for Legal Reporting and the Canadian Hillman Prize, for journalism in service of the common good. Starting as a breaking news reporter, she soon joined the investigative team writing on social justice, the environment, and the lives of people living in seniors' homes. Moira lives in Toronto, Ontario, with her family.